Luxemburger Juristische Studien –
Luxembourg Legal Studies

edited by

Faculty of Law, Economics and Finance
University of Luxembourg

Volume 26

Giovanni Chiapponi

Interfaces between National and EU Law

Time Limits in Cross-Border Civil Proceedings and Their Impact on the Free Circulation of Judgments

Nomos

The Deutsche Nationalbibliothek lists this publication in the Deutsche Nationalbibliografie; detailed bibliographic data are available on the Internet at http://dnb.d-nb.de

ISBN 978-3-7560-1799-7 (Print)
978-3-7489-4473-7 (ePDF)

British Library Cataloguing-in-Publication Data
A catalogue record for this book is available from the British Library.

ISBN 978-3-7560-1799-7 (Print)
978-3-7489-4473-7 (ePDF)

Library of Congress Cataloging-in-Publication Data
Chiapponi, Giovanni
Interfaces between National and EU Law
Time Limits in Cross-Border Civil Proceedings and Their Impact on the Free Circulation of Judgments
Giovanni Chiapponi
237 pp.
Includes bibliographic references.

ISBN 978-3-7560-1799-7 (Print)
978-3-7489-4473-7 (ePDF)

Online Version
Nomos eLibrary

1st Edition 2024

Alla nonna Rosy

Table of Contents

Acronyms and abbreviations

AG	Advocate General
Am. J. Comp. L.	The American Journal of Comparative Law
Art.	Article
AVAG	Anerkennungs- und Vollstreckungsausführungsgesetz (Recognition and Enforcement Act)
BGB	Buergerliches Gesetzbuch (German Civil Code)
Brussels Convention	1968 Brussels Convention on Jurisdiction and the Recognition and Enforcement of Judgments in Civil and Commercial Matters (1972) OJ L 299.
Brussels I Regulation	Council Regulation (EC) 44/2001 of 22 December 2000 on Jurisdiction and the Recognition and Enforcement of Judgments in Civil and Commercial Matters (2001) OJ L 12.
Brussels Ibis Regulation	Regulation (EU) 1215/2012 of the European Parliament and of the Council of 12 December 2012 on Jurisdiction and the Recognition and Enforcement of Judgments in Civil and Commercial Matters (Recast) (2012) OJ L 351.
Bull. Civ.	Bulletin Civil de la Cour de Cassation
Camb. Yearb. Eur. Leg. Stud.	Cambridge Yearbook of European Legal Studies
CFR	Charter of Fundamental Rights
CJEU	Court of Justice of the European Union
CMLR	Common Market Law Review
Cor. giur.	Il Corriere Giuridico
Cuad. der. trans.	Cuadernos de Derecho Transnacional
C.J.Q.	Civil Justice Quarterly
c.p.c.	Codice di Procedura Civile (Italian Code of Civil Procedure)

CPC	Code de Procédure Civile (French Code of Civil Procedure)
CPP	Κώδικας Πολιτικής Δικονομίας (Greek Code of Civil Procedure)
disp. att.	Dispozioni di Attuazione del Codice di Procedura Civile (Preliminary Rules of the Italian Code of Civil Procedure)
Droit et procédures	Droit et Procédures: La Revue des Huissiers de Justice
EC	European Community Treaty
ECHR	European Convention of Human Rights
ECtHR	European Court of Human Rights
EAPO Regulation	Regulation (EU) 655/2014 of the European Parliament and of the Council of 15 May 2014 Establishing a European Account Preservation Order Procedure to Facilitate Cross-Border Debt Recovery in Civil and Commercial Matters (2014) OJ L 189.
EEC	European Economic Community Treaty
EEO Regulation	Regulation 805/2004 Regulation (EC) 805/2004 of the European Parliament and of the Council of 21 April 2004 Creating a European Enforcement Order for Uncontested Claims (2004) OJ L 143.
E.L. Rev.	European Law Review
EPO Regulation	Regulation (EC) 1896/2006 of the European Parliament and of the Council of 12 December 2006 Creating a European Order for Payment Procedure (2006) OJ L 399.
ESCP Regulation	Regulation (EC) 861/2007 of the European Parliament and of the Council of 11 July 2007 Establishing a European Small Claims Procedure (2007) OJ L 199.
Eur. Rev.	Private Law European Review of Private Law
Foro it.	Il Foro Italiano
Gaz. Pal.	Gazette du Palais
Giur. it.	Giurisprudenza Italiana

Giust. civ.	Giustizia Civile
Giusto proc. civ.	Il Giusto Processo Civile
IJPL	International Journal of Procedural Law
INT'L LIS	Rivista di Diritto Processuale Internazionale e Arbitrato Internazionale
IPRax	Praxis des Internationalen Privat- und Verfahrensrechts
JCER	Journal of Contemporary European Research
J-CL Droit International	JurisClasseur Droit international
J-CL Europe Traité	JurisClasseur Europe Traité
JCMS	Journal of Common Market Studies
JDI	Journal du Droit International (Clunet)
JPIL	Journal of Private International Law
JPE	Journal of Political Economy
Judicium	Judicium Il Processo Civile in Italia e in Europa
LEC	Ley de Enjuiciamiento Civil (Spanish Code of Civil Procedure)
MJ	Maastricht Journal of European and Comparative Law
MLR	The Modern Law Review
NCPC	Nouveau Code de Procédure Civile (Luxembourgish Code of Civil Procedure)
NIPR	Nederlands Internationaal Privaatrecht
Unif. L. Rev.	Uniform Law Review
RCDIP	Revue Critique de Droit International Privé
RDIPP	Rivista di Diritto Internazionale Privato e Processuale
RIDC	La Revue Internationale de Droit Compare
Riv. es. forz.	Rivista dell'Esecuzione Forzata

Riv. trim. dir. e proc. civ.	Rivista Trimestrale di Diritto e Procedura Civile
Riv. dir. eu.	Rivista di Diritto Europeo
Riv. dir. proc.	Rivista di Diritto Processuale
RIW	Recht der Internationalen Wirtschaft
RTD civ.	Revue Trimestrielle de Droit Civil
RTD eur.	Revue Trimestrielle de Droit Européen
TFEU	Treaty on the Functioning of the European Union
Yb. PIL	Yearbook of Private International Law
ZIZ	Zakon o izvršbi in zavarovanju (Slovenian Code of Civil Procedure)
ZPO	Zivilprozessordnung (German Code of Civil Procedure)

Foreign legal terms

Bundesgerichtshof	German Supreme Court
Cancelleria	Registry of the Court (Italy)
Corte di Appello	Italian Court of Appeal
Cour d'Appel	French Court of Appeal
Corte di Cassazione	Italian Supreme Court
Cour de Cassation	French Supreme Court
Greffe	Registry of the Court (France)
Huissier de justice	French Bailiff
Landsgericht	German First Instance Court
Oberlandesgericht	Higher Regional Court (Germany)
Tribunal Judiciaire	French First Instance Court
Tribunale	Italian First Instance Court
Tribunal Supremo	Spanish Supreme Court
Ufficiale giudiziario	Italian Bailiff

Introduction

This research deals with time limits in cross-border civil proceedings at the EU level. The legal issues that arise are particularly insightful to study the interplay between national and EU law, an issue that has caught the attention of the EU legislator in recent years.

The interaction between time, more precisely time limits, and civil proceedings is a topical issue for all legislations. Time is indeed an absolute fixture that dictates the pace at which the procedures must unfold within a specific procedural framework where parties and judges must accomplish their activities in a logical and chronological order. Time limits are thus an essential tool that provide structure at the procedure. In practice, time limits impact the effective exercise of the procedural rights of the parties and determine the management of cases, the fairness of the proceedings, the prevention of delays, the efficiency of justice and the effect of *res judicata*. Against this background, the failure to comply with time limits entails irreversible consequences for the protection of parties' procedural rights that are even more far-reaching in cross-border cases.

In light of their fundamental role within civil proceedings, time limits figure prominently in the assessment carried out by national and EU legislators when attempting to strike a balance between legal certainty and parties' rights in every legal order. Domestic laws are deemed to grant parties fixed parameters for litigating at national level. These criteria generally provide litigants with a high degree of legal certainty with a view to effectively exercising their procedural rights. However, the scenario becomes much more complex when introducing a cross-border element to the dispute. Even within a harmonised legal system such as the one set up by the EU, time limits still differ from one country to another. To this date, time limits remain indeed mainly set by national law and this introduces elements of unclearness and legal uncertainty. In a philosophical dimension adapted to the object of this research, the above view might be interpreted as endorsing St. Augustine of Hippo's thought about time: *quid est ergo tempus? Si nemo ex me quaerat, scio* (time limits in a national setting); *si quarenti explicare velim, nescio* (time limits in a cross-border setting)[1].

Against this backdrop, it should be noted that the lack of uniformity regarding the regulation of time limits at the EU level raise challenges, as we will see, to the judicial cooperation in civil matters (Art. 81 TFEU). The divergent rules lead to an unequal exercise of rights in cross-border cases, and ultimately jeopardises the free circulation of judgments across the Member States. Time thus becomes relative. The absolute and fixed order of civil proceedings collapses and turns (as Salvador Dali perfectly represented in his masterpiece 'The Persistence of Memory') into limp watches, soft as cheese melting in the sun ('the camembert of time').

1 This sentence can be translated as follows: 'What then is time? If no one asks me, I know, if I want to explain it to someone who asks, I do not know'.

Under these circumstances, litigants in cross-border cases do not enjoy the same level of protection, as guaranted by Art. 6 ECHR and Art. 47 CFR, as litigants in national proceedings. In order to strengthen at EU level both the effective recognition and enforcement of judgments and the protection of parties' procedural rights, this research will explore possible EU legal solutions based on uniform standards which aim at promoting an objective interpretation of time limits in cross-border civil proceedings. The EU legislator could thus envisage some 'common foundations' -what in Claude Monet's painting 'the Rouen Cathedral' is represented by the absolute nature of the cathedral's architecture - for challenging the fragmentation between domestic time limits, which vary widely between the Member States, as the Rouen cathedral does in Monet's view depending on the light throughout the different hours of the day.

In order to better understand the divergences that arise under unharmonised time limits, it is helpful to consider the following hypothetical cases.

Case 1

X is an art dealer from Paris who sold a painting by Andy Warhol to Y, who is an art dealer domiciled in Italy, for 100,000 euros. X delivered the painting to Y, but received only half the money from Y. The contract provided for a choice-of-court clause establishing that the first instance court of Paris would be competent to decide any disputes arising out of their contractual relationship.

Given these facts, the following situations can be distinguished:

X sues Y before the Court of Paris. Y is served with the lawsuit and appears within the time limit of 2 months and 15 days. The Court of Paris renders a judgment against Y ordering him to pay the full amount. X serves the judgment on Y who can lodge an appeal against the judgment within 3 months from the date of service.

X sues Y before the Court of Paris. Y is served with the lawsuit and appears within the time limit of 2 months and 15 days. The Court of Paris renders a judgment against Y ordering him to pay the full amount. The judgment is not served on Y who can lodge an appeal against the judgment within 2 years from its rendering.

X sues Y before the Court of Paris. Y is served with the lawsuit and has 2 months and 15 days to appear. Y fails to appear. The Court of Paris renders a default judgment against Y ordering him to pay the full amount. X serves[2] the judgment on Y who can oppose the judgment within 3 months from the date of service.

Case 2

X is an art dealer from Milan who sold a painting by Andy Warhol to Y, who is an art dealer domiciled in France, for 100,000 euros. X delivered the painting to Y, but received only half the money from Y. The contract provided for a choice-of-court clause establishing that the first instance court of Milan would be competent to decide any disputes arising out of their contractual relationship.

2 The 2 years time limit does not concern default judgments, which must necessarily be served in order to achieve the *res judicata* effects.

Given these facts, the following situations can be distinguished:

X sues Y before the Court of Milan. Y is served with the lawsuit and appears in the proceedings within the time limit of 70 days. The Court of Milan renders a judgment against Y ordering him to pay the full amount. X serves the judgment on Y who can lodge an appeal against the judgment within 30 days from the date of service.

X sues Y before the Court of Milan. Y is personally served with the lawsuit and appears in the proceedings within the time limit of 70 days. The Court of Milan renders a judgment against Y ordering him to pay the full amount. The judgment is not served on Y who can lodge an appeal against the judgment within 6 months from its publication.

X sues Y before the Court of Milan. Y is served with the lawsuit and has 70 days to appear. Y fails to appear. The Court of Milan renders a default judgment against Y ordering him to pay the full amount. X serves the judgment on Y who can lodge an appeal against the judgment within 30 days from the date of service.

X sues Y before the Court of Milan. Y is served with the lawsuit and has 70 days to appear. Y fails to appear. The Court of Milan renders a default judgment against Y ordering him to pay the full amount. The judgment is not served on Y who can lodge an appeal against the judgment within 6 months from its publication[3].

These examples give some preliminary insights on the divergences between time limits in France and Italy that make the exercise of defendants' rights in a cross-border setting subject to a different treatment.

Under French law, a foreign defendant has 2 months and 15 days to react, under Italian law 70 days[4].

Further divergences arise when an appeal is brought on factual grounds in cross-border proceedings[5]. Under French law, the standard time limit of 1 month, which is extended by 2 months for foreign defendants, is running from the moment the judgment is served on the losing party, whereas the long time limit of 2 years applying in case the judgment is not served on the losing party, is running (it does not run in case of default judgments) from the moment the judgment is renderend. Under Italian law, the standard

3 If the defendant provides the Court of appeal with a proof of his illness demonstrating that his default was involuntary, the 6 months time limit does not apply.

4 For a detailed analysis on the time limits to react in Italy and France see (i) Time to react in general first instance proceedings.

5 For a detailed analysis on the time limits to appeal in Italy and France see (i) Time limits for lodging an appeal on factual grounds.

time limit of 30 days, which does not foresee any extension for foreign defendants, is running from the moment the judgment is served upon the losing parties, while the long time limit of 6 months applying in case of lack of service of the judgment, is running from the publication of the judgment (it generally runs also in case of default judgments except if it is proved that default is involuntary).

These cases illustrate that the setting, application and interpretation of time limits vary widely between Italy and France, two systems that are typically considered to be relatively similar, where one is surprised to find such divergences. This suggests that the divergences between the 25 other Member States should be even bigger. This fragmentation across the EU considerably impacts the exercise of parties' procedural rights in EU cross-border civil litigation, in particular the right to a fair trial. This situation, as further examined in Chapter 2[6], is at odds with the free circulation of judgments.

As discussed in Chapter 3[7], harmonising time limits at EU level could help mitigate these issues and represent one of the future challenges to address in the policy area of judicial cooperation in civil matters. In order to find the best policy option, the feasibility and desirability of EU action on time limits needs to be carefully balanced with national procedural autonomies, which limit to a certain extent the competence of the EU lawmaker in civil procedure.

A) Research question

The research aims at exploring possible legal solutions to remove the obstacles to the free circulation of judgments in the civil justice area that arise from the remarkably diverging national rules on procedural time limits within the EU. As shown by the case-law of the CJEU, time limits have recently come under closer scrutiny.

The interplay between national and EU law doubtlessly illustrates that time limits raise significant challenges to the right to a fair trial under Art. 6 ECHR and Art. 47 CFR – e.g. the effective recovery of claims, effective judicial protection, effective cross-border enforcement of judgments – which negatively impact EU cross-border civil litigation. With a view to

6 See Chapter 2: Effective judicial cooperation in civil matters and the right to a fair trial
7 See Chapter 3: Time limits from the perspective of the EU lawmaker

overcoming some of the weaknesses of the current legal framework governing the cross-border enforcement of judgments and strengthening the parties' fundamental procedural rights, this research intends to determine whether and, if so, to what extent time limits can be harmonised at EU level. EU action on time limits would indeed favour the speed, efficiency, and proportionality of cross-border proceedings without compromising the fairness of the judicial process and the equality of the parties.

Under these premises, this work intends to address the following research question: can time limits be harmonised at EU level and, if so, to what extent?

To answer this research question and assessing possible legal hypotheses the following sub-questions have been addressed:

(i) What practical issues do time limits raise in the policy area of judicial cooperation in civil matters?
(ii) Does the current regulation of time limits at EU level offer sufficient guarantees for protecting parties' rights in cross-border civil litigation?
(iii) Is it feasible and desirable to enact EU legislation on time limits or do the peculiarities of the national systems prevent such EU intervention?
(iv) Which specific policy recommendations could be issued?

In answering these questions, this research provides a comprehensive analysis of the key issues that time limits raise in national and CJEU case law.

When referring to national laws, the main focus is – without excluding by way of example references to other EU countries – to Italy and France, which are two systems with a very important historical legal tradition that has very relevant implications for the policy decisions of the EU lawmaker. Notably, the choice of mainly analysing Italian and French law finds its rationale in the need of pre-assessing, prior to dealing with a larger pool of legal systems, if there is room for harmonization at least between two similar procedural systems. This is a sort of 'pre-harmonization test' enquiring whether there are common grounds between the two systems at hand enabling harmonisation or if, on the contrary, the differences between them are so prominent to prevent full harmonisation and make necessary the pursuit of a different legislative strategy at the EU level. A preliminary assessment shows that time limits are premised on specific procedural activities requiring different degrees of complexity. This makes opting for common fixed time limits extremely burdensome. Even with two close legal systems belonging to the same legal tradition such as the French and the Italian ones, it seems practically impossible to provide for uniform general time limits as there are structural differences embeeded in complex and peculiar legal backgrounds that underlie the setting of time limits at national level.

B) Scope of the research

The time limits mainly dealt with in this work are: the time limits to react in general first instance proceedings; for opposing the issuance of payment orders; for challenging judgments (appeal on factual and legal grounds); for enforcing judgments; and for applying for *restitutio in integrum.*

An important *caveat* must be made regarding the scope of the research. For the sake of limiting the scope of the analysis to instruments applied within the area of judicial cooperation in civil matters, the research focuses on the study of a classical situation of cross-border litigation in the context of general first instance civil proceedings and payment order procedings without considering, instead, how cases are regulated in the context of other special civil proceedings.

The research thus addresses issues that originate from the interface between national procedural rules on time limits and the following European Regulations allowing for cross-border debt recovery across the Member States in civil and commercial matters: the Brussels Ibis Regulation, the EEO, EPO, ESCP and EAPO Regulations. On the contrary, the Regulations on (i) matrimonial matters, parental responsibility and child abduction, (ii) maintenance, (iii) succession, (iv) enhanced cooperation on matrimonial property, and (v) registered partnerships, do not fall under the scope of this research.

C) Methodology

In order to investigate the research questions above, a three-step methodological approach was adopted. Each step corresponds to one of the chapters. Firstly, the crucial role of time limits in the regulation of civil proceedings has been highlighted by focusing on their historical background, classification, and function in EU civil procedure. Secondly, the main issues that time limits raise in EU cross-border civil litigation are identified and critically assessed. In particular, their impact on the protection of the parties's procedural rights under Art 6 ECHR and Art. 47 CFR is examined.

Thirdly, specific policy recommendations and reforms proposals are made to address some of the challenges time limits pose to the current legal framework of cross-border enforcement of judgments in civil and commercial matters.

The chronological order of the three steps is justified by their purpose in the research. The choice of first tracing the evolution, classification, and function of time limits in civil proceedings (chapter 1) finds its rationale in the need to describe a comprehensive legal-historical framework that lays the foundations for dealing with the sub-questions that are examined in the following chapter. The second step (chapter 2) defines the research issues by addressing sub questions (i) and (ii). It proves, as such, how time limits are a practical obstacle to the free circulation of judgments in the area of civil justice. Based on these findings, the third step (chapter 3) finally tackles sub-questions (iii) and (iv) and examines whether some degree of harmonisation is desirable for considering EU legislative action on time limits.

Legal desk research[8] is the methodology chosen for identifying, synthetizing and analysing the meaning and content of time limits throughout the different chapters. A careful analysis of the collected case law made it possible to establish both the scientific background of each sub-question and the prerequisites for providing answers. Time limits are thus investigated through the discovery of primary and secondary sources.

Primary sources include the most relevant laws and the most pertinent cases of EU civil procedure (mainly related to the Brussels Ibis, EEO, EPO, ESCP and EAPO Regulations) which were selected both at national and EU level. In addition, primary sources include other sources of international law, such as the ELI-UNIDROIT Model European Rules of Civil Procedure and the ECHR.

The secondary sources rely on national and international literature dealing with EU civil procedure. Under the scope of this research, primary sources are of paramount importance because they contribute to identifying the issues which time limits raise in EU cross-border civil litigation and they contain the legal bases for enacting legislation at EU level. On the

8 For further details on the history and basis of this method see Terry Hutchinson, 'Doctrinal Research: Researching the Jury' in Dawn Watkins and Mandy Burton (eds), *Research Methods in Law* (Routledge Taylor and Francis Group 2013), 7–34; Terry Hutchinson, *Researching and Writing in Law* (4th edn, Thomson Reuters 2018), 49–67; Paul Chynoweth, 'Legal Research', in Andrew Knight and Les Ruddock (eds), *Advanced Research Methods in the Built Environment* (Wiley-Blackwell 2008), 28–39.

other hand, secondary sources play a fundamental complementary role to primary sources, since the future developments of EU civil procedure are foreshadowed by the most topical questions discussed in legal literature.

D) Structure of the research

This work is composed of three chapters.

Chapter 1 highlights the importance of time limits in civil proceedings for effectively protecting the parties' procedural rights. The chapter is thus structured along the three following sections focusing on the historical background (section A), classification (section B) and function (section C) of time limits in EU civil procedure.

Chapter 2 provides some practical examples showing how differences between domestic legal rules on procedural time limits preclude the circulation of civil and commercial judgments across Member States. The chapter is divided into the three following sections addressing specific deficiencies of the interplay between national and EU law in setting time limits.

In particular, Section A examines how national rules on the time limits to react in general first instance proceedings, for opposing payment orders, for challenging judgments (appeal and cassation) and for applying for *restitutio in integrum* impact the application of Art. 45 (1)(b) (subsection I) and, in a subsidiary way of Art. 45 (1)(a) (subsection II) Brussels Ibis refusal grounds.

Section B highlights how national rules regarding the time limits for enforcing judgments (Subsection I) and the time limits which shall elapse between the service of the Art. 53 Certificate of enforceability and the first enforcement measure (subsection II) might impair the effectiveness of the scheme laid down in the Brussels Ibis regime.

Section C analyses, on the one hand, some deficiencies regarding the regulation of the uniform time limits laid down within the EPO, ESCP and EAPO procedures (subsection I) and, on the other hand, underlines how the interpretation of EU standards of review under the EEO, EPO and ESCP review procedures might be overshadowed by the application of national time limits which fill in the gap left by lacking EU legislation (subsection II).

Chapter 3 addresses the question of EU action on time limits wondering, in particular, if harmonising time limits at EU level is both feasible and desirable. The arguments are presented in three following sections.

Section A focuses on the EU legislative competence in civil procedure which under the current institutional framework insists on the two following dimensions: an horizontal one based on Art. 81 TFEU (subsection I) and a vertical one based on Art. 114 TFEU (subsection II). Subsection III then presents Art. 81 TFEU as the most appropriate legal basis for the purpose of harmonising time limits under the scope of this research.

Section B assess whether it is desirable to deal with time limits at EU level or, rather, if this constitutes a national procedural matter where EU action would not be recommended. On the one hand, arguments that speak in favour of a higher level of harmonisation are the need to promote a level playing field in the internal market and reinforce parties' fundamental procedural rights (subsection I). On the other hand, criticism relates to the advantages deriving from procedural diversity and to reasons linked to the fact that dealing with time limits means considering some procedural rules which are deeply embedded in the national traditions of each Member State (subsection II).

Once proved that a certain degree of desirability is achievable, Section C finally sheds lights on the possible policy interventions by the EU legislator when enacting legislation on time limits. The work argues in favor of an an umbrella instrument on the computation of time (subsection I) combined with an approach addressing the issues regulation by regulation rather than in general terms in order to cover the deficiencies arising under the scope of the Brussels Ibis. EEO, EPO, ESCP and EAPO Regulations (subsection II).

The conclusion captures the findings of the research. It thus answers the main research question of this work by highlighting the proposed solutions contrasting the vastly diverging national rules on time limits. It is hoped that this research will contribute to a deeper understanding of the issues which time limits entail in EU cross-border civil litigation and raise awareness of the need to address them in the future legislative developments in EU civil procedure in order to reinforce the protection of parties' fundamental rights in civil proceedings, as enshrined in Arts 47 CFR and 6 ECHR.

Chapter 1: Background, classification and function of time limits in EU civil procedure

The following analysis will provide a general overview of the historical background, classification and function of time limits in EU civil procedure.

A) Time limits within civil proceedings

Civil proceedings are a method to solve legal disputes before an impartial and independent judge. They ensure that equality of arms between parties is respected and must be conducted within a reasonable time. It follows that all the activities carried out by the parties and judge in any proceedings are strictly connected with the concept of time. Proceedings develop, indeed, as a succession of judicial powers and acts[9] set in a logical and chronological order, which aim at rendering a final judgment in order to solve a legal dispute.

Time limits structure and 'pace' the course of proceedings, thus entailing a very strict regime which strongly influences the decision of the case[10]. The judge and parties will necessarily comply with fixed time limits when, respectively, exercising their procedural rights and conducting the proceedings. Time limits are an essential tool at the service of providing structure to procedure and, they ensure, as such, that specific activities of the proceedings are carried out within, or not before, a defined period[11]. Time limits are inherent to civil proceedings and they aim at guaranteeing that all different stages of proceedings are governed by 'order and legal certainty'[12].

9 Crisanto Mandrioli and Antonio Carratta, *Diritto Processuale Civile*, vol 1 (21st edn, Giappichelli Editore, 2019), 34.

10 Jacques Héron, *Droit Judiciaire Privé* (Montchrestien 1991), para 180.

11 Paolo Biavati, *Argomenti di Diritto Processuale Civile* (5th edn, Bononia University Press 2020), 254.

12 Gérard Cornu and Jean Foyer, *Procédure Civile* (11th edn, P.U.F. 1996), 546.

I) *Punctum temporis or distantia temporis*?

Time limits are traditionally considered to be an essential element of civil proceedings[13].

The study of time limits in civil proceedings stands at a crossroad between two different meanings. On the one hand, it deals with the 'moment' or 'the unity' (a precise day, month or year) at which a particular act shall or shall not happen (*punctum temporis*); on the other hand, it relates to the 'distance' (length or period of time) between one act and another act, within which the act at stake shall happen (*distantia temporis*)[14].

It follows that the first temporal dimension, because it considers the precise moment of an act, has a static nature[15]. On the contrary, the second temporal dimension, because it deals with the succession of judicial acts in the proceedings, has dynamic characteristics and, as shown below, raises the most topical issues on procedural time limits[16].

II) Time limits as an autonomous legal tool within the proceedings

The definition of procedural time limits is disputed in legal literature. In particular, academics wonder whether time limits are formal requirements of a procedural act[17] or whether they have an autonomous legal basis.

13 This is the so called 'Teoria dei termini processuali', see Remo Caponi, *La Rimessione in Termini nel Processo Civile* (Giuffrè Editore 1996), 15; Nicola Picardi, *La Successione Processuale*, vol 1 (Giuffrè Editore 1964), 63; Nicola Picardi, 'Per una Sistemazione dei Termini Processuali' (1963) 18 IUS, 209–233; Nicola Picardi and Roberto Martino, 'Termini', *Enciclopedia Giuridica Treccani*, vol 31 (1994). On the contrary, Carlo Edoardo Balbi, *La Decadenza nel Processo di Cognizione* (Giuffrè Editore 1983), 218.

14 In the same vein, German academics refer, on the one hand to 'Zeitpunkt' or 'Termin' regarding the precise moment the act shall occur, and to 'Zeitspane' or 'Frist' to identify the temporal distance from an act within which the act shall be accomplished. See James Goldschmidt, *Zivilprozessrech*t (Springer 1932), 108 as referred to in Francesco De Santis, *La Rimessione in Termini nel Processo Civile* (Giappichelli Editore 1997), 5 fn 14.

15 The question that the legal expert has to answer is 'when (day, month, year) must the act happen?', see De Santis (n.14), 6.

16 The question that the legal expert has to answer is 'how long is the time within which the act must happen?'; see De Santis (n.14), 6.

17 De Santis (n.14), 6; Giuseppe Chiovenda, *Saggi di Diritto Processuale Civile 1894–1937* (Giuffrè Editore 1993) 353; Piero Calamandrei, *Istituzioni di Diritto Processuale*

What naturally follows from the theory that makes time limits an *id est* of procedural acts is that these acts themselves are valid or invalid depending on the expiry of time[18]. Adhering to this theory requires, first, to establish if the time limits – which are in the middle between two different acts – refer to the procedural act *ad quem* or *a quo*[19].

Where time limits are deemed to be accomplished in a *punctum temporis,* one could argue that they refer to the procedural act *a quo* to be accomplished on a fixed day[20].

On the contrary, if time limits are considered in a dynamic perspective relating to the *distantia temporis* between two acts – as will generally be the case under the scope of this research – time limits do not refer to the previous procedural act, but to the subsequent one, i.e. the *dies ad quem* in the sequence of procedural acts[21].

It follows that acts and time limits cannot coexist at the same moment. On the hand, when the act is performed there are no more time limits to comply with; on the other hand, where time limits expire, the act has not been performed yet. Thus, time limits insist on a temporal and spatial domain different from that of acts[22].

Within a dynamic procedural perspective, time limits cannot therefore be considered as formal requirements of procedural acts because the acts themselves are valid or invalid depending on the expiry of time.

On the other hand, a dynamic approach requires time limits to be considered as an autonomous legal instrument within the series of procedural acts in chronological and logical order called proceedings[23]. This stresses their key role in the structure of proceedings as they accelerate or decelerate their course[24], e.g. time limits that allow proceedings to continue even in

---

Civile, vol 1 (Cedam 1941), 161; Marco Tullio Zanzucchi, *Diritto Processuale Civile,* vol 1 (6th edn, Giuffrè Editore 1964), 433; Ugo Rocco, *Trattato di Diritto Processuale Civile* (2nd edn, UTET Giuridica 1966), 264.

18 De Santis (n.14), 7.

19 Nicola Picardi, 'Art. 152' in Enrico Allorio, *Commentario del Codice di Procedura Civile,* vol 1 book 2 (2nd edn, UTET Giuridica 1973), 1535.

20 De Santis (n.14), 8.

21 De Santis (n.14), 8.

22 De Santis (n.14), 8.

23 Picardi (n.19), 1535.

24 See Enrico Redenti, 'Atti Processuali Civili' in Francesco Calasso, Costantino Mortati, Salvatore Pugliatti, Francesco, Santoro-Passarelli, Mario Talamanca and Angelo Falzea (eds), *Enciclopedia del Diritto,* vol 4 (Giuffrè Editore 1959), 105, where he distinguishes between 'termini ordinatori' and 'termini finali o acceleratori'; Cornu

the case of inactivity by the parties or time limits establishing a minimum period between the performance of two different acts.

Under the scope of this research, time limits will thus be considered autonomously within the proceedings in order to assess how national lawmakers choose to manage time limits and civil proceedings.

B) Classification of time limits

Against this backdrop, a general classification of time limits in EU civil procedure based on their source, purpose, legal consequences, and rigid or flexible character will follow.

I) Source: legal or judicial time limits

The first distinction deals with the source of time limits. Time limits within civil proceedings could indeed be fixed either by law or on a case by case basis by the judge. This a characteristic which mainly pertains to the nature of the system at stake. In common law systems (e.g. Ireland) time limits are generally fixed by the judge on a case by case basis in the course of proceedings. On the other hand, in civil law systems – e.g. Italy[25] and France[26] – time limits within civil proceedings are, except for few specific instances, established by law.

---

and Foyer (n.12), 418 distinguish between 'delais accelerateur' and 'delais freins'. The distinction between 'Handlungfristen' and 'Zwischenfristen' exists also in German law.

25 Under Italian law, according to Art. 152 c.p.c. procedural time limits are generally fixed by law, nevertheless, where the applicable law so provides, it is up to the judge to set time limits within the proceedings.
For instance, an important category of judicial time limits deals with the taking of evidence. The Italian code of civil procedure does not establish a rigid system for accomplishing such activities, but it allows for some flexibility by giving the judge a leading role to manage the taking of evidence.
Once the first hearing has been held, the judge establishes a detailed calendar of the proceedings in order to organize the taking of evidence (Art. 81 bis disp. att.). Depending on how complex and urgent the case at stake is, the judge, once having heard parties, fixes the calendar of hearings and time limits to be complied with to enable evidence-taking activities to be accomplished.

26 Under French law, time limits within civil proceedings are established by the lawmaker, except for some exceptions mainly dealing with evidence taking. Provided that

II) Rationale: acceleratory or dilatory time limits

Depending on the function of the proceedings and the practical result being pursued, both legal and judicial time limits establish either maximum deadlines within which certain procedural activities must be accomplished ('acceleratory time limits')[27] or minimum deadlines before which certain procedural activities cannot be accomplished ('dilatory time limits')[28].

Acceleratory time limits thus fix the maximum period between two acts in the proceedings; dilatory time limits fix, instead, the minimum period[29].

The rationale of acceleratory time limits is to avoid that proceedings continue for too long due to parties' inactivity[30]. Acceleratory time limits thus aim at preventing delaying tactics and procedural abuse of rights arising from parties' inactivity within the proceedings. These time limits are therefore deemed to accelerate the course of proceedings by avoiding, as such, any possible deadlock which might undermine the effectiveness of proceedings.

For instance, the time limits for lodging an appeal on factual and legal grounds fall within the category of acceleratory time limits. The shaping of time limits for filing appeals – i.e., their length, the way of determining their starting point and the possibility of restoring them – aims at guaranteeing the correctness of judgments by combining the two following different interests. On the one hand, there is a need for finality. The *res judicata* effects of judgments cannot be pending indefinitely, but must be limited to a definite period of time so that citizens can trust the functioning of judicial

---

time limits on the taking of evidence vary in light of the specific circumstances of the case at hand, the legislator does not establish fixed time limits for accomplishing such activities, but it grants to the judge the power to set flexible time limits in each specific case. The judge therefore acts as a sort of case manager by fixing time limits for the taking of evidence on a case by case basis depending on the nature, complexity and urgency of the circumstances at hand (Art. 764 CPC). In this respect, he generally establishes a specific calendar for the proceedings (Art. 764 (3) CPC), generally agreed with parties. This regulates the taking of evidence by fixing upcoming hearings, time limits to file pleadings, the date of closing of evidence, the date of oral debates and the date of rendering of the judgment.

27 E.g. these time limits are known as 'termini acceleratori' under Italian law and 'delais d'action' under French law.

28 E.g. these time limits are known as 'termini dilatori' under Italian law and 'delais d'attente' under French law.

29 Francesco Carnelutti, *Istituzioni del Processo Civile Italiano*, vol 1 (Foro Italiano 1956), 331; Calamandrei, (n.17), 181.

30 Redenti (n.24), 138.

systems. On the other hand, parties must be granted a period of time long enough to allow them to properly assess the facts of the case at hand so they can decide whether or not to file an appeal. The expiry of these time limits therefore 'accelerate' the course of proceedings leading either to the beginning of a new instance proceedings or to the finality of the judgment.

On the contrary, dilatory time limits providing for a *terminus post quem or ne ante quem* have the objective of making two different activities far enough apart in the course of proceedings[31]. They therefore slow down the course of proceedings by establishing a waiting period which forces one party to stay inactive while granting the other party a kind of 'truce'[32]. This period encourages reflexion by the parties and must be long enough to allow them to properly manage their procedural strategy. In addition to their main function of granting parties sufficient time to organise their defences, it should be noted that dilatory time limits also set a reverse maximum deadline which contributes to ensuring the effectiveness of judicial systems.

The main example regarding dilatory time limits is the time to react[33]. This establishes a fixed period of time before which the defendant cannot make his first appearance in the proceedings. Time is 'frozen' to allow the defendant to reflect on his defence strategy. The time granted to the defendant for this purpose depends on the system involved and is related to the difficulty of the first reaction he must deal with.

III) Legal consequences: peremptory or non-peremptory time limits

Having established the distinction between acceleratory and dilatory time limits, attention now turns to the legal effects[34] on parties' rights in the

31 Redenti (n.24), 138.

32 Jacques Héron, Tristan Le Bars and Karim Salhi, *Droit Judiciaire Privé* (7th edn, LGDJ 2019), para 233.

33 See below (i) Time to react in general first instance proceedings) for a more detailed analysis on the time to react.

34 According to the dominant opinion in the literature, the distinction based on the legal effects of time limits only applies to acceleratory time limits. In light of the function pursued in the proceedings, the expiry of dilatory time limits is independent and autonomous from this classification. For instance, the expiry of the time to react ends the mandatory waiting period and allows the claimant to continue proceedings, even default ones, see Mandrioli and Carratta (n.9), 466; Biavati (n.11), 257. On a different note, Eugenio Saracini, *Il Termine e le sue Funzioni* (Giuffrè Editore 1979), 180–189 affirms that both acceleratory and dilatory time limits must have a final or non-final

proceedings which follow on from non-compliance with acceleratory time limits[35].

On the one hand, time limits are provided under penalty of waiver (the so called 'peremptory' time limits)[36]. The expiry of time thus entails irreversible final consequences for the parties by definitely preventing them – except in the case of extraordinary relief – from dealing with procedural activities at a later stage of proceedings if they are no longer admissible. This is the consequence that Member States generally attach to the expiry of time limits for lodging appeals, thus granting judgments *res judicata* and finally concluding proceedings[37]. In particular, the expiry of a time limit may produce its effects either by the immediate operation of the law ('waiver' *ope legis*), or it may require an additional decision of the court ('waiver' *ope judicis*)

On the other hand, a more flexible approach is possible as the expiry of time limits does not necessarily entail such rigid and final consequences leading to the loss of the right they serve (the so called 'non-peremptory' time limits). Indeed, parties might still be allowed to comply with their normal procedural activities, but eventually they might have to bear procedural disadvantages arising from their delayed action[38].

---

character. It does not seem therefore justified to consider the distinction between acceleratory and dilatory time limits as a third *genus*.

35 See See Picardi (n.19), 1539; Dante Grossi, 'Termine Diritto Procesuale Civile' in Francesco Calasso, Costantino Mortati, Salvatore Pugliatti, Francesco, Santoro-Passarelli, Mario Talamanca and Angelo Falzea (eds), *Enciclopedia del Diritto*, vol 44 (Giuffrè Editore 1992), 234–252; Caponi (n.13), 16; Redenti (n.24), 139; Chiara Besso and Matteo Lupano, 'Atti Processuali. Disposizioni Generali Art. 121–162' in Sergio Chiarloni (ed), *Commentario Codice di Procedura Civile* (Zanichelli Editore 2016), 608–644; Luigi Viola 'La Perentorietà Tollerante dei Termini Ordinatori' (Judicium.com 26 Septmeber 2013) https://www.judicium.it/la-perentorieta-tollerante-dei-termini-ordinatori-processuali/.

36 E.g. under Italian law, time limits provided under penalty of waiver are classified as final or peremptory time limits ('termini perentori'). The time to appeal falls *inter alia* within the category. Under French law as well, time limits for lodging appeals are provided under penalty of waiver ('forclusion').

37 See below (cc) Appeal procedures) for a more detailed analysis on the time to appeal.

38 For instance, under Italian law, time limits not provided under penalty of waiver are expressly classified as non-final time limits ('termini ordinatori'). Non-final time limits – e.g. the time limit for admitting evidence outside the court's district or the time limit for serving and communicating acts to the party in default of appearance – do not have a homogenous character which means that there are no autonomous and fixed effects connected with their expiry. It has validly been argued that sanctions are assessed on a case by case basis by the judge. On the other hand, Member States do

Notably, the peremptory or non-peremptory nature of a time limit depends on the following circumstances:

i) the element for which the time limit has been established. In particular, time limits serving powers of the parties or of the court may be or may not be peremptory; on the contrary those serving duties are never to be peremptory as an unfulfilled duty is never to vanish because of the mere elapsing of the time limit when it was meant to have been used.
ii) the will of the law-maker. It is, indeed, a political choice to decide whether the expiry of a time limit must entail the loss of a power or whether the expiry of the time limit does not entail any loss of the power at all.

C) The function of time limits in the proceedings

Against this background, it is important to underline the fundamental function that procedural time limits play in civil litigation.

All modern legal systems establish a precise timeframe to ensure the protection of procedural rights which cannot be exercised irrespective of time limits. Time limits appear to be a mere technical question, but in fact they raise much broader issues that are at the heart of civil procedure, such as dealing with case management, fairness of the proceedings, prevention of delays, efficiency of justice, and *res judicata* effects.

As clearly shown from the above, the role of time limits in the development of proceedings is crucial as they provide structure to the procedure and aim at guaranteeing that the activities of parties and judges are completed within a definite temporal period. In particular, time limits can be established, on the one hand with respect to a right or a duty of the parties and, on the other hand, with respect to a power or a duty of the court.

I) The indissoluble link between time limits and parties' rights and duties

In shaping the exercise of procedural activities by affecting parties' powers and duties, the existence of time limits marks and defines parties' rights in the proceedings

---

not generally provide for a classification of time limits not provided under penalty of waiver, they are simply embedded in the normal development of proceedings.

The law thus encourages parties to comply with time limits by providing, on the one hand, for procedural advantages when parties act within and comply with time limits and, on the other hand, imposing procedural disadvantages – e.g. waiver of some procedural rights which have negative consequences on the possibility of obtaining a favourable final judgment – when parties do not act at all or do not act in time[39]. In particular, proceedings are meant to continue either if parties deal or do not deal in time with their procedural activities based on their freedom of choice. This makes possible that proceedings will reach in any case a final effect within a reasonable time.

II) The impact of time limits on judges' activities in the proceedings

Judges when conducting the proceedings (i.e. dealing with their powers and duties) must also comply with time limits and generally render a judgment within a reasonable time[40]. However, their failures and delays cannot be sanctioned by making it impossible to exercise their procedural rights – as happens when parties do not comply with time limits – as judges are not party to the proceedings and don't have any actual interest in the proceedings[41]. This entails that *error iudici est error partis*. Effective remedies for judges' persistent inactivity might be, for instance, replacing them at the parties' request during proceedings or subjecting them to disciplinary proceedings while granting parties the right to damages[42].

III) Competing interests underlying time limits

Time limits are at a crossroad between two compelling and conflicting interests which makes it particularly cumbersome for legislators to provide rules on time limits at domestic and EU level

On the one hand, time limits are necessary to ensure the structured development of proceedings and to achieve finality of judgments, which are

39 Caponi (n.13), 17, 18.

40 Nowadays this principle is widely recognized by Arts 6 ECHR and 47 CFR.

41 Mauro Di Marzio, 'La Disciplina dei Termini' in Sergio Matteini Chiari and Mauro Di Marzio (eds), *Le Notificazioni e i Termini nel Processo Civile* (Giuffrè Editore 2019), 79.

42 Caponi (n.13), 19, 20.

both required by the public interest in legal disputes being resolved swiftly, so as not to create a source of uncertainty, or unfairness or increased costs of litigation (*interest rei publicae ut sit finis litium*). On the other hand, it is hard for a party to accept that he has lost a right just because a time limit has elapsed. In particular, it is manifestly unjust to hold a party accountable if he was unable or could not reasonably be expected to exercise his rights (assuming that he acted without any fault).

The nature of legal consequences firmly impacts both on the fairness of parties' rights in the proceedings and on formal justice: parties could take advantage of the counterparty's errors in the proceedings (e.g. non-compliance with time limits), but this could be detrimental to formal justice whose interpretation might be undermined when judicial decisions are based on such errors.

In principle, parties are able to exercise their rights when they fulfil the following conditions[43]. First, they must be able to validly assess their own conduct in the proceedings, i.e. deciding if they should act or not. Second, they must concretely be aware that the procedural right exists and understand how it can be exercised. Third, they must effectively be in the position to deal with their procedural right.

Nevertheless, it might happen that material obstacles hinder parties' procedural activities, precluding, as such, the exercise of a right. Under exceptional circumstances an application for relief restoring the rights of the party damaged can be justified.

In principle, only obstacles that a party is not responsible for, e.g. those falling within the definition of force majeure or unforeseeable circumstances, can justify an application for relief. Nevertheless, parties' conduct in the proceedings could be full of ambiguities: their inactivity could be the result of a voluntary procedural choice on their part or it could stem from facts they are not responsible for.

In particular, it is not an easy task for the judge dealing with the case to discern whether the party itself is responsible for the obstacle or whether the obstacle falls, for instance, within the meaning of force majeure or unforeseeable circumstances. Such assessment, which could arguably be based

43 Caponi (n.13), 19, 20.

on parties' 'self-responsibility'[44], presents many difficulties in national and especially in cross-border proceedings.

What emerges is that conflicting interests underlie time limits: on the one hand, the necessity to respect parties' rights and, on the other hand, the necessity for legal certainty required at two different layers: the national and the European one. All legislators try to strike a fair balance between these interests, improving in such a way the efficiency of civil proceedings. Establishing such a balance is complicated and how each country has weighed and balanced those competing interests varies considerably. A too rigid application of time limits could prevent the exercise of parties' rights, while a more extensive solution could reduce the legitimate expectations of citizens in a proper administration of justice at national and EU level.

44 The assessment by the judge must attribute to the parties the consequences of a fact which does not undermine the interests of others, but their own interests. Caponi (n.13), 19, 20.

Chapter 2: Effective judicial cooperation in civil matters and the right to a fair trial

Recently, European civil procedural law has gradually become quite predominant. The procedural systems of EU Member States are becoming increasingly coordinated and interlinked by various EU instruments.

Each Member State aims at ensuring to the greatest possible extent the efficiency, proper functioning and fairness of civil proceedings in its own legal order and in the European one. This means guaranteeing 'a due process of law (proper procedural order) that, on the one hand, secures procedural rights – including fundamental rights – and, on the other fosters procedural efficiency'[45].

When assessing the relationship between parties' interests and public concerns in the regulation of domestic and European litigation, the following guideline should be observed: 'if the interest of a polity is on the side of one party (either the plaintiff or the defendant), such a situation should not be detrimental to the essence (Wesengehalt) of the fair trial guarantee and thereby damaging to the counterparty'[46].

It follows that the basis of any procedural system should be that of fair trial. Establishing a set of clear and fair procedural rules in each Member State has significant implications not only at national level, but also for ensuring the free movement of judgments within the EU, which raises profound practical questions concerning the protection of parties' fundamental procedural rights. The principle of mutual recognition and enforcement of judgments should not result in any breach of parties' fundamental procedural rights.

The interest of the EU in strengthening and enhancing judicial cooperation in civil matters should be combined with the need to guarantee the parties' right to a fair trial in the proceedings, as envisaged by Art. 6 ECHR and Art. 47 CFR. The creation of an effective regime for the free movement

---

45 Xandra Kramer, 'The Structure of Civil Proceedings and Why it Matters: Exploratory Observations on Future ELI-UNIDROIT European Rules of Civil Procedure' (2014) 19 Unif. L. Rev., 218.

46 Remo Caponi, 'Transnational Litigation and Elements of Fair Trial' in Peter Gottwald and Burkhard Hess (eds), *Procedural Justice* (Gieseking 2014), 507.

of civil judgments across the Member States requires striking a balance between the protection of parties' rights in the proceedings and facilitation of recognition and enforcement formalities: 'a true internal market between ... the States will be achieved only if adequate legal protection can be secured'[47].

Apart from a few exceptions, it is up to the Member States to regulate time limits. Each Member State has its own specific rules on time limits, which underlie a tension in the proceedings between parties' rights and legal certainty. Some systems are more rigid as they tend to have one-size-fits-all time limits, while others allow a more tailored organisation of deadlines. Each legislation establishes its own balance between the interests at hand, managing differently the efficiency of civil proceedings. Solutions vary widely between Member States systems: 'the disparity may refer to the starting point of the computation of time; the expiration of time periods; the reciprocal effect of service; the calculation of calendar years, months and weeks; the relevance of intermediate legal holidays ('clear' versus unqualified days); the extension or abridgment of time; the impact of force majeure on time limits'[48].

In this respect, the lack of uniformity regarding some time limits is 'eminently counter-productive to the smooth functioning of an integrated market'[49] and might represent a practical hurdle for foreign litigants when different national systems interact at the EU level. This might hamper their access to justice in cross-border civil proceedings and prevent the achievement of the objectives put forth by EU instruments.

Time limits must comply with the standards of protection of due process embedded in Art. 6 ECHR and Art. 47 CFR[50]: the length, starting point, interruption, and suspension of time limits in the proceedings must allow parties to effectively exercise their rights. Where, on the contrary, rules on time limits entail a breach of parties' procedural rights, this stifles the free circulation of civil judgments within the EU.

---

47 Paul Jenard, 'Report on the Convention on Jurisdiction and the Enforcement of Judgments in Civil and Commercial Matters (Signed at Brussels, 27 September 1968)' (1979) OJ C-59/1.

48 Konstantinos Kerameus, 'Political Integration and Procedural Convergence in the European Union' (1997) 45 Am. J. Comp. L., 927, 928.

49 Kerameus (n.48), 928.

50 The importance of Art. 47 CFR for judicial cooperation in civil matters increased with the entry into force of the Lisbon Treaty which granted to the CFR a full normative status.

What emerges is that time limits play a key role in strengthening and reinforcing judicial cooperation in civil matters: setting clear and reasonable rules on time limits in a cross-border scenario could increase the level of protection of parties' rights in the proceedings, so favouring a swift free circulation of judgments across the Member States.

Against this background, some paradigmatic examples as to how time limits can practically hinder judicial cooperation in civil matters will follow. These examples will prove that setting and defining time limits is currently a topical issue in European civil litigation and will give insights on some of the recurrent problems that time limits entail for the recognition and enforcement of judgments between the Member States.

In particular, some sensitive issues which time limits raise in cross-border civil litigation will be looked at under the scope of the Brussels Ibis, EEO, EPO, ESCP and EAPO Regulations[51].

First, it should be noted that under the Brussels I*bis* Regulation decisions are recognized and enforceable *ipso iure* within the territory of the EU, without any special procedure being required (Art. 39)[52]: decisions given by the courts of any Member State are automatically enforceable in the territory of the EU[53].

Notwithstanding an intense discussion in the literature about the review of the Brussels I Regulation, the Recast maintains the possibility for the debtor to attack the judgment at the enforcement stage on grounds of non-recognition (Arts 45 and 46)[54]. While these grounds are the same as previously provided under the Brussels I Regulation, in contrast to the former regime, in the context of the Brussels I*bis* Regulation it is the inter-

51 The EEO, EPO, ESCP and EAPO Regulations are known in academia as the so-called 'second generation' of EU Regulations, see Burkhard Hess, 'The State of the Justice Union' in Burkhard Hess, Maria Bergström and Eva Storskrubb (eds), *EU Civil Justice Current Issues and Future Outlook* (Bloomsbury 2016), 1–4.

52 This regime has replaced the one provided by the Brussels Convention and the Brussels I Regulation, which were based on a simple, harmonised, intermediate procedure to obtain a declaration of enforceability in the Member State where enforcement was sought (i.e., the *exequatur* procedure).

53 Regarding its territorial scope, the Brussels Ibis Regulation applies between all Member States of the EU including Denmark. See Agreement between the European Community and the Kingdom of Denmark on jurisdiction and the recognition and enforcement of judgments in civil and commercial matters (2005) OJ L299.

54 The choice by the EU legislator to retain the grounds of refusal in the enforcement stage as a safeguard for the protection of parties' rights, as enshrined in Arts 6 ECHR and 47 CFR, depends on the fact that the Brussels Ibis regime operates with respect to different national judicial systems (and not to a uniform procedure).

ested party who has to apply for a refusal of recognition or enforcement in the requested Member State.

On the other hand, the second generation instruments are based on the same basic principle[55]: once a title has been obtained within these uniform and harmonised procedures[56], it can be directly enforced in other EU Member States[57] without any traditional ground available to refuse its enforcement[58]. Instead of providing the possibility to apply for refusal in the enforcement State, these instruments entrust the courts of the Member State of origin with the task of checking whether the rights of the defence have been guaranteed.

Against this backdrop, time limits will be analysed as follows.

Issues dealing with the time to react (also including the time to oppose the issuance of payment orders) arise from the notion of sufficient time under Art. 45 (1)(b) Brussels I*bis* Regulation.

Similar issues regarding the time limits for challenging judgments emerge from the second part of Art. 45 (1)(b) which aims at checking that defendants were granted an effective opportunity to challenge judgments in the Member State of origin.

Moreover, Art. 45 (1)(a) could exceptionally encompass issues on time limits preventing recognition and enforcement of judgments.

Further issues dealing with time limits concern the interactions between national time limits and the Brussels Ibis enforcement regime (Arts. 39–44). In particular, some questions regarding the time limits to proceed to the enforcement of foreign judgments and the time limits which shall elapse between the service of an Art. 53 Certificate and the first enforcement measure will be analysed.

On the other hand, some deficiencies on the setting and practical application of time limits could emerge under the scope of the second generation Regulations.

---

55 Michele Angelo Lupoi, 'Di Crediti non Contestati e Procedimenti di Ingiunzione: le Ultime Tappe dell'Armonizzazione Processuale in Europa' (2008) 71 Riv. trim. dir. e proc. civ., 174.

56 In particular, the EEO permits the cross-border direct enforcement of uncontested claims (especially of default judgments); the EPO addresses the cross-border enforcement of monetary contractual claims; the ESCP contains a procedure for all civil claims below € 5,000 and the EAPO allows to freeze funds held in bank accounts that are located in several Member States.

57 Regarding their territorial scope, these Regulations apply in all EU countries except Denmark.

58 See nevertheless Art. 21 EEO; Art. 22 EPO and Art. 22 ESCP.

First, the application of the uniform time limits within the EPO, ESCP and EAPO procedures could raise issues regarding the lack of protection of defendants' rights in cross-border civil litigation.

Second, the uniform setting and national pre-understandings of time limits within the EEO, EPO and ESCP review proceedings could entail deficiencies and inconsistencies under the scope of these EU instruments.

A) Time limits and grounds for refusal under the Brussels Ibis Regulation

I) Time limits and default judgments under Art. 45 (1)(b)

Art. 45 (1)(b) Brussels Ibis Regulation, read in conjunction with Art. 6 ECHR and Art. 47 CFR, provides for a ground of refusal of recognition and enforcement which specifically aims at protecting defendant's procedural rights with regard to judgments issued in default proceedings[59]. Such refusal ground applies where the two following cumulative conditions are met: the defendant 'was not served with the document instituting the proceedings or with an equivalent document in sufficient time and in such a way as to enable him to arrange for his defence, and he did not fail 'to commence proceedings to challenge the judgment when it was possible for him to do so'.

The objective of Art. 45 (1)(b) is to guarantee that the defendant has been able to properly organize his defence in the Member State of origin even when judgments have been rendered *in absentia*.

In this respect, Art. 45 (1)(b) refers to an autonomous definition of default judgments. In particular, judgments given in default of appearance are those judicial decisions rendered without the legal participation – either in person or through a representative – of the defendant[60]. This definition, as

59 Art. 45 (1)(b) finds its origin in Art. 34 (2) Brussels I Regulation and Art. 27 (2) Brussels Convention. The importance of this ground for refusal of recognition and enforcement has been stressed by Burkhard Hess, Thomas Pfeiffer and Peter Schlosser, *The Brussels I-Regulation (EC) No 44/2001: The Heidelberg Report on the Application of Regulation Brussels I in 25 Member States (Study JLS/C4/2005/03)* (Beck 2008), 239 which affirms that 'in practice, the most important provision for objecting to the recognition of a foreign judgment is still Art. 34 (2)' (now repealed in its new version in Art. 45 (1) (b)). This provision mainly applies to default judgments, which occur frequently in the European Judicial Area.

60 See Vincent Richard, *Le Jugement par Défaut dans l'Espace Judiciaire Européen* (Droit Université Panthéon-Sorbonne – Paris I 2019), 28–41; Chiara Enrica Tuo,

interpreted by the CJEU in its settled case law[61], also encompasses payment order procedures, which are considered in European law to be a particular type of default judgment[62].

Against this backdrop it should be noted that time limits underlie a very sensitive balance between the defendant's rights and legal certainty, which entails relevant implications for the recognition and enforcement of default judgments under the Brussels Ibis regime.

As we will see below, rules on time limits firmly impact on the assessment which courts make when verifying the requirements for applying the Art. 45 (1)(b) refusal ground. Art. 45 (1)(b) insists on two different layers, thus leading courts to check, on the one hand, if the defendant has been granted effective and adequate time limits to properly defend himself and to challenge judgments and, on the other hand, if the expiry of these time limits was or was not the defendant's fault. Based on this assessment, courts will refuse recognition and enforcement of default judgments under Art. 45 (1)(b) when both the defendant was not given enough time to properly organize his defences and the expiry of time limits was involuntary, i.e. he did not have any effective possibility to challenge the judgment in the Member State of origin.

1) Service of the documents instituting the proceedings

According to the text of Art. 45 (1)(b), the court of the Member State where recognition and enforcement of a judgment is being sought should check, first, that the defendant was effectively served with the document instituting the proceedings or with an equivalent document 'in sufficient time and in such a way' as to enable him to adequately prepare his defence.

As a preliminary condition, it should be noted that the meaning of documents instituting the proceedings or equivalent documents is autonomously defined under the scope of Art. 45 (1)(b).

La Rivalutazione della Sentenza Straniera nel Regolamento Bruxelles I: tra Divieti e Reciproca Fiducia (Cedam 2012), 174–186.

61 In particular, see Case C-166/80 *Peter Klomps v Karl Michel* (1981) EU:C:1981:137; Case C-474/93 *Hengst Import BV v Anna Maria Campese* (1995) EU:C:1995:243.

62 See Richard (n.60), 44–55; Claudio Consolo, 'La Tutela Sommaria e la Convenzione di Bruxelles: la "Circolazione" Comunitaria dei Provvedimenti Cautelari e dei Decreti Ingiuntivi' (1991) 27 RDIPP 593–626; Janek Nowak and Vincent Richard, 'Art. 45' in Marta Requejo Isidro (ed), *Brussels I Bis. A Commentary on Regulation (EU) No 1215/2012* (Edward Elgar Publishing 2022), para 45.17.

Notably, the three following criteria established by the CJEU in its case law[63] are used to identify documents instituting the proceedings: 'first, the documents must be served on the defendant before an enforceable judgment is given; second, they must enable the defendant to understand the content of the claim and, third, they must enable the defendant to understand that the documents are of a legal nature and that legal proceedings have been initiated against him'[64].

a) Effective service

The original version of the 1968 Brussels Convention in Art. 27 (2) provided that the document instituting the proceedings had to be duly served and in sufficient time for the defendant to organise his defence. These two conditions were independent and cumulative: the CJEU in its case law considered that recognition and enforcement should be refused where service was not duly effected – i.e. made lawfully – even when the defendant became aware of the proceedings in sufficient time to organize his defence. This requirement gave rise to extensive discussion in legal literature as it was particularly 'difficult to conduct and led to the refusal of recognition to many default judgments, which sometimes led to rewarding avoidance strategies employed by defendants'[65]. In light of this, the EU legislator removed the latter requirement from the text of Art. 34 (2) of the Brussels I Regulation and it also does not appear in the Brussels Ibis Regulation. What arises from the amended provisions and from CJEU case law is that Arts 34 (2) and 45 (1)(b) do not necessarily require the document which instituted the proceedings to be duly served but they do require that the rights of the defence are 'effectively respected'[66].

It would appear then that the effective and adequate organization of the right of defence in the Member State of origin depends on the manner and

63 See *Hengst Import* (n.61); Case C-14/07 *Ingenieurbüro Michael Weiss und Partner GbR v Industrie- und Handelskammer Berlin* (2008) EU:C:2008:264.

64 Nowak and Richard, (n.62), para 45.19.

65 Nowak and Richard, (n.62), para 45.20.

66 Case C-283/05, *ASML Netherlands BV v Semiconductor Industry Services GmbH (SEMIS)*, (2006) EU:C:2006:787; Elena D' Alessandro, 'Irregolare Notifica del Decreto Ingiuntivo e Possibilità di Invocare, nello Stato Richiesto dell'Esecuzione, il Motivo di Diniego di Riconoscimento di cui all'Art. 34 n. 2 Reg. n. 44/2001: il Punto di Vista del Bundesgerichtshof Tedesco, Nota a BGH, Beschluss 21 Gennaio 2010 – IX ZB 193/07' (2010) 3/4 INT'L LIS, 144.

timeliness of service of the claim: the service of the document instituting the proceedings must be effected according to Art. 45 'in sufficient time and in such a way as to enable him to arrange for his defence'.

The latter modifications aim at ensuring that 'a mere formal irregularity in the service will not debar recognition or enforcement if it has not prevented the debtor from arranging for his defence'[67]. By removing the condition of due service, the Regulation abandoned the legal analysis and kept only the factual one: the court of the requested State is thus bound neither by the provisions of the law of the State of origin nor by the time limit rules of its own legislation[68].

b) Sufficient time

Addressing the question of sufficient time requires striking a balance between the two following contrasting interests: on the one hand, ensuring a rapid and efficient cross-border debt recovery and, on the other hand, preserving the right of defence.

What matters in the analysis of the court in the requested State is that the defendant was granted *in concreto* a period of time long enough to enable him to arrange for his defence. Art. 45 (1)(b) Brussels Ibis does not fix rigid deadlines to react, but adopts instead a flexible approach based on the notion of 'sufficient time'.

In assessing this requirement, the court considers the time elapsed between the service of the lawsuit and the first hearing or the time running until the issue of a default judgment. This assesment thus focusses on domestic time limits to react[69], i.e. those time limits governing the entering of appearance of the defendant and eventually the submission of his first statement of defence.

Whether the time granted is sufficient to enable the defendant to organise his defences is a question of fact left to a case-by-case determination by

---

67 As affirmed by the Commission in the Proposal for a Regulation of the European Parliament and of the Council on jurisdiction and the recognition and enforcement of judgments in civil and commercial matters COM 20110/0748 final 23.

68 Case C-49/84, *Leon Emile Gaston Carlos Debaecker and Berthe Plouvier v Cornelis Gerrit* Bouwman (1985) EU:C:1985:252, para 27.

69 It should be noted that the time for the defendant's first reaction refers both to the time to react in general first instance proceedings and to the time to oppose the issuance of payment orders.

the adjudicating court. Factual and legal circumstances vary from jurisdiction to jurisdiction among Member States. This situation reflects the high diversity of rules on time limits for the first reaction by the defendant within the EU, which can be an obstacle to the free circulation of judgments[70].

The requested court thus checks both the defendant's and claimant's conduct in the proceedings by making a sort of analysis of parties' burden of proof[71] in order to determine if the defendant is responsible or not for his lack of appearance[72].

In this regard, specific difficulties arise from Member States' domestic case law in deciding if the deadline granted to the defendant in the Member State of origin can be considered sufficient from the perspective of the Member State of enforcement. Even if the enforcement court carries out only an indirect review of foreign time limits without applying them directly, its general pre-understanding is certainly determined by the perspective on time limits in its own jurisdiction.

Against this backdrop, practical issues in assessing and interpreting the notion of sufficient time under Art. 45 (1)(b) might arise with regard to the *dies a quo,* expiry and length and of the time to react.

aa) *Dies a quo* of the time to react

The adjudicating court has to assess the actual date on which the documents were served on the defendant for the purpose of Art. 45 (1)(b) – notwithstanding the legal date of service indicated by the court of origin – which marks the *dies a quo* of the time to react.

According to CJEU settled case law[73], what matters when assessing the above date is to check if the defendant could defend his case from the beginning of the proceedings, not the possibility of contesting an enforceable decision already adopted after a unilateral procedure[74].

---

70 E.g. the length of the time to react under Italian and French law varies widely and this depends on the factual and legal circumstances at hand in each system, see below bb) The time to react.

71 See Richard (n.60), 412.

72 *Debaecker* (n.68).

73 Klomps (n.61), paras 9 and 10; Case C-123/91 *Minalmet GmbH v Brandeis Ltd* (1991) EU:C:1992:432, para 19.

74 Peter Mankowski, 'Art. 45' in Ulrich Magnus and Peter Mankowski (eds), *Commentary Brussels I bis Regulation* (2nd edn, Ottoschmidt 2023), para 51.

In particular, to comply with the right of defence under the Brussels Ibis Regulation, the time to react starts to run from the date on which the defendant is (or is supposed to have been) validly served with the claim at his habitual residence or elsewhere, even in public. The date on which the defendant receives (or is supposed to have received) the documents instituting the proceedings and thus becomes aware of them, is crucial.

Nevertheless, it should be noted that under these conditions some issues arise when courts serving a document abroad either according to national law or under the scope of the Service Regulation Recast[75] have to determine the date on which the defendant was served with the claim under Art. 45 (1)(b).

i) *Dies a quo* under national law

In spite of national general rules calculating this date from the day on which the document is validly served on the defendant, under some systems the judge could take into account another *dies a quo,* e.g. the date on which the documents are sent, or the date when the documents are deemed to have been served a certain number of days after they are sent. In such a case, the date of service to be taken into account under of Art. 45 (1)(b) is 'when the defendant received the document, and it could be completely different from the legal date of service in the country of origin'[76].

Similarly, when the date of service is the date on which the documents were received by a third person and not by the defendant himself – when this third person is not entitled to receive documents on behalf of the

75 Regulation (EU) 2020/1784 of the European Parliament and of the Council of 25 November 2020 on the service in the Member States of judicial and extrajudicial documents in civil or commercial matters (service of documents) (recast) (2020) OJ L 405. This Regulation recently recasted Regulation (EC) 1393/2007 of the European Parliament and of the Council of 13 November 2007 on the service in the Member States of judicial and extrajudicial documents in civil or commercial matters (service of documents), and repealing Council Regulation (EC) 1348/2000 (2007) OJ L 324. The rules concerning the service of judicial and extrajudicial documents in civil and commercial matters within the EU also apply to Denmark, see Agreement between the European Community and the Kingdom of Denmark on the service of judicial and extrajudicial documents in civil or commercial matters (2005) OJ L 300,

76 Nowak and Richard (n.62), para 45.21.

defendant – 'the date of reception may not be considered as the actual date of service for the purpose of Art. 45(1)b)'[77].

ii) *Dies a quo* under the Service Regulation Recast

Further issues in determining the *dies a quo* of time limits under Art. 45 (1)(b) might emerge when a document is served abroad under the scope of the Service Regulation Recast. In this regard, the interpretation of Arts 12 and 13 of the Service Regulation Recast might be problematic.

α) Date of service under Art. 13[78]

The Service Regulation Recast does not establish a formal date of service. Instead, Art. 13 (1) only provides for a conflict-of-laws rule according to which the date of service 'shall be the date on which the document was served in accordance with the law of the Member State addressed'.

The defendant will therefore receive notification of the claim according to the law of the Member State addressed. However, this rule might be problematic to the extent that it leads the authorities of the State of origin effecting service to deal with some foreign procedural rules that might raise some sensitive issues of interpretation.

For instance, the rule in Art. 13 (1) of the Service Regulation Recast might raise some interpretative doubts in those systems laying down different rules for domestic and cross-border service. When the service of documents has to be carried out in Luxembourg, for example, the foreign authorities must opt for one of the two following dates provided for under Luxembourgish law. The court could consider that service was carried out either on the date the defendant was effectively served – in accordance with the rule applicable to domestic service ('remise en main propre') under Art. 155 (3) NCPC – or it could take into account the date on which the documents were dispatched – in accordance with the rule applicable to international service set out in Art. 156 (2) NCPC. The application of the

77 Nowak and Richard (n.62), para 45.21.

78 Art. 13 of the Service Regulation Recast replaced Art. 9 without introducing any substantial change regarding the conflict of laws rule. See Vincent Richard, 'La Refonte du Règlement sur la Notification des Actes Judiciaires et Extrajudiciaires' (2021) 111 RCDIP, 357.

latter rule would shorten the defendant's time to react: the time required to practically carry out the service would unreasonably be apportioned on defendant's side, thus, reducing the effective length of the time to react provided by law[79].

It follows that Art. 13 (1) might raise issues of compatibility under the scope of the Brussels Ibis Regulation where the enforcement court, on the basis of the lack of sufficient time to react, might uphold the Art. 45 (1)(b) refusal ground and deny recognition and enforcement of the foreign judgments.

In light of the foregoing, when the claim is served cross-border according to the Service Regulation, doubts about the starting point of the time to react might emerge, thus negatively impacting both on the organisation of the defendant's defence and on the assessment which courts make when applying the Art. 45 (1)(b) Brussels Ibis refusal ground.

β) Art. 12

Some sensitive questions regarding the *dies a quo* of the time limits to refuse service of a document under Art. 8 of the Service Regulation (now replaced by Art. 12 of the Service Regulation Recast) arose in the case *C-7/21 LKW Walter*[80].

In 2019, a Slovenian court issued a default enforcement order against an Austrian company, based on authentic documents, written in Slovenian. The debtor's lawyers lodged their opposition 12 days after the order was received, thus failing to comply with the 8 days Slovenian time limit. When the opposition was rejected, the Austrian company sued its lawyers before the competent Austrian court for professional misconduct. The lawyers argued that the Slovenian time limit was incompatible with EU law. The Austrian court submitted a request for a preliminary ruling before the CJEU. The referring court asked, in essence, whether the starting point and the length of the Slovenian time limit granted to foreign defendants for opposing a national enforcement order issued *in abstentia* violated

79 Richard (n.60), 140; Thierry Hoscheit, 'La Transmission des Actes vers l'Étranger' (2013) 28 Journal des tribunaux (Luxembourg), 89.

80 Case C-7/21 *LKW WALTER Internationale Transportorganisation AG v CB and Others* (2022) EU:C:2022:527.

Art. 45 (1)(b)[81], 46 of the Brussels Ibis Regulation, or Art. 8 of the Service Regulation[82], read in conjunction with Art. 47 CFR, or the principle of non-discrimination laid down in Art. 18 TFEU.

The reasoning of the CJEU is premised on the addressee's right to refuse service of a document written in a language that he does not understand either at the time of service or within 1 week[83], under Art. 8 Service Regulation, as forming part of his fundamental rights of defense, whose effective judicial protection must be ensured pursuant to Art. 47 CFR.

The Court noted that the starting point of the Slovenian time limit and of the time limit to refuse service of a document practically overlapped. According to the Court, this prevented the addressee from fully and effectively enjoying both procedural rights in accordance with Art. 47 CFR, as he was not able to devote the whole respective 8 days and 1 week period to the exercise of these distinct rights.

The Court also held that, regardless of the duration of the time limit to oppose the enforcement order, the overlapping of the starting point of the two time limits leads to discriminatory effects between national and foreign parties. Foreign addressees who do not understand the language of the document served must not only file their opposition – as national addressees do – but also assess their right to refuse service. This places foreigners at a procedural disadvantage contrary to the objective of avoiding any discrimination between those two categories of addressees, pursuant to Art. 8 (1) Service Regulation.

The Court also underlined that, by allowing the starting point of the two time limits to overlap, parties could be encouraged to refuse service of the documents to automatically gain some time for their defence. However, this

81 In particular, the following question, as reformulated by AG Pikamae, arises with regard to Art. 45 (1)(b): is the Slovenian time limit granted to foreign defendants for opposing a national enforcement order issued *in abstentia* long enough to ensure the defendants' rights under Art. 45 (1)(b) are respected? See Opinion of AG Pikamäe Case C-7/21 *LKW WALTER Internationale Transportorganisation AG v CB and Others* (2022) EU:C:2022:185.

82 In particular, the following question regarding Art. 8 of the Service Regulation, read in conjunction with Art. 47 CFR arises: when documents instituting the proceedings are served in a language that addressees do not understand, does the Slovenian time limit granted to foreign defendants to oppose a national enforcement order issued *in abstentia* start to run on the day of its service on the addressee or after the expiry of the 1 week time limit provided for in Art. 8 of the Service Regulation for refusing to accept the document to be served?

83 It should be noted that this time limit has been extended by Art. 12 of the Service Regulation Recast to 2 weeks.

contradicts one objective of the Service Regulation which is to facilitate the expedited transmission of documents.

The Court concluded – contrary to AG Pikamäe's opinion[84] – that Art. 8 Service Regulation, read in conjunction with Art. 47 CFR, precludes national legislation providing that the 1 week time limit to refuse service of a document starts to run at the same time as the national time limit for filing remedies against that document.

A general rule arises from the present judgment: when documents instituting the proceedings are served in a language that addressees do not understand, domestic time limits for seeking remedies against these documents should not begin to run as long as the 1 week period provided for in Art. 8 of the Service Regulation has not expired. Such rule applies irrespective of whether the law of the Member State of origin already provides more favourable rules to compensate for linguistic deficiencies in cross-border cases.

This ruling has very broad implications at the national level, in that it will likely lead Member States to reconsider the setting of their domestic time limits to file remedies when parties are served with a document instituting the proceedings drafted in a language they do not understand[85]. The effects on national time limits are set to be even more important as the deadline for refusing the document has been recently extended to 2 weeks by Art. 12 of the Service Regulation Recast.

84 According to AG's opinion, it generally arises from Arts 8 and 9 of the Service Regulation, read in conjunction with Art. 47 CFR, that if the addressee is aware and does not voluntarily exercise his right to refuse to accept the service of documents instituting the proceedings, time limits for seeking remedies start running from the date on which documents are effectively served on the addressee. The right of defence is indeed already ensured by the possibility granted to the addressee to refuse the service of a document written in a language he does not understand. In the case at hand, there was therefore no need to postpone the *dies a quo* of the Slovenian time limit, See Opinion of AG Pikamäe *LKW Walter* (n.81), para 51.

85 Giovanni Chiapponi, 'Postponing the *Dies a Quo* of Domestic Time Limits to Ensure Effectiveness of the Right to Refuse Service of Documents: Some Insights from LKW WALTER (C-7/21)' (EU Law Live 27 July 2022) https://eulawlive.com/analysis-postponing-the-dies-a-quo-of-domestic-time-limits-to-ensure-effectiveness-of-the-right-to-refuse-service-of-documents-some-insights-from-lkw-walter-c-7-21-by-giovanni-ch/.

bb) Expiry of the time to react

When checking if the defendant has been granted sufficient time under Art. 45 (1)(b), requested courts must consider the *dies ad quem* of the time limits to react.

Time limits to react generally expire on the date defendants must enter their first appearance in the proceedings[86], e.g. when the defendant must appoint his lawyer, appear before the court, file his defences or oppose payment orders[87]. Nevertheless, in some proceedings this date does not represent a peremptory time limit, provided that late appearances before the judge can still be taken into account.

In any case, these time limits expire when the judgment is rendered[88].

cc) The length of the time to react

Once the *dies a quo* and *dies ad quem* of time limits to react are determined, the adjudicating court must concretely verify on a case by case basis if these time limits are long enough to ensure the defendant's procedural rights under Art. 45 (1)(b), read in conjunction with Art. 47 CFR.

This check on the sufficiency of time, other than from the length of time limits themselves, depends on the legal and factual circumstances currently at stake in each specific case, i.e. which activities of defence the defendant could file to validly exercise his right of defence[89].

---

86 For further details on the rules governing defendants' first appeareance in different systems see below bb) The time to react.

87 With respect to payment order proceedings, the CJEU ruled in *Klomps* that the requested judge, when considering if the defendant has been granted sufficient time to react under Art. 45 (1)(b), shall only take into account the time limits for submitting an objection to the payment order ('Widerspruch') available to the defendant for the purposes of preventing the issue of a judgment in default which is enforceable under the Brussels Ibis regime. See *Klomps* (n.61), paras 9 and 10.

88 In this respect, it should be noted that time limits for challenging judgments are deemed to be excluded from the latter analysis of the judge. See Richard (n.60), 410; Nowak and Richard (n.62), para 45.26; on the contrary Wendy Kennet, 'Reviewing Service: Double Check or Double Fault' (1992) 11 C.J.Q., 115.

89 E.g. short time limits can be justified where a simple opposition without any further motivation is required to contest a payment order; on the other hand longer time limits can be required for appointing a foreign lawyer or filing defences under foreign law. Richard (n.60), 410.

For instance[90], the court could take into account the fact that the defendant actually appeared in the proceedings[91], even if service was irregular[92]; or the fact that the parties knew or should have known the foreign time limit since they opted for the application of foreign law, even if such time limit was very short if compared to the one under domestic procedural law[93]; or the fact that that the defendant should have been granted the time to ask for a translation of the document instituting the proceedings which was drafted in a foreign language[94].

Against this backdrop, it should be noted that numerous national court decisions exist on the sufficiency or insufficiency of the time limits for the defendant to submit his first reaction. What generally follows is that a period of 1 month is held, in principle, to be sufficient for the foreign defendant to prepare his defences; however, it seems that a period of time shorter than 10 days is insufficient for the protection of the rights of the defendant domiciled abroad[95].

---

90 Francesca Villata, Lidia Sandrini, Marco Farina, Gabriele Molinaro, Valeria Giugliano, Michele Casi and Denisa Docaj, *Report on Italian Case-Law in Towards More Effective EnFORcemenT of ClaimS in Civil and Commercial Matters within the EU EFFORTS (Project JUST-JCOO-AG-2019-881802)*, 34.

91 Italian Supreme Court 18–11–2016, n. 23561; Cour of Appeal of Metz 20.03.2018, n. 16/04164. See Villata, Sandrini, Farina, Molinaro, Giugliano, Casi and Docaj (n.90), 34; Marco Buzzoni, *Report on National Case-Law: France in Towards More Effective EnFORcemenT of ClaimS in Civil and Commercial Matters within the EU EFFORTS (Project JUST-JCOO-AG-2019–881802)*, 11.

92 Court of Appeal of Milan 26.04.2010 in (2010) 46 RDIPP, 764. See Villata, Sandrini, Farina, Molinaro, Giugliano, Casi and Docaj (n.90).

93 Italian Supreme Court 16.07.2014, n. 16272. See Villata, Sandrini, Farina, Molinaro, Giugliano, Casi and Docaj (n.90), 18, 19.

94 Court of appeal of Lyon 18–04–1978 with case note of Dominique Holleaux (1979) JDI, 380; See Richard (n.60), 410 fn. 1925.

95 See the list of cases ranging from 1978 to 2000 in Alexander Layton and Hugh Mercer, *European Civil Practice*, vol 1 (2nd edn, Thomson, Sweet and Maxwell 2004), para 26.039; see also the list of German case law referred to in Fernando Gascón Inchausti and Marta Requejo Isidro, 'A Classic Cross-border Case: the Usual Situation in the First Instance' in Burkhard Hess and Pietro Ortolani (eds), *Impediments of National procedural Law to the Free Movement of Judgments* (Beck-Hart-Nomos 2019), para 136 fn 82; Richard (n.60), 411 fn. 1927; see also the list of cases referred to in Villata, Sandrini, Farina, Molinaro, Giugliano, Casi and Docaj (n.90); Buzzoni (n.91).

dd) Practical cases on the lack of sufficient time

Some practical examples will follow in order to show how under specific circumstances national courts might consider time limits to react insufficient for protecting defendants' rights under Art. 45 (1)(b).

i) *LKW Walter*: open question on the length of the time limit

In addition to the issue described above under Art. 8 of the Service Regulation, some doubts existed on the compliance of the 8 days Slovenian time limit with Art. 45 (1)(b) Brussels Ibis read in conjunction with Art. 47 CFR arose in *LKW Walter*.

Nevertheless, the Court, contrary to AG Pikamäe[96], did not rule on the compatibility of the Slovenian time limit with Art 45 (1)(b) Brussels Ibis Regulation. It can be argued that the Court's choice not to answer this question was due to its hypothetical character: given the applicant decided to settle his debt in Slovenia, no enforcement proceedings were initiated in Austria against the final enforcement order.

Hence, the question whether an 8 days time limit to oppose the issuance of a default enforcement order complies with Art. 45 (1)(b) Brussels Ibis Regulation, interpreted in the light of Art. 47 CFR, remains open, just when

96 AG Pikamae considered that in light of the complex character of the circumstances at hand in Slovenian opposition proceedings, the 8 days Slovenian time limit was deemed to be too short to effectively protect the exercise of the right of defence. In addition, the AG further justified his conclusions by referring to and establishing a comparison with the *Profi Credit Polska* judgment where the CJEU ruled that a 2 weeks time limit granted under Polish law to consumers for lodging a reasoned statement of opposition against payment orders did not comply with Directive 93/13/EEC as it made excessively difficult the exercise of consumers' right of defence. The AG indicated that similar circumstances were at stake in *LKW Walter*. According to his view the fact that in *LKW Walter* the payment order was not addressed against a consumer, but against a business company did not change the final outcome. In light of these arguments, AG Pikamae considered that the 8 days Slovenian time limit (even shorter than the Polish one) combined with the alleged complexity of Slovenian opposition proceedings (the conditions for opposing payment orders are very similar to the Polish ones) was deemed to be too short to effectively protect the exercise of the right of defence. The insufficiency of the Slovenian time limit to oppose payment orders would therefore justify refusal of recognition and enforcement of foreign judgments under Art. 45 (1)(b) Brussels Ibis, read in conjunction with Art. 47 CFR. Opinion of AG Pikamäe *LKW Walter* (n.81), paras 69–93; Case C-176–17 *Profi Credit Polska S.A. w Bielsku Białej v Mariusz Wawrzosek* (2018) EU:C:2018:711.

the Court's reply to this topical issue currently affecting EU cross-border litigation, would be more than welcome[97].

Let's slightly modify the facts at hand in *LKW Walter* to make the preliminary ruling admissible and deal with the question of sufficient time *in concreto*. Let's imagine that enforcement proceedings have been initiated in Austria and the defendant applied for refusal of recognition and enforcement. Under these circumstances the preliminary ruling would be admissible allowing the CJEU to interpret Art. 45 (1)(b).

What matters here is to verify if Slovenian rules on time limits to oppose the issuance of payment orders ensure effective exercise of the defendant's rights or if, on the contrary, they preclude or make excessively difficult the exercise of their right to lodge an opposition.

The assessment on the question of sufficient time thus needs to deal, first, with the structure of opposition proceedings under Slovenian law, i.e. which activities of defence shall be carried out to validly contest and prove the inadmissibility of the claim.

In particular, under Slovenian law, opposition proceedings to contest payment orders are structured as follows: opposition must be justified by legally significant facts and evidence, otherwise it shall be deemed to be unfounded; representation by a lawyer is optional and decided by the defendant depending on the complexity of the case; the payment of some judicial fees is required by law to proceed.

It follows that for the foreign addressee to validly oppose the Slovenian payment order, he shall within the 8 days Slovenian time limit (Art. 9 ZIZ) accomplish the following activities of defence: become aware of the served documents, decide to appoint a lawyer or not, pay judicial fees required by law to proceed, flie his defences, eventually ask for the translation of some documents, and finally lodge a statement of opposition justified by facts and proofs. Lodging an opposition under Slovenian law is therefore an activity which entails a certain degree of complexity.

One could thus argue – similarly to what the AG stressed in his conclusions in *LKW Walter*[98] – that under these circumstances the 8 days time limit granted to foreign defendants to oppose the issuance of the Slovenian

97 Chiapponi (n.85).

98 In spite of the AG's opinion, the legal and factual circumstances at hand under Slovenian law are analyzed alone. One could argue that the comparison with *Profi Credit Polska* as an additional argument of refusal can barely be justified because such judgment was rendered in the field of consumer law, which generally establishes more protective rules than business law.

payment order makes particularly burdensome an effective exercise of the right of defence. Such time limit could therefore be considered too short for protecting the right of defence under Art. 45 (1)(b). This could justify refusal of recognition and enforcement of foreign judgments according to Art. 45 (1)(b) Brussels Ibis, read in conjunction with Art. 47 CFR.

ii) Defective service[99]

The Court of Appeal of Versailles[100] refused to enforce an Italian payment order issued against a French company on the basis (*inter alia*) of Art. 45 (1)(b) because the defendant had not been granted sufficient notice and time to arrange for his defence.

In particular, the court considered that the foreign debtor had not validly been served with the payment order as he only received notice of the order by registered letter with acknowledgement of receipt. The court thus underlined that service was defective in light of the following circumstances: service by letter did not identify with certainty the type of act which was served on the defendant; the document instituting the proceedings was not translated into French; the defendant was not informed of his right to refuse the service of the document instituting the proceedings (previous Art. 8 Service Regulation) which was not translated into French.

Under these circumstances, the Court of Versailles concluded that the time to oppose the issuance of the Italian payment order was insufficient: indeed, it never started to run without granting the defendant a possibility to properly organise his defences as required by Art. 45 (1)(b)[101].

---

99 The cases referred to below wrongly qualified as falling within the public policy exception (Art. 45 (1)(a)) can reasonably be related to this list of cases regarding defective service under Art. 45 (1)(b), see below a) Wrong qualification of the public policy ground for refusal.

100 Court of Appeal of Versailles 09-01-2020, n. 17/08693. See Buzzoni (n.91), 17–19.

101 Similarly, a German court refused the recognition and enforcement of a foreign judgments based on Art. 27 (2) Brussels Convention because it considered that a time to react of 13 days was not sufficient to allow a German defendant to properly organize his defences before a Belgian court when the document instituting the proceedings was served in Dutch, which was a language the defendant could not understand. Translations from such specialised language required the help of an expert legal translator. Under these circumstances, a 13 days time limit has been deemed to be too short and insufficient. See Higher Regional Court of Hamm 07-03-1979, n. 20 W 29/78. Under the same premises, recognition and enforcement of foreign judgments has been refused under Art. 27 (2) Brussels Convention in

iii) Running of time limits during the summer period

The Court of Appeal of Milan[102] refused the recognition and enforcement of a German judgment based on Art. 27 (2) Brussels Convention because it considered a 25 days time limit to react insufficient to allow a defendant domiciled in Milan to prepare his defence before the German court of Stuttgart. In particular, the court's reasoning was premised on the fact that the latter time limit ran during August when the machinery of justice was not fully working and the defendant's business was closed; however, such period of time would have been appropriate under different circumstances, e.g. a different moment of the year.

c) Redefining the notion of sufficient time under Art. 45 (1)(b)?

What ultimately arises from these cases is that the discrepancies between time limits to react at national level could constitute a practical hurdle to the free circulation of judgments when courts concretely interpret the sufficiency of time under Art. 45 (1)(b)[103]. There is therefore a compelling need for redefining the notion of sufficient time under Art. 45 (1)(b) in order to reduce the margin of appreciation of courts. This would promote a more consistent and uniform interpretation between the Member States on the grounds for refusing recognition and enforcement under the Brussels Ibis regime, which would probably decrease cases of refusal of recognition and enforcement of judgments in civil and commercial matters[104].

German Supreme Court 23-01-1986, n. IX ZB 38/85; Higher Regional Court of Dusseldorf 11-10-1999, n. 3 W 258/99; Court of Appeal of Milan 29-09-1978, *Officina Costruzioni Meccaniche S.r.l. v S.A. Ets Jean Ivens* in (1980) 26 RDIPP, 53–56.; Court of Appeal of Naples 20-02-1982, *Trans-Atlantica S.p.A. v. Soc. Vertom Shipping and Trading Corporation B.V.* in (1983) 29 RIDPP, 128–135.

102 Court of Appeal of Milan 28 September 1976, *Soc. Ingg. S and Agostino Belotti S.r.l v Veeder Root GmbH.*

103 Thus 'we may conclude that the discrepancies concerning the time limits for service and defense constitute a significant obstacle to the circulation of judgments'. See Gascón Inchausti and Requejo Isidro (n.95), para 132.

104 Giovanni Chiapponi, 'Can Harmonized Time Limits in European Civil Procedure Enhance the Effectiveness and Enforcement of EU law?' (2020) 12 Cuad. der. trans., 548.

2) The lacking possibility to challenge the judgment in the Member State of origin

Once the latter requirements for effective service of the document instituting the proceedings have been verified, the court of the Member State where enforcement is sought for applying Art. 45 (1)(b) refusal ground should further assess whether the defendant has had an opportunity to react to his involuntary default in the Member State of origin.

Where, under the law of the Member State of origin, the defendant was in a position to appeal the decision given in default but did not do so due to his fault, recognition and enforcement of foreign judgments cannot be denied[105].

This situation was regulated differently under the Brussels Convention of 1968. The CJEU in its jurisprudence[106] prior to the Brussels I and Ibis Regulations also did not mention any positive obligation on the defendant to challenge his default of appearance in the Member State of origin before he could raise the objection at the enforcement stage. Regardless of this case law, the Brussels I (Art. 34 (2)) and Ibis (Art. 45 (1)(b)) Regulations have adopted a different and more restrictive approach[107]: the defendant who could have challenged the default judgment in the Member State of origin, but did not do so, loses the possibility to contest the recognition and enforcement of the default judgment in the Member State of enforcement. The CJEU reinforced this approach in *Apostolides*[108] ruling that 'a default judgment given on the basis of a document instituting the proceedings which was served on the defendant in sufficient time and in such a way as to enable him to arrange for his defence must be recognised if he did not take the initiative to appeal against the judgment when it was possible for him to do so'.

---

105 See for instance Court of Appeal of Paris 14.02.2019, n. 17/22771, where the Court of Appeal of Paris reiterated, in the context of the enforcement of an Italian order for payment, that the enforcement of a foreign default judgment cannot be refused if the defendant had the opportunity to challenge it before the courts of the State of origin. See Buzzoni (n.91), 15.

106 *Minalmet* (n.61). See also Jonathan Fitchen, 'Art. 45'. in Andrew Dickinson and Eva Lein (eds), *The Brussels I Regulation Recast* (Oxford University Press 2015), para 13.279.

107 Paolo Biavati, *Europa e Processo civile: Metodi e Prospettive* (Giappichelli Editore 2003), 75.

108 Case C-429/07, *Meletis Apostolides v David Charles Orams and Linda Elizabeth Orams* (2009) EU:C:2009:271.

It follows that the defendant who was aware of default proceedings initiated against him but did not appear, cannot wait until the stage of recognition and enforcement to object to the judgement; he must, indeed, challenge the default decision at the time at which proceedings are initiated in the Member State of origin. Thus, the defendant must have made use of any remedy available in the Member State of origin in order to prove that his default was involuntary under Art. 45 (1)(b)[109].

The Brussels Ibis Regulation aims at concentrating litigation in the Member State of origin[110]: all procedural issues should be examined by priority in the State where proceedings were initiated and whose courts are better placed for assessing them[111]. This also prevents abuses which derive from a 'type of strategic default' by the defendant: he might take advantage of his inactivity by intentionally failing to appear and not challenging the default of appearance in the Member State of origin, but simply raising the violation of his right to a fair hearing at the stage of enforcement.

Art. 45 (1)(b) does not explicitly refer to any specific type of proceedings to challenge judgments. This has then been interpreted as covering 'any general possibility to challenge the judgment or the payment order as well as any specific procedure aiming at setting aside the default judgment. However, this does not mean that all possibilities should be accepted at all times'[112].

Thus, the requested court should concretely check whether challenging the judgment in the State of origin was both possible and reasonable. In assessing this criterion, the requested court, as emerges from ECtHR[113] case law, should have examined the burden of proof regarding the existence and availability of a remedy in the Member State of origin and given a reasoned decision on this point[114].

109 The compliance of this principle with Art. 6 ECHR has recently been confirmed by the ECtHR in *Avotiņš v Latvia* App no 17502/07 (ECtHR 23 May 2016). In particular, the ECtHR considered that the requirement to exhaust remedies arising from the mechanism provided for in Art. 45 (1)(b) Brussels Ibis (Art. 34 (2) Brussels I) is not in itself problematic in terms of the guarantees of Art. 6 (1) of the Convention. See also *Avotiņš v Latvia* App no 17502/07 (ECtHR 25 February 2014); Marta Requejo Isidro, 'On Exequatur and the ECHR: Brussels I Regulation before the ECtHR' (2015) 35 IPRax, 69–74.

110 As explained in the Commission proposal, Commission proposal (n.67), 7, 21, 24.

111 Mankowski (n.74), para 57.

112 See Nowak and Richard (n.62), para 45.28.

113 See *Avotiņš v Latvia* 23 May 2016 (n.109), para 121.

114 See Nowak and Richard (n.62), para 45.30.

It follows that the check of the requested court shall insist on conditions of service of default judgments which – as arises from CJEU settled case law[115] – are the same than those relating to the service of documents instituting the proceedings. What matters is the manner and timeliness of service of default judgments: these must be served on the defendant in sufficient time and in such a way as to enable him to effectively lodge his challenges before the courts of the State in which the judgment was given.

On the one hand, this means that defendants should have been properly acquainted with the content of judgments in a language they understand[116]. It is crucial to verify that the defendant had sufficient information to challenge the judgment[117]. Such information must allow the defendant to lodge his challenge without going beyond normal diligence in the defence of his rights[118].

On the other hand, the requirement of sufficient time shall be analysed with regard to the time limits for challenging judgments and to the conditions for being relieved from the expiry of these time limits provided for under the law of different Member States.

a) General time limits for challenging judgments

Rules on these time limits – e.g. dealing with their length and *dies a quo* – vary considerably across the EU. This leads national courts to interpret on a case by case basis the sufficiency or insufficiency of time limits for challenging judgments. If the time limits are deemed to be insufficient, this might be one of the reasons preventing defendants from effectively challenging default judgments which might justify refusal of recognition and enforcement of foreign judgments under the Brussels Ibis regime[119].

115 Case *ASML* (n.66), para 100.
116 A simple formal irregularity in the service of the judgment does not necessarily prevent defendants from being considered unable to challenge the decision, see above a) Effective service.
117 See Nowak and Richard (n.62), para 45.29.
118 Case *ASML* (n.66), para 39.
119 See Nowak and Richard (n.62), para 45.28.

b) Restoring original time limits to challenge a judgment: the *Lebek* case

A different situation arises where the defendant has not been able to defend himself because he did not know that proceedings were initiated against him in the Member State of origin. This is when the defendant was not made aware of the issuing of a default judgment against him and time limits to appeal against that judgment expired without any fault on his side. In such a case, the defendant can lodge an application for relief at the stage of recognition and enforcement which would restore his right to appeal. This then allows him a new time limit, identical to the original one, to bring a new challenge against the default judgment in the Member State of origin.

In the case of cross-border service of documents, Art. 22 (4) of the Service Regulation Recast applies to the application for relief from the effects of the lapsed time limit for appeal. On the other hand, if there is no cross-border service, the domestic law of the Member States will regulate the conditions under which the defendant can apply for relief. If the defendant is exempted from the expiry of the time limit, proceedings are brought back to the moment at which he should have appeared to show his first reaction to the claim and he could conduct new proceedings.

Against this backdrop, the following general questions arise: when the judge relieves the defendant from the expiry of the time to appeal, could an application for relief be examined as an ordinary challenge falling within the meaning of 'proceedings to challenge the judgment' provided for in Art. 45 (1)(b)? Is the defendant applying for relief in the same position as the defendant lodging an appeal prior to the expiry of time limits? Under these circumstances, could the defendant be considered to have had an opportunity to properly defend himself in the Member State of origin according to the Brussels Ibis Regulation?[120]

These issues were brought before the CJEU in the *Lebek*[121] judgment where the Court stated that an application for relief restoring the right of the defaulting defendant after the expiration of time limits, allowing him to

120 Giovanni Chiapponi, 'Time Limits and Default Judgments in European Cross-border Civil Litigation: Minimum Standards?' (2020) 12 Cuad. der. trans, 974, 975.

121 Case C-70/15, *Emmanuel Lebek v Janusz Domino* (2016) EU:C:2016:524. For further details on this judgment see Etienne Leroy, 'L'Exequatur aux Confins de la Coopération Judiciaire Européenne et du Respect des Droits de l'Homme ou le Paradigme de l'Homme Avisé mais pas Informé' (2016) Ius & Actores, 439–453; Laurence Idot, 'Motifs de Refus de Reconnaissance' (2016) 10 Europe. 40,41; Cyril Nourissat, 'Reconnaissance et Exécution: la Cour de justice de l'Union européenne Conforte sa

bring a new challenge, falls within the meaning of 'proceedings to challenge the judgment' laid down in Art. 34 (2) of the Brussels I Regulation (now repeated in the same wording by Art. 45 (1)(b) of the Brussels Ibis Regulation).

Nevertheless, contrasting interests underlie this solution and the interpretation of the wordings 'proceedings to challenge the judgment'.

On the one hand, it is important to stress the objective of the Brussels Ibis Regulation, which is to foster the broadest recognition and enforcement of judgments between the Member States by removing further formalities. Art. 45 (1)(b) therefore has to be interpreted extensively so as to also include relief proceedings as being within the meaning of 'proceedings to challenge the judgment'.

On the other hand, it should be underlined that according to its wording Art. 45 (1)(b) refers to 'proceedings to challenge the judgment'; relief proceedings do not strictly qualify as such. Relief proceedings, indeed, are set to allow the defendant, who did not exercise his right due to the expiry of the provided time limit without any fault on his part, to restore his position and subsequently initiate the relevant proceedings. When relief proceedings are successful, they give to the defendant a new time limit within which he can lodge a second appeal. This means that the defendant would be afforded two proceedings, which would seriously disrupt the equality of arms between the parties insofar as the defendant after the *restitutio in integrum* would have the possibility to conduct an additional proceeding to defend his interests[122].

Therefore, the CJEU in *Lebek* promoted an autonomous definition of 'proceedings to challenge the judgment' which includes relief proceedings. The Court distinguished between two different hypotheses depending on whether or not the deadline to submit an application for relief has elapsed.

First, recognition and enforcement of foreign judgments should not be refused if the 'defendant has not made use of his right to apply for relief when it was possible for him to do so'. This solution results from the wording of Art. 45 (1)(b) and from the CJEU's case law, precluding the defaulting defendant from applying for refusal of enforcement if he had an opportunity to previously defend himself in the Member State of origin.

Nouvelle Construction sur la Purge des Procédures dans l'État d'Origine' (2016) 12 Procédures, 24,25.

122 In this regard, see Opinion of AG Kokott Case C-70/15, *Emmanuel Lebek v Janusz Domino* (2016) EU:C:2022:777.

Conversely, a default judgment should not be recognised and enforced if the defendant submitted an application for relief which has subsequently been dismissed (even though the requirements set out for that application were met). It will be up to the Member State addressed to verify if the application has been dismissed correctly or not.

The distinction established by the Court perfectly reflects the wording of Art. 45 (1)(b) which draws a distinction based on the defendant's responsibility. Thus, an application for relief can lead to the denial of recognition and enforcement of judgments only if the defendant acted without any fault on his part and the time limit to apply for relief was respected[123].

The ruling of the CJEU focusses on the due diligence of the defendant: when his default of appearance is involuntary and not attributable to him, the recognition and enforcement of judgments can be denied. The CJEU's statement is very strict and severe. The purpose of the Court is to avoid the possibility that the defendant has derived any advantage from his default by using it as a procedural strategy to cause delays in the proceedings and hampering the free circulation of judgments within the EU[124].

A possible third situation that the CJEU did not take into account in *Lebek* could arise if the time limit to apply for relief is still running when enforcement is sought in another Member State. In such a case, the defendant should of course apply for relief in the Member State of origin and make recourse in the Member State of enforcement to the provision of Art. 44 (2) of the Brussels Ibis Regulation, which requires the court to suspend the enforcement proceedings if the enforceability is suspended in the Member State of origin[125].

This mechanism is based on the pre-condition that the pendency of an application for relief could entail the suspension of the enforceability of the judgment under the law of the Member State where enforcement is sought. On the other hand, where the enforceability of the judgment is not automatically suspended in the Member State of origin, the mechanism laid down in Art. 44 (2) could not work. Nevertheless, the defendant applying

123 Chiapponi (n.120), 976.

124 Chiapponi (n.120), 976.

125 Fernando Gascón Inchausti, 'Service of Proceedings on the Defendant as a Safeguard of Fairness in Civil Proceedings: in Search of Minimum Standards from EU Legislation and European Case-Law' (2017) 13 JPIL, 502 fn 79.

for relief in the Member State of origin might ask for limitation or suspension of enforcement proceedings according to Art. 44 (1)[126].

What emerges from *Lebek* is that the CJEU interpreted in an extensive way the wording 'proceedings to challenge the judgment' laid down in Art. 45 (1)(b) by also including relief proceedings in its meaning. This puts a defendant who commences proceedings to challenge a judgment before the expiry of the time limits for challenging it, and a defendant whose time limit has involuntary expired and thus must first apply for relief before initiating the relevant proceedings to appeal, on the same level[127].

Conditions for applying for relief are therefore analysed by requested courts when assessing if defendants have been granted sufficient time to challenge default judgements rendered against them under the law of the Member State of origin. The setting of time limits for applying for *restitutio in integrum* vary between the Member States. These differences could entail some interpretative issues when enforcement courts must decide on refusal grounds and on suspension or limitation of enforcement proceedings.

aa) Time limits for filing an action under the Service Regulation Recast

In this respect, a practical issue concerning the time limits within which applications for relief may be brought under the scope of the Service Regulation further arose in *Lebek*.

When a default judgment is served cross-border, the requirements of Art. 22 (4) of the Service Regulation Recast should be respected.

The defendant may thus apply for relief if the deadline to appeal has expired and the following two conditions are fulfilled: (a) the defendant, without any fault on the defendant's part, did not have knowledge of the

126 It should be noted that it is also possible that the defendant applies for relief according to the national law of the State of origin without applying for refusal of recognition and enforcement under Art. 45 (1)(b). In such case, he might require suspension of enforcement proceedings pursuant to Art. 41 (2).

127 Despite the interpretation of the CJEU in *Lebek*, one may wonder if, under these circumstances the right of the defaulting defendant to a fair trial faces a serious challenge which might prevent recognition and enforcement of judgments within the EU. Including relief proceedings in the meaning of 'proceedings to challenge the judgment' (Art. 45 (1)(b)) could entail, indeed, a high risk of disrupting the equality of arms between the parties as long as the defendant after having applied for relief has to conduct additional proceedings to defend properly his interests, see Chiapponi (n.120), 977.

document in sufficient time to enter a defence or did not have knowledge of the judgment in sufficient time to appeal; and (b) the defendant has raised a *prima facie* defence to the action on the merits[128].

Further, Art. 22 (4) sets a deadline to submit an application for relief: such an application 'may be filed only within a reasonable time after the defendant has knowledge of the judgment'.

bb) The notion of reasonable time

What 'a reasonable time' might be remains unclear[129]. However, the EU legislator introduces a minimum standard specifying that the length of this period shall in no case be less than 1 year following the date of the judgment. The precise determination of the period is then left to the discretion of each Member State, which shall communicate its decision to the Commission according to Art. 33 (1) of the Service Regulation Recast.

Against this background, the CJEU ruled in *Lebek* that, where the cross-border service of documents is at stake under the provisions of the Service

---

128 It should be noted that Art. 22 (4) corrected the following linguistic issues which derived from the previous version of Art. 19 (4) of the Service Regulation. As referred in Florian Scholz, Katharina Auernig, Julius Schumann and Paul Oberhammer, 'Default Procedures and Judgments in Cross-border Settings' in Burkhard Hess and Pietro Ortolani (eds), *Impediments of National Procedural Law to the Free Movement of Judgments* (Beck-Hart-Nomos 2019), para 105 'Art.19 (4)(a) of the English version of the Regulation sets out the following requirements: the defendant, without any fault on his part, did not have knowledge of the document in sufficient time to defend, or knowledge of the judgment in sufficient time to appeal. The German version, however, requires that both conditions (no knowledge of the document in sufficient time and no knowledge of the judgment in sufficient time) have been met at the same time (the German version uses the word "und" which translates as and). While the English version is in accordance with e.g. the French, the Italian and the Spanish one, the German text seems to be better in line with the purpose of the provision, to grant an extraordinary remedy in cases where the defendant did not have knowledge of the document initiating the proceedings in time. When taken literally, the English text would allow for relief of the defendant also in cases where fault can be attributed to him either for the failure to enter into the proceedings or for the failure to lodge an appeal against the judgment, when only the other omission can be attributed to the lack of information and has happened without any fault on his part. Hence, in an extreme situation, the English text of Art. 19 para 4 – if taken literally – would allow for *restitutio in integrum* in cases where the defendant has gained knowledge of the document initiating the proceedings in time and only did not learn of the default judgment in time to lodge an appeal'.

129 See Scholz, Auernig, Schumann and Oberhammer (n.128), para 106.

Regulation, the only time limit that is applicable to an application for relief is the one provided for in Art. 19 (4) of the Service Regulation (the same time limit now applies under Art. 22 (4) of the Service Regulation Recast) as specified by the Member States in their communication to the Commission according to Art. 23 (1) (now repealed by Art. 33 (1) of the Service Regulation Recast).

In this way, the CJEU prevents the defendant, when submitting an application for relief based on Art. 22 (4) of the Service Regulation Recast, from alternatively choosing the most favourable time limit laid down either in national law or at the EU level[130].

As EU Regulations are binding and directly applicable in all the Member States, the time limits provided for in the text of the Service Regulation are the only possible option for the defendant seeking *restitutio in integrum.* The application of national law, even if it provides for a longer time limit for bringing an application for relief, is excluded. This situation, indeed, 'could potentially lead to an unjustified discrimination of parties who reside in a different Member States, since they might be time-barred from bringing an application for relief, while a domestic party in the same situation would still be able to do so'[131].

In light of the above, the EU legislator in Art. 22 (4) of the Service Regulation Recast has set a minimum standard that the defendant applying for relief must comply with. Each Member State decides autonomously this absolute time limit, which cannot be shorter than 1 year, and notifies the Commission of it.

Even if the scope of Art. 22 (4) is limited to cases of cross-border service of documents, the purpose of the EU legislator is likely far reaching[132] as it provides common minimum standards for applying time limits at EU level. This uniform interpretation seems to reinforce the parties' right to a fair trial in cross-border proceedings and strengthen judicial cooperation in civil matters.

---

130 Chiapponi (n.120), 977.

131 Scholz, Auernig, Schumann and Oberhammer (n.128), para 107.

132 As further examined below (aa) Interpreting the notion of sufficient time under Art. 45 (1)(b)), Art. 22 (1)(a) will be used as reference for making concrete proposal for a EU action on time limits.

c) Possible breach of the right of defence?

What arises from the above is that the requested court when assessing the possibility of the defendant to challenge the judgment in the Member State of origin under the scope of Art. 45 (1)(b) shall identify both the time limits for bringing challenges and the rules for being relieved from the expiry of these time limits provided for under the law of the Member State of origin. Making this evaluation on time limits for the purpose of Art. 45 (1)(b) is a complex activity which raises questions on the fairness of the proceedings, as embedded in Art. 6 ECHR and Art. 47 CFR, and shall be balanced on a case by case basis with the objective of enhancing the free circulation of judgments in civil and commercial matters between the Member States.

Such balance established under Art. 45 (1)(b) leads to different outcomes. On the one hand, it could occur, as happened in *Lebek*, that the need to reinforce and strengthen judicial cooperation in civil matters is prioritized at the cost of some procedural guarantees of the defendant connected with the length, *dies a quo* and expiry of time limits to challenge judgments in the Member State of origin; on the other hand, if the due process guarantees of the defendant related to the setting of the above time limits prevail, this could hamper the recognition and enforcement of civil judgments under the Brussels Ibis Regulation[133].

It follows that the setting of national time limits for challenging judgments including relief proceedings strongly impact on the assessment which the requested courts makes to decide on the application of Art. 45 (1)(b). Notably, national rules on these time limits differ considerably across the Member States. This lack of uniformity could have negative repercussions for the free movement of civil judgments within the EU and needs to be addressed in future reforms by the EU legislator.

II) Time limits and public policy under Art. 45 (1)(a)

1) The public policy exception

In addition to Art. 45 (1)(b), the public policy exception (Art. 45 (1)(a)) could under exceptional circumstances and in a subsidiary way – i.e. when the conditions set out in Art. 45 (1)(b) are not met – protect, as well,

133 Chiapponi (n.120), 977.

parties' rights in the proceedings, as embedded in Art. 6 ECHR and 47 CFR. Its application is therefore possible only when the violation does not already fall under the scope of Art. 45 (1)(b)[134].

According to Art. 45 (1)(a), the recognition and enforcement of judgments might be refused if this is 'manifestly contrary to public policy in the member State addressed'.

The main function of public policy is to protect the fundamental values of the legal order of the requested Member State against unacceptable results which could follow either from the application of foreign law or from the recognition and enforcement of foreign judgments under the Brussels Ibis regime[135].

Public policy works as a '"safety valve", "handbrake", "sheet-anchor"'[136], which Member States could activate when the recognition and enforcement of a foreign judgment manifestly contradicts their fundamental values.

What is *in concreto* assessed are the effects of such recognition or enforcement and not the content of the judgment itself[137].

The public policy clause must be interpreted strictly[138] and applied only under exceptional circumstances[139]. In particular, 'the exceptional character of public policy is derived from the underlying assumption of private in-

---

134 Elena D'Alessandro, *Il Riconoscimento delle Sentenze Straniere* (Giappichelli Editore 2007), 138–143.

135 Burkhard Hess and Thomas Pfeiffer, *Interpretation of the Public Policy Exception as Referred to in EU Instruments of Private International and Procedural Law (Study 15-06-2011 on the interpretation of the public policy execption)*, 27.

136 Fitchen (n.106), para 13.279.

137 Nowak and Richard (n.62), para 45.64.

138 See Case C-414/92 *Solo Kleinmotoren GmbH v Emilio Boch* (1994) EU:C:1994:221, para 20; Case C-7/98 Dieter *Krombach v André Bamberski* (2000) EU:C:2000:164, para 21; Case C-38/98 *Régie nationale des usines Renault SA v Maxicar SpA and Orazio Formento* (2000) EU:C:2000:225, para 26; Case C-559/14 *Rudolfs Meroni v Recoletos Limited* (2016) EU:C:2016:349, para 38; and Case C-386/17 *Stefano Liberato v Luminita Luisa Grigorescu* (2019) EU:C:2019:24, para 55.

139 Jenard Report (n.47), 44; Case C- 145/86, *Horst Ludwig Martin Hoffmann v Adelheid Krieg* (1988) EU:C:1988:61, para 21; Case C-78/95 *Bernardus Hendrikman and Maria Feyen v Magenta Druck & Verlag GmbH* (1996) EU:C:1996:380, para 23; *Krombach* (n.138), para 21; *Renault* (n.138), para 26; Hess and Pfeiffer (n.135), 28; Andrew Dickinson, *The Rome II Regulation. The Law Applicable to Non-Contractual Obligations* (Oxford University Press 2009), para 15.10.

ternational and procedural law that foreign law and foreign decisions in general have the same value as their domestic counterparts'[140].

Public policy is not defined at EU level. There is indeed no common definition of public policy established by the EU legislator[141] and the CJEU in its case law[142] has repeatedly held as well that it has no power to positively define the concept of public policy within the meaning of Art. 45 (1)(a).

In spite of not defining positively public policy, the CJEU sets the boundaries within which Member States must interpret and apply the public policy clause for refusing recognition and enforcement of a foreign judgment[143].

Public policy is thus a national concept made up of a substantial and procedural component which is premised under the scrutiny and guidance of the CJEU[144].

Notably, public policy can be activated by national courts when a foreign judgment infringes a fundamental principle of the Member State addressed, which constitutes 'a manifest breach of a rule of law regarded as essential in the legal order of the State in which enforcement is sought or of a right recognized as being fundamental within that legal order'[145].

It must be noted that in any case such assessment cannot result neither in a mere difference of national procedures nor in any review of the foreign judgment as to its substance (Art. 52 Brussels Ibis Regulation), which would otherwise be contrary to the principle of mutual trust between Member States.

140 Hess and Pfeiffer (n.135), 28; Bernd Von Hoffmann, *Internationales Privatrecht: einschließlich der Grundzüge des Internationalen* (Verlag C.H. Beck 2022), para 6.142.

141 The absence of such a common definition has further been stressed by the Brussels Ibis Recast which, by maintaining the public policy as refusal ground, implicitly confirmed that important differences on this point continue to exist between the Member States. See Nowak and Richard (n.62), para 45.67; Louis D'Avout, 'L'Efficacité Internationale des Jugements. Après la Refonte du Règlement Bruxelles I' (2015) 5 IJPL, 251; Marco De Cristofaro, 'The Abolition of Exequatur Proceedings: Speeding up Free Movement of Judgments While Preserving the Rights of the Defense' (2011) 1 IJPL, 451.

142 *Apostolides* (n.108), para 57; *Meroni* (n.138), para 40.

143 Case C-629/10 *Trade Agency Ltd v Seramico Investments Ltd* (2012) EU:C:2012:531, para 49; *Meroni* (n.138), para 40.

144 Nowak and Richard (n.62), para 45. 67.

145 *Renault* (n.138), para 30

In addition to the parameters fixed by the CJEU in its case law, the following driving forces are pushing public policy towards a trends of Europeanisation[146].

First, it should be noted that the growing harmonisation of EU civil and commercial substantive law considerably reduces the risk that the national systems are not based on similar legal foundations: 'the more national systems are harmonised, the more the divergences are reduced and the corresponding danger that the application of the substantive law of other EU Member States will lead to unacceptable results[147].

Moreover, the procedural component of public policy is more and more influenced by the fundamental right to a fair trial, as embedded in Art. 6 ECHR and Art. 47 CFR.

Once the CFR received full normative status with the entry into force of the Lisbon Treaty, the CJEU made clear in its case law that, under the scope of the Brussels Ibis Regulation, proceedings leading to the delivery of judicial decisions must take place in such a way that the rights of the defence enshrined in Art. 47 CFR are observed[148].

It follows that the public policy exception will be activated when the procedural guarantees laid down in the legislation of the State of origin and in the Brussels Ibis Regulation are insufficient to protect the defendant from a manifest breach of his right to defend himself before the court of origin, as embedded in Art. 6 ECHR and Art. 47 CFR[149].

The need to protect the fundamental right to a fair trial, as enshrined in Article 6 ECHR and Article 47 CFR, is thus emerging as a benchmark common to all EU Member States which allows the CJEU 'to play a bigger role in spelling out the contours of the public policy concept'[150].

Under these premises, time limits, which are at the very heart of each procedural system as they are intrinsically connected with the protection of parties' fundamental rights in the proceedings, contribute to define the procedural public policy of each Member State under the scope of Art. 45 (1)(a).

National courts shall thus determine on a case by case basis whether foreign judgments comply with the principles and rules defining the pro-

146 Nowak and Richard (n.62), para 45.69.

147 Hess and Pfeiffer (n.135), 170.

148 Case C-112/13 *A v B and others* (2014) EU:C:2014:2195, para 51; *Meroni,* (n.123), paras 42–45.

149 See *Krombach* (n.138), para 44.

150 Nowak and Richard (n.62), para 45.69.

cedural public policy of the requested Member State (Art. 45 (1)(a)), i.e. if the application of foreign time limits ensured compliance with the fundamental right of defence, as guaranteed by Art. 6 ECHR and Art. 47 CFR. Under these circumstances, the recognition and enforcement of the foreign judgment might be refused under Art. 45 (1)(a), read in conjunction with Art. 6 ECHR and Art. 47 CFR and, if the application of foreign time limits entails effects manifestly contrary to the procedural public policy of the Member State addressed.

The following examples will practically prove how time limits could exceptionally fall under the scope of Art. 45 (1)(a) and justify refusal of recognition and enforcement of foreign judgments.

2) Practical issues

a) Wrong qualification of the public policy ground for refusal

The Higher Regional Court of Nurnberg[151] has held that an informal notification of a Romanian maintenance order which set a 15 days deadline for lodging a remedy against that order did not ensure the defendant's procedural rights, as embedded in Art. 6 ECHR and Art. 47 CFR. Under these circumstances where both service of the order did not clearly expose that its receipt was relevant for calculating the time limit to contest it, and the period of appeal was considerably short for challenging a foreign decision, the enforcement court refused to recognize and enforce the Romanian maintenance order pursuant to Art. 45 (1)(a) read in conjunction with Art. 34 No. 2 EuGVVO.

Based on the violation of defendant's procedural rights falling within German public policy, the Higher Regional Court of Nurnberg therefore refused to recognise and enforce the Romanian judgment under Art. 45 (1)(a). In spite of this interpretation, one could argue that the Higher Regional Court of Nurnberg wrongly applied Art. 45 (1)(a) as the conditions for applying Art. 45 (1)(b) – service was not effected in such a way and in sufficient time for allowing the defendant to prepare his defence – were at hand.

151 Higher Regional Court of Nurnberg 14-04-2014, n. 2 W 1488/11.

In a similar case, the Court of Appeal of Bordeaux[152] refused to enforce a Spanish decision under Art. 45 (1)(a) considering that there was no proof under the circumstances of the case that the defendant had validly been summoned to appear before Spanish courts. In particular, the certificate of enforceability provided for in Art. 53 of the Brussels Ibis Regulation did not mention the date of service and, further, the service letter delivered to the defendant did not refer to the decision for which enforcement in France was sought (there were indeed several decisions among the same parties in Spain and the claimant referred to the wrong one when applying for enforcement).

Based on these considerations, the Court of Appeal of Bordeaux thus found a violation of the adversarial principle, as embedeed in Art. 6 ECHR and Art. 47 CFR, which defines French procedural public policy under Art. 45 (1)(a). Neverthless, one could argue that given that service was not effectively carried out and the time to react never began to run, the conditions for applying Art. 45 (1)(b) were complied with. Art. 45 (1)(b) should have justified refusal of recognition and enforcement without making recourse to the public policy execption.

b) Expiry of time limits to appeal without prior service of the judgment on the defendant[153]

An exceptional case (created *ad hoc*) dealing with time limits which could eventually lead to refusal of recognition and enforcement under the public policy exception (Art. 45 (1)(a)) is the following one.

An Italian default judgment became *res judicata* after the expiry of the 6 months (long) time limits to appeal (Art. 327 c.p.c.) without prior service of it on the defendant. The creditor applied for the recognition and enforcement of this judgment in France.

Under French law, long time limits to appeal do not run with respect to default judgments and judgments could be enforced only after having been served on the defendant (Art. 503 CPC).

152 Court of Appeal of Bordeaux 31-03-2016, n. 14/05833.

153 This example finds inspiration in the situation regarding the Brussels I regime referred to by Etienne Pataut, 'Notifications Internationales et Règlement Bruxelles I' in Tristan Azzi and Hélène Gaudemet Tallon (eds), *Vers de Nouveaux Équilibres entre Ordres Juridiques: Liber Amicorum Hélène Gaudemet-Tallon* (Dalloz, 2008), 377–395.

Under these circumstances, could the Italian judgment be recognised and enforced in France or, must its recognition and enforcement be refused under Art. 45 (1)(a) because the Italian judgment did not effectively ensure defendant's right of appeal as embedeed under French law?

Under these circumstances, French courts could have wondered whether the Italian default judgment violated the defendant's procedural rights with respect to the lack of service of the judgment prior to its enforcement which is a condition effectively ensuring the right of appeal of defaulting defendants under French law.

The solution of this question depends on the actual qualification of the service of the judgment under French law.

If service is deemed to be a condition regarding the enforceability of the judgment, the recognition and enforcement of the Italian default judgment must be refused under Art. 45 (1)(a) because the defendant's right of appeal as embedded under French law is not effectively ensured due to the lack of service of the judgment.

However, if service is considered to pertain to the enforcement in the strict sense, the Italian judgment could be recognised and enforced in France as long as the Italian judgment prior to being enforced in France is served on the defendant as provided for in the Brussels Ibis Regulation.

3) No need to address the issue in future reforms

Under these premises, one could argue that time limits do not raise any recurrent issue falling under the scope of Art. 45 (1)(a). The above examples[154] show indeed that the cases of refusal of recognition and enforcement coming under Art. 45 (1)(a) are generally already covered by Art. 45 (1)(b). Only under very exceptional circumstances, could Art. 45 (1)(a) be the only ground for refusal applicable[155].

It arises that it is hardly possible to clearly identify any specific issue related to time limits and covered by the public policy exception. There are no time limits' deficiencies – other than those already indentified under

154 See above (a) Wrong qualification of the public policy ground for refusal) the cases decided by the Higher Regional Court of Nurnberg and the Court of Appeal of Bordeaux.

155 See above (b) Expiry of time limits to appeal without prior service of the judgment on the defendant) the case created *ad hoc* concerning the expiry of time limits to appeal without prior service of the judgment on the defendant

Art. 45(1)(b) – that can be categorised as generally violating fundamental procedural rights under Art. 45 (1)(a).

Thus, no specific change is envisaged under Art. 45 (1)(a). Any potential reform of Art. 45 (1)(b) might nevertheless have the indirect effect of further limiting the recourse to the public policy exception as it would reduce divergences between national laws with respect to a topical issue of each procedural system like time limits.

B) Domestic time limits and enforcement under the Brussels Ibis Regulation

The Brussels Ibis Regulation provides a procedural framework, according to which the *exequatur* has been abolished and the declaration of enforceability is no longer required to enforce a foreign judgment within the territory of EU Member States. According to Art. 39, decisions given by the courts of any Member State are automatically enforceable in the territory of the EU.

The Brussels *Ibis* Regulation[156] does not create any uniform procedure for the enforcement of judgments within the EU. The legislator has just set some common rules on specific aspects (Arts. 39–44). For the rest, enforcement is governed by *the lex fori* of the Member State addressed (Art. 41 (1)). Accordingly, parties can immediately proceed to the enforcement of a judgment abroad, by directly addressing themselves to the competent authorities in the Member State of enforcement where the debtor has assets.

Under these premises, the following interactions between some domestic procedural rules on time limits and the Brussels Ibis enforcement regime might negatively impact on the free circulation of judgments.

I) Time limits and the principles of equivalence and effectiveness

Art. 41 (1) of the Brussels Ibis Regulation provides that the procedure for the enforcement of judgments given in another Member State is governed by the law of the Member State addressed.

Since Art. 41 (1) refers to the procedural autonomy of Member States for determining the rules of enforcement, it will be interpreted and applied by national courts in accordance with the EU general principles of equivalence

156 Neither did the Brussels Convention nor the Brussels I Regulation.

(which here translates into the same level of protection between national and foreign creditors) and effectiveness (ensuring in practice the protection guaranteed by the Regulation)[157].

Member States are therefore free to determine their own enforcement rules as long as these rules are no less favourable than those governing similar domestic cases and do not make it practically impossible or excessively difficult to exercise the rights conferred by EU law.

1) Non-discrimination of national and foreign defendants

Following the principle of equivalence, Art. 41 (1) requires that the enforcement of a foreign judgment (even provisional enforcement) under Brussels Ibis be carried out 'under the same conditions' as a judgment given in the Member State addressed. The domestic procedural rules of the Member State addressed must apply to the enforcement of foreign judgments in the same way as they apply to the enforcement of national ones; in short, when it comes to the rules of procedure, no discrimination is admissible between domestic and foreign enforceable decisions[158].

Hence, national legislation of the Member State addressed cannot require the creditor who proceeds to the enforcement of a foreign judgment to comply with additional formalities, be subjected to shorter time limits, or additional costs, or otherwise complicate his access to enforcement[159].

In this scenario it should be noted that deviations from the usual rules resulting in a (at first sight) better treatment of foreign parties have been envisaged by some Member States. In fact, the special rules aim at compensating for difficulties arising from the cross-border nature of a case.

For instance, when implementing the Brussels Ibis regime in its own system[160], the Netherlands established that the service of documents for

---

157 Giovanni Chiapponi, 'Art. 41' in Marta Requejo Isidro (ed), *Brussels I Bis. A Commentary on Regulation (EU) No 1215/2012* (Edward Elgar Publishing 2022), para 41.08.

158 Arnaud Nuyts, 'La Refonte du Reglement Bruxelles I' (2013) 103 RCDIP, 23, 24; Sergio Carbone and Chiara Tuo, *il Nuovo Spazio Giudiziario Europeo in Materia Civile e Commerciale. Il Regolamento UE n. 1215/2012* (Giappichelli Editore 2016), para 17.3.

159 Chiapponi (n.157), para 45.17.

160 Art. 9 of the Implementation Act of the EU Enforcement Regulation and Lugano Convention ('Uitvoeringswet EU-executieverordening en Verdrag van Lugano') No 40/2014 of 30 January 2014.

enforcement needs to take place at least 4 weeks before the enforcement when the person against whom enforcement is sought has domicile in the Netherlands, and 8 weeks when he is domiciled abroad[161].

France provides as well for more favourable time limits to oppose enforcement proceedings for foreign debtors with the purpose of balancing their distance, linguistic deficiencies and inexperience with French law. As a general rule, these time limits are extended either by 1 month for debtors living in French oversea territories (Art. 643 (1) CPC) or 2 months for debtors living abroad (Art. 643 (2) CPC).

2) Divergent time limits as obstacles to the free circulation of judgments

Domestic enforcement rules must not impair the effectiveness of the scheme laid down in the Brussels Ibis Regulation, i.e., they should not run counter to the objective of facilitating the free circulation of judgments within the EU[162].

a) *Al Bosco* and the time limits to enforce foreign judgments

Issues concerning the application of a national rule establishing a time limit to apply for the enforcement (Section 929 (2) ZPO)[163] of a foreign decision (a preventive attachment order issued in Italy) arose in the *Al Bosco* case.

Al Bosco involved an Italian property company (Al Bosco) that obtained from an Italian district Court (Gorizia) a preventive attachment (or freezing) order authorizing it to seize the debtor's movable and immovable, tangible and intangible assets. The regional Court of Munich, pursuant

161 Gascón Inchausti and Requejo Isidro (n.95), para 235.

162 *Hoffmann* (n.139), para 29; Hélène Gaudemet-Tallon and Marie-Élodie Ancel, *Compétence et Exécution des Jugements en Europe: Matières Civile et Commerciale: Règlements 44/2001 et 1215/2012, Conventions de Bruxelles (1968) et de Lugano (1988 et 2007)* (6th ed, LGDJ 2018), paras 503,511.

163 According to German law a preventive attachment order is enforced through the registration of a debt-securing mortgage in the Land Register (Section 932 (1) ZPO) within the time limit of 1 month provided for in Section 929 (2) ZPO. This was the wording of Section 929 (2) when the preliminary question has been brought before the CJEU. Nowadays, the 1 month time limit has been extended to 2 months if enforcementt of a foreign preventive attachment order is sought in Germany, see fn 172.

to Brussels I Regulation, declared that preventive attachment order enforceable in Germany. However, the claimant applied for its enforcement after the time limit of 1 month, provided under Section 929 (2) ZPO, had already elapsed. On this ground, the Local Court of Munich rejected the application. This rejection was, subsequently, confirmed by the Higher Regional Court of Munich. Nevertheless, Al Bosco appealed against the decision arguing that the time limit for enforcement of the attachment laid down in the law of the Member State in which that instrument was issued (Art. 675 Italian c.p.c.[164]) had been complied with. In light of these arguments, Al Bosco considered that the German time limit (Section 929 (2) ZPO) was not relevant for the enforcement of the Italian attachment order whose validity only depends on Italian law.

Thus, with regard to these facts the following preliminary question was brought before the CJEU: does it comply with the Brussels I/Ibis enforcement regime to apply a time limit for the enforcement of a provisional measure (that of Section 929(2) ZPO) which is laid down in the law of the State in which enforcement is sought (Germany), to a preventive attachment instrument issued in another Member State (Italy) and recognized and declared enforceable in the State in which enforcement is sought (Germany)? Or do the time limits for enforcement provided for by the law of the Member State of origin (Italy) apply?[165]

The CJEU was thus asked to determine whether the time limits to proceed to enforcement pertain to the enforceability of judgments (the order authorizing a preventive attachment) issued by a court of a Member State other than the Member State in which enforcement is sought, or whether they come within the scope of enforcement in the strict sense. It is a subtle distinction, but the implications are very relevant for the cross-border enforcement of judgments under the Brussels regime.

In his conclusions, AG Szpunar stressed that the German time limit, in spite of its classification under domestic law, must be interpreted as a condition for the enforceability of judgments under EU law[166]. The AG justified this autonomous interpretation by considering that the time limit laid

164 In order to enforce a preventive attachment order, Art. 675 Italian c.p.c. provides for a time limit of 30 days starting from the rendering of the decision.

165 See Chiapponi (n.104), 545.

166 See See Opinion of AG Szpunar, Case C-379/17 Proceedings brought by *Società Immobiliare Al Bosco Srl* (2018) EU:C:2018:472, para 46.

down in Section 929 (2) ZPO impacts on the legal validity of judgments and cannot be applied in isolation, irrespective of its origin[167].

The AG finally concluded the German time limit should not be applied in order to avoid a lack of judicial protection as the preventive attachment order was still a valid title in Italy whereas in Germany enforcement was barred[168]. This might undermine the effectiveness of the Brussels I/Ibis enforcement regime preventing in such a way the free circulation of judgments in civil and commercial matters[169].

Contrary to the AG's opinion, in the view of the CJEU, the German time limit restricted the enforcement of a preventive attachment order, but not its legal validity. As this time limit affected only the enforcement of a title which had already been recognized and declared enforceable, the CJEU stated that it certainly belonged to the phase of enforcement in the strict sense[170].

Based on these arguments, the CJEU affirmed that the time limit laid down in Section 929 (2) ZPO applied to the Italian provisional measure, which was thus recognized and declared enforceable in Germany. The CJEU further considered that the starting point of this time limit was calculated from the date on which the declaration of enforceability was notified to the creditor[171]. This meant that the effectiveness of the Brussels/Brussels Ibis regime was not undermined by the application of the time limits laid down in Section 929 (2) ZPO[172].

To sum up, following the reasoning of the CJEU in *Al Bosco*, the applicable time limit to proceed to enforcement is not governed by the law of the Member State of origin under Art. 39, but it belongs to the remit of the rules of enforcement and, consequently, falls under the scope of the law of the Member State addressed.

---

167 See Opinion of AG Szpunar *Al Bosco Srl* (n.166), para 53.

168 See Opinion of AG Szpunar *Al Bosco Srl* (n.166), para 72.

169 See Chiapponi (n.104), 546.

170 Case C-379/17 *Proceedings brought by Società Immobiliare Al Bosco Srl* (2018) EU:C:2018:806, paras 31 and 32.

171 *Al Bosco* (n.170), para 50.

172 As a consequence of this ruling the German lawmaker decided nevertheless to amend Section 929 (2) ZPO. He considered indeed that 1 month was a too short period to enforce foreign peventive attachment orders in Germany under the conditions of the Brussels Ibis Regulation in which the exequatur procedure was not required anymore. Thus, the the time limit laid down in Section 929 (2) ZPO has been exetended from 1 to 2 months if direct enforcement of a foreign preventive attachment order is sought in Germany.

Thus, for example, if the law of the Member State addressed foresees a maximum period of 4 years to ask for the enforcement of a domestic judgment, this very same time limit shall be the one that must be taken into account when it comes to the enforcement of a foreign judgment under Brussels Ibis, no matter what the law of the Member State of origin says.

In spite of this ruling, one could argue that the arguments of the CJEU in *Al Bosco* are not fully convincing[173]. The compatibility of this interpretation with the scheme of the Brussels I/Ibis Regulation might indeed be debatable.

The time limit under examination in *Al Bosco* related to the requirements under which a preventive attachment can be ordered in Germany. Its purpose is to ensure that a preventive measure is not enforced after a (relatively) long period, having in mind that the circumstances could have changed in the meantime. Its application in a cross-border setting raised doubts.

The CJEU held that, under the Brussels I Regulation, the *dies a quo* to lodge an application for enforcement was the date the declaration of enforceability was notified to the creditor.

After the abolition of the *exequatur* procedure under the Brussels Ibis regulation, no specific rule has been provided for. Each State is therefore free to calculate the starting point to lodge an application for enforcement in accordance either with the law of the State of origin or with the law of the enforcement State.

---

173 The CJEU solution has been extensively discussed in academia, see Wolfgang Hau, 'The Dialogue on the European Law of Civil Procedure' in Burkhard Hess and Koen Lenaerts (eds), *The 50th Anniversary of the European Law of Civil Procedure* (Nomos 2020), 175; Bettina Rentsch, 'Die Grenzüberschreitende Vollziehung Einstweiliger Maßnahmen: Im Zweifel Für Die Lex Fori' (2020), 40 IPRax, 337–342; Dominique Foussard, 'Délai d'Exécution d'une Ordonnance de Saisie Conservatoire Émise par un État Membre et Revêtue du Caractère Exécutoire sur le Territoire d'un Autre État Membre' (2019) 109 RCDIP; Chiapponi, (n.104), 543–548; Caterina Silvestri, 'L'Esecuzione Forzata nella Prospettiva UE. Il Caso Al Bosco: Sovvertiti i Principi alla Base dello Spazio Giudiziario Europeo?' (2019) Le Pagine de l'Aula Civile, 824–826; Rafael Arenas García, 'Plazo para la Ejecución en un Estado Miembro de una Medida Cautelar Dictada en Otro Estado' (2018) 65 La Ley Unión Europea, 86–102; Alexander Steinmetz, 'Anwendbarkeit der Ausschlussfrist in der Spanischen ZPO auch auf Ausländische Vollstreckungstitel?' (2009) 55 RIW 304. In *Al Bosco*, however, the setting was the opposite one – the time limit established under the law of the Member State addressed was shorter than the time limit foreseen by the law of the Member State of origin – and that issue did not arise.

In spite of few national exceptions, the time limit to ask for enforcement is generally deemed to start to run on the day on which the certificate issued pursuant to Art. 53 Brussels Ibis Regulation is served on the person against whom enforcement is sought[174].

Nevertheless, it could happen that the creditor, once a preventive attachment order in the Member State of origin has been obtained, does not immediately seek enforcement in the Member State addressed. As a consequence, the starting point of the time limit provided for in Section 929 (2) ZPO would be delayed, and the function this section pursues in the German system disregarded, so precluding its application in a cross-border scenario[175].

The creditor must therefore request a new preventive attachment in the Member State of origin. It could, however, occur that this new application is inadmissible in the Member State of origin due to some specific reasons proper to the system at hand, e.g. the previous preventive attachment order has not been annulled or has not lost its legal validity[176].

Under these circumstances the creditor would be unable to proceed both in the Member State of origin and in the Member State of enforcement. This would create a 'deadlock'[177] which puts future free circulation of judgments in civil and commercial matters at risk.

Even though this was not the case in *Al Bosco*, the following issue remains open for the future: applying a national enforcement rule designed for national cases to foreign decisions could entail a situation of uncertainty

174 This seems to be the most reasonable solution. However, some Spanish courts in their case law considered the relevant moment for the mentioned delay to run is the finality of the decision in the Member State of origin, Spanish Supreme Court 16-10-2014 (Sala Civil, Sección 1a). For a closer look at this issue see Giovanni Chiapponi (n.104), 548; Jean-Paul Beraudo and Marie-Josèphe Beraudo, 'Convention de Bruxelles, Conventions de Lugano, Règlement (CE) No 44/2011, Règlement (UE) No 1215/2012 – Exécution des Décisions Judiciaires, des Actes Authentiques et des Transactions Judiciaires' (2020) Fasc. 633 J-CL Droit International, para 24; Rentsch (n.173), 341, 342; Marta Requejo Isidro, 'The Enforcement of Monetary Final Judgments under the Brussels Ibis Regulation (A Critical Assessment)', in Vesna Lazić and Steven Stuij (eds), *Brussels Ibis Regulation Changes and Challenges of the Renewed Procedural Scheme* (Springer 2017), para 4.4.2.1; Arenas García (n.173), 94–96.

175 Giovanni Chiapponi, 'Art. 39' in Marta Requejo Isidro (ed), *Brussels I Bis. A Commentary on Regulation (EU) No 1215/2012* (Edward Elgar Publishing 2022), para 39.22; Opinion of AG Szpunar *Al Bosco* (n.166), paras 54–59.

176 Opinion of AG Szpunar *Al Bosco* (n.166), paras 70, 71.

177 Chiapponi (n.104), 548; Opinion of AG Szpunar *Al Bosco* (n.166), paras 72–76.

for parties litigating across the EU which could undermine the effectiveness of the scheme laid down in the Brussels Ibis Regulation[178]. Based on the principle of effectiveness, if the time limits established by domestic law undermine the system set out in the Brussels regime, those time limits might become inapplicable[179].

b) Overruling the *Al Bosco* solution?

What further arises from the *Al Bosco* ruling in stating that the time limit to proceed to enforcement of provisional measures shall be governed by the law of the Member State addressed is that, if the time limit in the State addressed is longer than the time limit in the State of origin, enforcement is no longer possible in the State of origin, whereas it still is in the State addressed.

It should be noted that these uncertainties do not only deal with the enforcement of provisional measures, as further doubts emerge also with regard to general enforcement settings. For instance, EU Member States provide for different prescription periods regarding the enforcement of (final) judgments. As a result, a judgment coming from Germany remains enforceable for 30 years whereas a judgment given by a French court is enforceable for 10 years. These differences entail legal uncertainty, as it is unclear whether the French prescription period applies to the German judgment in France and vice versa[180].

Such uncertain result could undermine the rationale of Art. 39 and the *res judicata* effects attached to the judgment rendered in the Member State of origin[181].

It could be inferred from Art. 39 that as the law of the Member State of origin allows for enforcement, the foreign judgment must be enforced in the State addressed, regardless of whether the law of this latter State allows for the enforcement of similar judgments or not.

---

178 Chiapponi (n.104), 548. On the other hand, in academia it has been argued that the situation of uncertainty depends on a creditor's fault and seems thus justified, see Foussard (n.173).

179 Chiapponi (n.175), para 39.21.

180 Burkhard Hess, 'Reforming the Brussels Ibis Regulation: Perspectives and Prospects' (2021) 8 Max Planck Research Paper Series, 16.

181 Foussard (n.173), 172, 173.

It follows that the most appropriate solution to comply with Art. 39 would be to argue that the time limit to proceed to enforcement pertains to the enforceability of judgments[182]: where such time limit has not elapsed under the law of the State of origin, enforcement would also be possible in the State addressed regardless of what is the equivalent time limit in this latter State.

To further support this solution, if one looks at the Art. 53 certificate, it seems apparent that one of its objectives is to allow the court of the Member State addressed to proceed to enforcement without having to investigate as to the enforceability of the foreign judgment in the Member State of origin.

As arises from the wording of the Art. 53 form ('the judgment is enforceable in the Member State of origin without any further conditions having to be met'), all the relevant information regarding enforceability should be provided by the court issuing the certificate in application of its own law[183].

The lack of any reference to the time limits to proceed to enforcement could be seen as a shortcoming in the form of the Art. 53 certificate to be amended in the future in order to overcome the uncertainty that arises therefrom[184].

It might thus be advisable to include in the Art. 53 certificate a reference to the *dies a quo* and *dies ad quem* of the applicable time limit to proceed to enforcement in the State of origin[185]. On the contrary, if the future Recast of the Brussels Ibis will not refer to this issue, this might regrettably be seen as a confirmation of the view according to which time limits pertain to enforcement and therefore the law of the Member State addressed applies[186].

II) Service of the certificate prior to the first enforcement measure

According to Art. 43 (1) of the Brussels bis Regulation, a person seeking to enforce a judgment given in another Member State must serve the certifi-

182 Hess (n.180), 16; Chiapponi (n.175), para 39.22.

183 Enrique Vallines Garcia, 'Art. 53' in Marta Requejo Isidro (ed), *Brussels I Bis. A Commentary on Regulation (EU) No 1215/2012* (Edward Elgar Publishing 2022), para 53.06.

184 Chiapponi (n.175), para 39.23.

185 Rentsch (n.173), 341, 342; Chiapponi (n. 104), 548; Requejo Isidro (n.174), para 4.4.2.1; Maria López de Tejada, *La Disparition de l'Exequatur dans l'Espace Judiciaire Européen* (LGDJ 2013), paras 366–368.

186 Chiapponi (n.175), para 39.23.

cate issued pursuant to Art. 53 on the person against whom enforcement is sought prior to the first enforcement measure. The certificate shall be accompanied by the judgment, if not already served on that person.

It follows that no enforcement measures can be taken by the court of the Member State addressed if service on the debtor of the Art. 53 certificate and, if needed, of the judgment, has not taken place[187].

Such an obligation has been introduced as a counterbalance to the abolition of the *exequatur* in order to ensure the respect of the debtor's rights. Making the defendant aware that he is a party to pending proceedings before the starting of enforcement represents indeed one of his fundamental procedural rights, forming part of his right to a fair trial as guaranteed by Arts 6 ECHR and 47 CFR[188].

In Recital 32 the EU legislator makes it clear that Art. 43 (1) aims at the debtor being informed in 'reasonable time' that the enforcement of a judgment in another Member State is sought against him[189]. Service facilitates any challenge the defendant can bring against the enforcement[190]. Nevertheless, the impact of the service on the right of defence varies depending on whether the Art. 53 certificate is served alone or accompanied by the judgment[191].

Where the defendant was not aware of the judgment, the service of the certificate and of the judgment in due time plays a key function in respecting his right of defence. There is indeed a concrete risk that service of the judgement has not taken place, provided that the Brussels Ibis Regu-

187 As arises from *Al Bosco* (n.170), the service of the Art. 53 certificate seems to mark the starting point to calculate the *dies a quo* to lodge an application for enforcement according to national enforcement rules.

188 In order to make defendants' rights more effective it would have been desirable to also mention in which other Member State enforcement has been sought. See Gilles Cuniberti, 'Art. 43' in Ulrich Magnus and Peter Mankowski (eds), *Commentary Brussels I bis Regulation* (2nd edn, Ottoschmidt 2023), para 2; Xandra Kramer, 'Art. 43' in Andrew Dickinson and Eva Lein (eds), *The Brussels I Regulation Recast* (Oxford University Press 2015), para 13.238.

189 Under the previous regime, the service of the declaration of enforceability had as well the function of strengthening the right of defence, see Case C-3/05, *Gaetano Verdoliva v J. M. Van der Hoeven B, Banco di Sardegna and San Paolo IMI SpA* (2006) EU:C:2006:113.

190 See Francesco Salerno, *Giurisdizione ed Efficacia delle Decisioni Straniere nel Regolamento (UE) n. 1215/2012 (Rifusione)* (4th ed, Wolters Kluwer Cedam 2015), 392.

191 Giovanni Chiapponi, 'Art. 43' in Marta Requejo Isidro (ed), *Brussels I Bis. A Commentary on Regulation (EU) No 1215/2012* (Edward Elgar Publishing 2022), para 43.15.

lation does not contain any rule qualifying the service of the judgment as pertaining either to the law of the Member State of origin or to the law of the Member State of enforcement, and this can give rise to a negative conflict on the applicable law.

Under these circumstances, Art. 43 (1) thus enables the defendant to become aware of the judgment. In particular, it allows him, on the one hand, to contest the judgment either in the Member State of origin or in the State of enforcement before suffering the effects of the first enforcement measure and, on the other hand, it gives him the opportunity of complying with the judgment voluntarily before the beginning of enforcement proceedings[192].

Conversely, where the judgment has already been served on the defendant, service of the certificate under Art. 43 (1) has the main function of simplifying that the defendant can challenge the judgment in the State of enforcement, based on a – quite unlikely – discrepancy between the content of the judgment and the certificate[193]. One could argue that as the debtor is in principle already aware that enforcement measures are about to be taken, the delivery of the Art. 53 certificate in such case represents a mere simplification of enforcement formalities and would not be mandatory in order to respect the right of defence[194].

192 Chiapponi (n.191), para 43.16.

193 Even if inconsistencies between the judgment and the certificate are limited to very few cases, some national judges have claimed that 'there is a great risk on discrepancy between the reproduction of the content of the decision on the form of Art. 53 and the content of the judgment', see Gascón Inchausti and Requejo Isidro (n.95), para 254 fn 189. It should also be noted that errors in the certificate (e.g. it is issued wrongfully or to a wrong person) could occur. As the Brussels Ibis is silent about these issues, one could infer that these errors will be challenged and corrected according to the remedies available under the national law of each Member State, see Paolo Biavati, 'L'Esecutorietà delle Decisioni nell'Unione Europea alla Luce del Reg. UE n. 1215/2012' in Roberta Tiscini, Bruno Capponi, Bruno Sassani, Alfredo Storto (eds), *Il Processo Esecutivo (Liber Amicorum Romano Vaccarella)* (UTET Giuridica 2014), 194; Darius Bolzanas, Egidija Tamošiuniene, Dalia Vasariene and Remigijus Jokubauskas, 'Certification of Enforceability in the Member State of Origin: Service of Certificate' in Vesna Rijavec, Wendy Kennett, Tomaž Keresteš, Tjaša Ivanc (eds), *Remedies Concerning Enforcement of Foreign Judgments Brussels I Recast* (Wolters Kluwer 2018), para 6.03 (A),(B); Chiapponi (n.191), para 43.17.

194 See Fernando Gascón Inchausti, 'La Reconnaissance et l'Exécution des Décisions dans le Règlement Bruxelles I bis' in Emmanuel Guinchard (ed), Le Nouveau Règlement Bruxelles I bis Règlement n°1215/2012 du 12 Décembre 2012 Concernant la Compétence Judiciaire, la Reconnaissance et l'Exécution des Décisions en Matière Civile et Commerciale (Bruylant, 2014), 233, 234; Burkhard Hess, David Althoff, Tess Bens, Niels Elsner, and Inga Järvekülg, 'The Reform of the Brussels Ibis Regu-

On a different note, the fact that service must be done – as required by Recital 32 – in reasonable time before the first enforcement measure could remove the creditor's 'surprise effect' advantage which automatic enforcement normally entails and render enforcement measures largely ineffective[195].

This condition thus challenges, at least to a certain extent, the meaning of automatic enforcement[196] and led some authors to wonder why the debtor should receive any additional protection: 'by definition, he was ordered to pay the money by an enforceable judgment, which means that he could not convince the foreign court; he still does not want to pay, which forces the creditor to initiate enforcement proceedings; finally, the debtor may be taking step to dispose of his assets'[197]. This all begs the question of why EU law should afford him such additional safeguard which by removing the surpise effect of enforcement measures is eminently counterproductive to the direct enforcement of Member States' judgments within the EU[198].

1) Uncertain time limits

Under the current institutional framework, the following issues on interpreting the notion of reasonable time arise.

Art. 43 (1) does not provide for any minimum period; Recital 32 refers to a 'reasonable time' without further elaboration. How long prior to the first

---

lation' (2022) 9 Max Planck Research Paper Series, 26, 27; Gilles Cuniberti, 'French Supreme Court Rules Certificate Provided for in Article 53 Brussels I bis May Be Served 5 Minutes before Enforcement' (EAPIL Blog 21 February 2023) https://eapil.org/2023/02/21/french-supreme-court-rules-certificate-provided-for-in-article-53-brussels-i-bis-may-be-served-5-minutes-before-enforcement/.

195 Burkhard Hess, 'Article 43 EuGVVO' in Peter Schlosser and Burkhard Hess (eds), *Europäisches Zivilprozessrecht* (5th ed, C.H.Beck 2021), para 1; Burkhard Hess, *Eu-Zivilprozessrecht* (2nd ed, De Gruyter 2021), para 6.224; Hess, Althoff, Bens, Elsner, and Järvekülg (n.194), 26, 27.

196 This is the reason why protective measures are excluded from the scope of Art. 43. In particular, it should be noted that protective measures ordered in ex parte proceedings in the Member State of origin are not characterised as 'judgments' for the purpose of Article 2(a) of the Brussels Ibis Regulation and cannot circulate under its regime, unless the judgment containing the measure is served on the defendant prior to enforcement. See Chiapponi (n.191), para 43.37; Hess, Althoff, Bens, Elsner, and Järvekülg (n.194), 26, 27.

197 Cuniberti (n.194)

198 Hess, Althoff, Bens, Elsner, and Järvekülg (n.194), 26, 27; Cuniberti (n.194).

enforcement measure must the certificate be served on the debtor has been widely discussed in academia during the legislative process for adopting the Brussels Ibis Regulation.

In this regard, the parliamentary Draft Report suggested a period of 7 or 14 days before the first enforcement measure[199]. Nevertheless, the Brussels Ibis did not finally comply with such proposal and reduced it to the current wording.

The absence of a uniform time limit at the EU level and the vagueness of the expression 'reasonable time' are apt to raise doubts and uncertainties across the Member States. The value of this expression is thus unclear[200].

2) Interpreting the notion of reasonable time

In particular, some issues could arise from the practical interaction between Art. 43 and the procedural law of the Member State of enforcement. One may wonder how the notion of reasonable time will be interpreted and whether the first enforcement measure needs to occur immediately after the service of the certificate or, on the contrary, it can be postponed[201].

---

199 European Parliament Committee on Legal Affairs, 'Draft Report on the proposal for a regulation of the European Parliament and of the Council on jurisdiction and the recognition and enforcement of judgments in civil and commercial matters (recast)' (2010/0383(COD)), amendment 114; See Andrew Dickinson, 'Surveying the Proposed Brussels I *bis* Regulation: Solid Foundations but Renovation Needed' (2010) 12 Yb. PIL, 268; Philippe Hovaguimian, 'The Enforcement of Foreign Judgments under Brussels I *Bis*: False Alarms and Real Concerns' (2015) 11 JPIL, 235.

200 Marco Buzzoni and Carlos Santaló Goris, *Report on Practices in Comparative and Cross-Border Perspective in Towards More Effective EnFORcemenT of ClaimS in Civil and Commercial Matters within the EU EFFORTS (Project JUST-JCOO-AG-2019-881802)*, 21; Chiapponi (n.191), para 43.22.

201 In this vein, it should be noted that Art. 43 (1) and Recital 32 arguably do not prevent the enforcement authority of the Member State addressed from ordering the first enforcement measures before service of the certificate, but only from implementing them without giving the defendant the opportunity to react against the proceedings. Accordingly, it is not contrary to the rationale of Art. 43 (1) and Recital 32 that the law of the Member State addressed allows the competent authorities to issue a decision ordering enforcement measures at the same time the service of the certificate takes place. This interpretation explains, for example, why the Spanish system (rule 1 of Section 3 of Final Disposition 25 LEC) where the decision ordering first enforcement measures is served at the same time as the certificate, has been regarded as respecting the Brussels Ibis requirements. Gascón Inchausti (n.194), para 131; Chiapponi (n.191), para 43.23.

The Regulation does not provide a clear answer and one could argue that by applying by analogy CJEU case law regarding criminal proceedings that the notion of reasonable time is to be determined on a case by case basis by the competent court in the light of all of the circumstances specific to each case[202]. The notification must thus be performed in accordance with domestic time limits, provided that depending on the specific circumstances at hand the right of defence is duly respected, i.e. that the time limits established by national law give the defendant sufficient time to react against the enforcement proceedings – even by way of complying with the judgment voluntarily – before he suffers the effects of the first enforcement measures[203].

For instance, the question whether the defendant had been served with the Art. 53 Certificate in reasonable time before the first enforcement measure, as required by Recital 32 read in conjunction with Arts 6 ECHR and 47 CFR, recently arose in the two following cases.

In a case pending before the enforcement judge in Paris, it was held[204] that the enforcement of a foreign judgment can be carried out even though the certificate of Art. 53 Brussels Ibis was served on the debtor only the day before the first enforcement measure was carried out. The enforcement judge thus highlighted that French law (Art. 503 CPC) – the law actually governing the enforcement of the foreign judgment – does not provide for any fixed time limit which shall elapse between service of the judgment and the first enforcement measure. Based on these considerations, the enforcement judge explicitly rejected the debtor's argument regarding Recital 32 holding, in particular, that neither the Regulation nor French domestic law requires a specific waiting period between the service of a court decision and the carrying out of enforcement measures. This assumption was further reinforced by the fact that the judgment to be enforced had already

202 In the context of criminal proceedings, the CJEU recently stated in Case C-612/15 *Criminal proceedings against Nikolay Kolev and Others* (2018) EU:C:2018:392, that the reasonableness 'must be assessed in the light of all of the circumstances specific to each case'. See Chiapponi (n.191), para 43.22 fn 20.

203 It has been argued In Italian academia that the time limit (not less than 10 days) laid down in Art. 482 Italian c.p.c. seems to comply with the requirement of reasonable time set out in Recital 32, See Carbone and Tuo (n.158), para 17.2 fn 30; Alberto Malatesta and Nicolò Nisi, 'Le Novità in Materia di Riconoscimento ed Esecuzione delle Decisioni' in Alberto Malatesta (ed), *La Riforma del Regolamento di Bruxelles I. Il Regolamento (UE) n. 1215/2012 sulla Giurisdizione e l'Efficacia delle Decisioni in Materia Civile e Commerciale* (Giuffrè Editore 2016), para 3.2.

204 Tribunal of Paris 01-07-2021, n. 21/80506.

been served on the defendant 19 days before requiring him to pay his debts by a specific date and time which had already lapsed prior to the service of the certificate.

The very same conclusion has further been confirmed and extended by the French Supreme Court[205] in a case where service of the Art. 53 certficate was effected only 5 minutes before the first enforcement measure. Here, the judges considered that even a time period of 5 minutes was sufficient to comply with the notion of reasonable time under Recital 32.

It follows that the notion of reasonable time provided for in Recital 32 is interpreted so broadly that even a period of 5 minutes is sufficient to comply with defendants' right to react against enforcement proceedings, as enshrined in Art. 6 ECHR and Art. 47 CFR. Under these circumstances, defendants cannot effectively challenge enforcement proceedings before suffering the effects of the first enforcement measure and this circumvent the meaning of Art. 43 (1).

Finally, the Regulation does not provide any sanctions if the first enforcement measure takes place without the prior service of the certificate[206]. Some authors rightly argue that the lack of service of the certificate shall entail the suspension of enforcement proceedings and the annulment of the enforcement measures currently taken: as Art. 43 (1) sets out some requirements ensuring the validity of enforcement proceedings there is no reason to not require compliance with them[207]. Nevertheless, making an enforcement measure null can prove extremely difficult[208].

3) Need for clarification?

As it is apparent from the above, the absence of a uniform definition at the European level of the time limits which shall elapse between the service of the Art. 53 certificate and the first enforcement measures has already

205 French Supreme Court 11–01–2023, n. 21–17092 in Bull. civ. 2023.

206 Chiapponi (n.191), para 43.24.

207 Malatesta and Nisi (n.203), para 4.2. On the other hand, Gascón Inchausti does not agree with the latter solution. He argues that the suspension of enforcement proceedings is justified only if the judgment (and not even the certificate) is not served prior to the first enforcement measure, Gascón Inchausti (n.194), 233.

208 Gaudemet Tallon and Ancel (n.162), para 510.

sparked litigation which might eventually lead to divergent interpretations across the Member States[209].

In this vein, one may thus wonder about the rationale of keeping Art. 43 (1) in force under the following conditions where service of the Art. 53 certficate could occur even 5 minutes before the first enforcement measure without giving to the defendant a real opportunity to react against enforcement prior than suffering its actual effects and, no sanctions are attached to the lack of service in reasonable time.

On a different note, one may raise some concerns about the abolition of the obligation to serve the judgment on the defendant prior to enforcement under Art. 43 (1), which could entail a serious risk of undermining the right of defence in case service of the judgment has not previously taken place.

To prevent this undesirable result, it would be necessary, together with the abolition of Art. 43 (1), to integrate service as an element which falls within the standards of protection of public policy. It would, then, be up to the enforcement court to check if service has validly been carried out in light of the specific circumstances of the case at hand.

Should the EU lawmaker in the future recast of the Brussels Ibis Regulation not delete Art. 43 (1) – and as emerges from the above this is certainly the most recommended proposal in academia[210] – it will be necessary to clarify both the meaning of reasonable time and the sanctions attached to its violation in order to increase transparency and legal certainty and make the defendants' rights ensured by Art. 43 (1) effective[211].

C. Time limits under the second generation instruments

I) Uniform time limits for filing remedies within the EPO, ESCP and EAPO Regulations

Within the EPO, ESCP and EAPO procedures, the EU legislator has established uniform procedural rules balancing creditors' and debtors' interests, e.g. the time limits for lodging a statement of opposition against an EPO, the time limits governing the different stages of the ESCP procedure or the time limits regulating the *ex parte* adoption of an EAPO.

209 Buzzoni and Santaló Goris (n.200), 21.
210 Hess, Althoff, Bens, Elsner, and Järvekülg (n.194), 26, 27; Cuniberti (n.194).
211 Kramer (n.188), para 13.238.

The setting of these uniform time limits play a key role in simplifying, accelerating and reducing costs in cross-border disputes, while preserving defendants' procedural rights as envisaged by Arts 6 ECHR and 47 CFR.

In this respect, some issues on their compatibility with fundamental procedural rights of defence arise in national and CJEU case law.

1) Time limits for opposing the issuance of the EPO

Opposition is an essential mechanism to contest a European payment order which is issued by the judge *inaudita altera parte.* The defendant's option of lodging a statement of opposition is thus designed to compensate for the fact that the system established by Regulation 1896/2006 does not provide for the defendant's participation in the EPO procedure, by enabling him to contest the claim after the EPO has been issued[212].

The defendant becomes aware of the order only when this is served on him, and from this moment he has 30 days to lodge a statement of opposition with the court that issued the EPO (Art. 16 (2) EPO Regulation). Notably, the statement of opposition shall be brought by filing standard form F[213] and sending it back[214] to the court. In his statement of defence the defendant must simply[215] indicate that he contests the claim, without having to specify the reasons for this[216].

On the contrary, if the defendant does not lodge a statement of opposition within the latter 30 days time limit, the issuing court will declare the EPO enforceable according to standard form G[217].

---

212 Case C-144/12 *Goldbet Sportwetten GmbH v. Massimo Sperindeo* (2013) EU:C:2013:393, para 30.

213 Form F has a fully standardized text and its translation in all the EU official languages can be found on the e-justice portal.

214 The statement of opposition is submitted either in paper form or by any other means of communication, including electronic.

215 See Lupoi (n.55), 200.

216 If the defendant oppose the payment order, proceedings will continue according to the law of the Member State of origin. For further details see Elena D'Alessandro, 'Il Procedimento Monitorio Europeo con Particolare Riferimento alla Fase di Opposizione ex Art. 17 Reg. n. 1896/2006' (2011) 6 Giusto proc. civ., 722.

217 For further information see Giacomo Porcelli, 'Art. 16' in Paolo Biavati 'Reg. CE n. 1896/2006 del Parlamento europeo e del Consiglio che Istituisce un Procedimento Europeo d'Ingiunzione di Pagamento' (2010) 33 Le nuove leggi civili commentate, 442.

a) *Dies a quo*

It follows that the 30 days time limit provided for in Art. 16 (2) EPO Regulation starts running once the European payment order has been served on the debtor.

The respect of the right of defence is then connected with the effective knowledge of the issuance of the EPO: the debtor has to be confronted with a document that he is able to understand and consequently contest before than the title becomes enforceable[218].

Service of the EPO is performed in accordance with national procedural law, but it must comply with some minimum requirements laid down in the EPO Regulation: 'of among the possible service procedures set out in national law, only those that follow one of the modalities or methods considered acceptable by EU legislation may be used'[219]. These rules aim at eliminating the use of methods that do not provide sufficient guarantees that service effectively took place[220].

In particular, the EPO must be served on the defendant (or on his representative)[221] according to one of the following methods of service: either service with proof of receipt (Art. 13 EPO Regulation) or service without proof of receipt (Art. 14 EPO Regulation).

Where service of the EPO is not consistent with the minimum standards laid down in Arts 13 to 15 EPO Regulation[222], 'the period within which to send a statement of opposition in Art. 16 (2) thereof does not start to run, so that the validity of the procedures which depend on the expiry of that period, such as the declaration of enforceability referred to in Art. 18 or the

---

218 Gascón Inchausti (n.125), 487; Marco Velicogna, Giampiero Lupo and Elena Alina Ontanu, 'Simplifying Access to Justice in Cross-Border Litigation, the National Practices and the Limits of the EU Procedures. The Example of the Service of Documents in the Order for Payment Claims' (2017) 7 IJPL, 93.

219 Gascón Inchausti (n.125), 487.

220 Elena Alina Ontanu, *Cross-Border Debt Recovery in the EU. A Comparative and Empirical Study on the Use of the European Uniform Procedures* (Intersentia 2017), 38.

221 See Art. 15 EPO Regulation.

222 The irregularity of service also includes the case in which the defendant is not informed of his right to refuse service of an untranslated document, as required by Art. 12 (1) of the Service Regulation Recast. See Case C-21/17 *Catlin Europe SE v O. K. Trans Praha spol. s.r.o.* (2018) EU:C:2018:675.

application for review in Art. 20, even if they have already been initiated, is affected'[223].

b) Interruption and suspension of time limits according to national law (C-18/21)

The time limit to oppose the issuance of payment orders – as arises from Recital 28 EPO Regulation – should be calculated pursuant to Regulation 1182/71 of 3 June 1971 determining the rules applicable to periods, dates and time limits[224].

In particular, Art. 3 of Regulation 1182/71 reads as follows. The *dies a quo* of the time limit must not be considered in the calculation (*dies a quo non computatur in termino); the dies ad quem* is instead counted. The time period[225] – including public holidays[226], Sunday and Saturday if expressed in calendar days or not including public holidays, Sunday and Saturday if expressed in working days – starts to run at the beginning of the first hour of the first day and ends with the expiry of the last hour of the last day of the period. Where the time limit expires on a public holiday, Sunday or Saturday, the deadline expires on the next working day.

In this respect, issues on the calculation of the 30 days time limit for opposing payment orders recently arose in *Uniqa Versicherungen*[227]. Notably, the question at hand was whether the 30 days time limit for opposing a European payment, as provided for in Art. 16 (2) of the EPO Regulation might be interrupted by paragraph 1 (1) of the Austrian Law on Covid-19,

223 Cases C-119/13 and C-120/13, *Eco cosmetics GmbH & Co. KG and Raiffeisenbank St. Georgen reg. Gen. mbH v Virginie Laetitia Barbara Dupuy and Tetyana Bonchyk* (2014) EU:C:2014:2144. Further see below aa) Absolute lack of service of the documents instituting the proceedings.

224 Regulation (EEC, Euratom) 1182/71 of the Council of 3 June 1971 determining the rules applicable to periods, dates and time limits (1971) OJ L 124. In this regard, it should be noted that some Member States (e.g. France and Spain) explictly refer to Regulation 1182/71 for calculating time limits, while others (e.g. Italy) do not provide any specific rule. In order to comply with the rationale of the EPO Regulation it seems clear, even without any specific reference, that time limits must be calculated according to the rules laid down in Regulation 1182/71.

225 It should be noted that the time limit to oppose the issuance of payment orders under Art. 16 (2) EPO Regulation is expressed in calendar days.

226 Public holidays are those days designated as such by the Member State in which the action is to be taken, See Art. 2 of Regulation 1182/71.

227 Case C-18/21 *Uniqa Versicherungen AG v VU* (2022) EU:C:2022:682.

pursuant to which all procedural periods in proceedings in civil cases for which the event triggering the period occurred after 21 March 2020 or which had not yet expired by that date were to be suspended until the end of 30 April 2020 and were to begin to run anew from 1 May 2020.

In this regard, it should be noted that the EPO Regulation does not provide any specific rule governing the interruption or suspension of the mentioned 30 days time limit while this is running. Without uniform procedural rules on this matter, it is for the national legal order of each Member State – as arises from Art. 26 EPO Regulation – to establish rules on the interruption and suspension of the Art. 16 (2) time limit as long as they comply with the EU principles of equivalence and effectiveness.

In *Uniqa Versicherungen* the CJEU thus noted, first, that the Austrian Covid-19 legislation appears to ensure equal treatment of order for payment procedures under national law and similar procedures under the EPO Regulation.

Second, the CJEU indicated that interrupting the running of the 30 days period laid down in Art. 16 (2) appears justified by the objective of ensuring compliance with the defendant's rights of defence without making its exercise excessively difficult in practice.

In light of the above, the CJEU concluded that the Austrian Covid-19 legislation, which interrupted procedural periods in civil matters for approximately 5 weeks, applied to the 30 days time limit laid down in Art. 16 (2) EPO Regulation.

c) The alleged shortness of the time limits in consumer law proceedings

The choice of the EU legislator to set in Art. 16 (2) EPO Regulation a 30 days period to lodge a statement of opposition against the issuance of an EPO is a pragmatic solution which aims at combining characteristics proper to the different national payment order procedures existing across the EU, i.e. documentary and non-documentary models[228].

The EPO Regulation opted for a 'hybrid' model where the court's examination on the merits of the claim – based solely on the partial information included in standard form A – is rather superficial and makes the issuance of an EPO semi-automatic. The EU legislator, in order to compensate for

228 See below (ii) Time to oppose the issuance of payment orders) for further information on the characteristics of documentary and non-documentary procedures.

a partial examination of evidence, thus opted for a 30 days time limit to oppose the EPO, which can be considered as a compromise between the short and long time limits provided for in documentary and non-documentary procedures.

In this respect, some doubts arose in *Bondora*[229] regarding whether the alleged shortness of the 30 days time limit was sufficient to ensure effective protection of consumers' procedural rights within the EPO procedure. In the case at hand, AG Sharpston[230] raised – *inter alia*[231] – the question whether the 30 days period for opposing the issuance of an EPO was sufficient to ensure effective protection of consumers' rights, as embedded by Directive 93/13[232]. According to AG's view a 30 days time limit was too short for effectively protecting consumer's rights within the EPO procedure in light of the following arguments.

First, the AG referred to *Banco Espanol de Credito*[233]. Here, the CJEU stated that the 20 days time limit provided for under Spanish procedural law to oppose national payment orders within a documentary procedure did not comply with European consumer law (in particular with Directive 93/13). When comparing the EPO to the Spanish procedure, it appears that a documentary procedure like the Spanish one allows a consumer to acquaint himself more easily with the evidence relied on against him, unlike the model on which the European order for payment procedure is based. A time limit only 10 days longer than that provided for in a documentary procedure – clearly better protecting consumers' rights in accessing evidence – does not seem sufficient to protect properly consumers' rights within the EPO procedure, where evidence is not fully produced, but only summarily described.

In addition, the AG appreciated the shortness of the 30 days time period with respect to the information made available to consumers within the EPO procedure. When an EPO is issued against consumers, they are generally unaware of the extent of their rights deriving from Directive 93/13,

229 Cases C-453/18 and C-494/18, *Bondora AS v Carlos V. C. and XY* (2019) EU:C:2019:1118.

230 Opinion of AG Sharpston, Cases C-453/18 and C-494/18 *Bondora AS v Carlos V. C. and XY* (2019) EU:C:2019:921.

231 The case raised further issues on the proection of consumer law which are not dealt with here.

232 See Council Directive 93/13/EEC on unfair terms in consumer contracts (1993) OJ L 95.

233 CJEU Case C-618/10 *Banco Español de Crédito, SA v Joaquín Calderón Camino* (2012) EU:C:2012:349.

and are not in the position to assess the unfair terms of a contract due to the limited information provided for in the EPO. Under these complex circumstances, a 30 days period is not deemed to be sufficient for effectively ensuring the rights of consumers when lodging a statement of opposition against an EPO.

Contrary to the AG's conclusions, the CJEU did not consider any specific issue connected with the excessive shortness of the 30 days time limit granted to consumers for opposing the issuance of an EPO[234].

In spite of this judgment, academic debates are still ongoing and it has reasonably been argued that in the present state of affairs, the 30 days time limit to oppose an EPO is not sufficient to effectively protect consumers' procedural rights in cross-border cases[235]. As arises from CJEU case law, consumers' rights deserve indeed a special *status quo* within the EPO procedure which requires additional safeguards compared to general cases. Providing consumer defendants with longer deadlines to oppose payment orders might be one of these safeguards.

2) Time limits within the ESCP Regulation

The ESCP Regulation sets specific time limits governing the different stages of proceedings to ensure their swift commencement, conduct and conclusion.

a) Uniform time limits governing ESCP proceedings

Art. 5 ESCP Regulation provides for the following specific timeframe for accomplishing procedural activities.

---

234 On a different note, the CJEU in *Bondora* (n.229) stated that a court seized of an EPO can 'request from the creditor additional information relating to the terms of the agreement relied on in support of the claim at issue, in order to carry out an ex officio review of the possible unfairness of those terms and, consequently, that they preclude national legislation which declares the additional documents provided for that purpose to be inadmissible'.

235 Burkhard Hess, 'Towards a More Coherent EU Framework for the Cross-Border Enforcement of Civil Claims' in Jan Von Hein and Thalia Kruger (eds), *Informed Choices in Cross-Border Enforcement. The European State of the Art and Future Perspectives* (Intersentia 2021), 400; Hess (n.180), 15.

It should be noted that according to Recital 24 ESCP Regulation[236] time limits should be calculated pursuant to Regulation 1182/71 determining the rules applicable to periods, dates and time limits[237].

The court receiving the claim form[238] shall within 14 days of its reception serve a copy of it together with the answer form[239] on the defendant (Art. 5 (2) ESCP Regulation).

According to Art. 13 (1) ESCP Regulation service of these forms shall in principle be carried out by postal service with acknowledgement of receipt including the date of receipt, or, on equal terms, by electronic means[240] that also generate acknowledgement of receipt including the date of receipt[241].

However, where service in accordance to one of these methods is not possible, Art. 13 (4) ESCP Regulation refers to any of the service methods provided for in Arts 13 and 14 of the EPO Regulation[242].

Finally, if none of the mentioned methods is available, Member States are free to establish an additional rule of service, provided that Arts 13 and 14 EPO Regulation refer to national law[243].

From the moment of service of the claim and answer forms, the defendant has 30 days to show his reaction to the claim by filling in the answer

---

236 In this regard, it should be noted that some Member States (e.g. Spain) explictly refer to Regulation 1182/71 for calculating time limits, while others (e.g. Italy and France) do not provide any specific rule. In order to comply with the rationale of the ESCP Regulation it seems clear, even without any specific reference, that time limits must be calculated according to the rules laid down in Regulation 1182/71.

237 See above (b) Interruption and suspension of time limits according to national law (*C-18/21*)) for further details on the rules on calculation of time limits as determined by Art. 3 of Regulation 1182/71. It should be noted that under the scope of the ESCP Regulation time limits are expressed in calendar days.

238 See standard form A attached to the ESCP Regulation.

239 See standard form C attached to the ESCP Regulation.

240 The admissibility of electronic means is subject to the two following requirements under the law of the Member State where service is effected: '(i) where such means are technically available and admissible in accordance with the procedural rules of the Member State in which the European Small Claims Procedure is conducted and, if the party to be served is domiciled or habitually resident in another Member State, in accordance with the procedural rules of that Member State; and (ii) where the party to be served has expressly accepted in advance that documents may be served on him by electronic means or is, in accordance with the procedural rules of the Member State in which that party is domiciled or habitually resident, under a legal obligation to accept that specific method of service'.

241 Gascón Inchausti (n.125), 489.

242 See above a) *Dies a quo*.

243 Richard (n.60), 478.

form (or alternatively in any other appropriate way) and sending it back to the court, accompanied by any relevant supporting document (Art. 5 (3) ESCP Regulation).

Where the defendant in his reply files a counterclaim, the claimant will have 30 days from its service to react to it (Art. 5 (6) ESCP Regulation).

Art. 7 ESCP Regulation further structures the procedure as follows. The court shall render a decision within a period of 30 days from 1) the moment of receiving the parties' response, or 2) after having received all the information necessary for giving the decision, or 3) from the oral hearing when this is deemed to be necessary.

As arises from Art. 14 ESCP Regulation, where the court sets a time limit for accomplishing a procedural activity, the parties concerned shall be informed of the consequences of not complying with it. The problem is that Art. 14 is vague and does not specify which procedural sanctions follow from the failure to act within the set time limit. In the answer form, it is simply indicated that if the defendant does not react to the claim within 30 days the judge shall give a judgment[244]. This suggests that the parties that did not react in time are precluded from showing their reaction later in the proceedings and a judgment will be rendered against them[245].

The ESCP procedure seems to work smoothly; its average length is approximately 5 months and this points to a significant decrease in the timeframe for small claims litigation across the EU[246].

b) The lack of a unform time limit to appeal

The ESCP Regulation does not contain any uniform rules on appeal proceedings. The availability of an appeal and the time limits to appeal an ESCP judgment are governed by national law. Solutions differ considerably between Member States' procedural systems[247].

---

244 Richard (n.60), 480.

245 Ontanu (n.220), 48.

246 Ontanu (n.220), 48.

247 E.g. under Italian law, two levels of appeal ('appello' and 'ricorso in cassazione') are generally available. The defendant can lodge an appeal on factual grounds within a 30 days time period from the service of the judgment, and can lodge an appeal on legal grounds within 60 days from the service of the appeal judgment. Under French law only one level of appeal – provided that appeal on factual grounds ('appel') is available only for claims over €5000 not included under the scope of the ESCP

In this respect, one could argue that the lack of harmonisation of appeal proceedings under the ESCP procedure is undesirable as different national rules apply to a uniform procedure that is intended to have one single outcome[248]. This weakens the ESCP uniform procedure leading to an unequal level of protection of parties' rights across the EU[249].

It follows that the availability of an appeal and the time limits for lodging it in the framework of a European procedure like the ESCP should lie with the EU legislator: 'If a mere procedure for refusal of enforcement[250] may be appealed as a matter of EU law, then *a fortiori* a fully European procedure shall be subject to the same principle'[251].

This assertion is further supported by the fact that within the ESCP Regulation the availability of an appeal is demeed to be taken for granted. The ESCP Regulation indeed establishes in its wording that some decisions cannot be contested separately – i.e. the refusal of a party's request to hold an oral hearing (Art. 5 (1)) and the decision whether the value of the claim falls within the scope of the Regulation (Art. 5 (5)) – which means that 'such decisions can only be contested when the judgment itself is contested, that is to say, by means of appeal'[252].

---

procedure – is generally available ('recours en cassation'). Appeals on legal grounds shall be lodged within 2 months from the service of the judgment. Only if the ESCP judgment is rendered in default, there are two levels of appeal available ('opposition' and 'recours en cassation'). Opposition shall be filed within 1 month from the service of the judgment and the appeal on legal grounds shall be lodged within 2 months from the service of the opposed judgment. Under Romanian law only one degree of appeal is possible. The ESCP judgment is subject to appeal before the tribunal within 30 days from being served. See Ontanu (n.220), 48, 139, 231, and 303; Frédérique Ferrand, 'Procédure Européenne de Règlement des Petits Litiges' in Serge Guinchard, *Droit et Pratique de la Procedure Civile* (10th edn, Dalloz 2021), para 449.32; Elena D'Alessandro, *Il Procedimento Uniforme per le Controversie di Modesta Entità* (Giappichelli Editore 2008), 93–96.

248 Cristian Oro Martinez, 'The Small Claims Regulation: on the Way to an Improved European Procedure' in Burkhard Hess, Maria Bergström and Eva Storskrubb (eds), *EU Civil Justice Current Issues and Future Outlook* (Bloomsbury 2016), 135.

249 Ontanu (n.220), 51; Oro Martinez (n.248), 136.

250 See in this regard Art. 49 (1) of the Brussels Ibis Regulation

251 Oro Martinez (n.248), 136.

252 Oro Martinez (n.248), 136.

3) Time limits within the EAPO Regulation

The EAPO Regulation introduces a European procedure for the preliminary preservation of bank accounts within the EU. Among its uniform rules, the EAPO Regulation establishes precise time limits for the different steps of the procedure.

In particular, the EAPO procedure is structured as follows.

On the one hand, the procedure for issuing, recognizing, enforcing and implementing the EAPO is conducted *inaudita altera parte*, i.e. without debtors having knowledge of the EAPO before its adoption. In order to ensure that the EAPO is issued swiftly and without delays[253] – delays would indeed further undermine the debtor's right of defence – the EU legislator foresaw strict time limits within which the parties and courts must, respectively, exercise their procedural rights and conduct the proceedings.

On the other hand, the respect of the right of defence is ensured when the EAPO is served on the debtor after its adoption. Based on the common grounds (including also possible deficiencies deriving from the lack of compliance with time limits) provided for in the Regulation, debtors can challenge the issue and enforcement of the EAPO within a unifom procedure subject to appeal. Both the time limits to challenge the issue or enforcement of the EAPO and those for appealing the latter decision are determined according to the applicable national law.

Therefore, the analysis first deals with the role of time limits in the *ex parte* procedure for issuing and enforcing the EAPO; second, with the time limits to challenge the EAPO.

As a preliminary observation, it should be noted – as Recital 38 EAPO Regulation makes clear – that under its scope periods and time limits should be calculated according to Regulation 1182/71[254].

253 See Recital 17 EAPO Regulation.

254 See above b) Interruption and suspension of time limits according to national law (*C-18/21*)) for further details on the rules on calculation of time limits as determined by Art. 3 of Regulation 1182/71. It should be noted that under the scope of the EAPO Regulation, save where explicitly indicated, time limits are expressed in calendar days.

a) Time limits governing the *ex parte* adoption of the EAPO

The following timeframe governing the *ex parte* adoption of the EAPO differs depending on whether the creditor has already obtained a title on the substance of the matter proving his claim.

aa) Proof of having initiated proceedings

What follows from Art. 10 (1) EAPO Regulation is that the creditor who applied for a preservation order without a title on the substance of the matter must provide proof that proceedings which lead to the adoption of a judgment on the merits have been initiated[255] within 30 days of the date on which he lodged the application for an EAPO or within 14 days of the date of the issue of the order. As these dates may diverge, the time limit will expire on whichever date is the later[256]. In this respect, the court may also extend the time limit at debtor's request, e.g. in order to reach a settled solution of the claim[257]. The rationale of the rule laid down in Art. 10 (1) is to prevent a situation in which the debtor's legal position is impacted by a protective measure without an enforceable title or the existence of ongoing proceedings capable of leading to an enforceable title[258].

The *dies a quo* of the time limit expressed in calendar days is on the day on which the creditor lodged the application (30 days) or the date of the issue of the order (14 days)[259].

---

255 The moment at which proceedings are initiated is determined according to Art. 10 (3) EAPO Regulation.

256 In light of the strict timeframe provided for under Art. 18 EAPO Regulation, the later date is generally 30 days from the application. Neverthless, some factors may slow down the procedure, making 14 days after the Issuing of the EAPO the later date to be taken into account. See Gilles Cuniberti and Sara Migliorini, *The European Account Preservation Order: A Commentary* (Cambridge University Press 2018), 145.

257 'The pressure to initiate proceedings within a short time limit may discourage parties from entering into negotiation, or lead to failure of ongoing negotiations'. Fernando Gascón Inchausti, 'Art. 10' in Elena D'Alessandro and Fernando Gascón Inchausti (eds), *Commentary of Regulation No 655/2014* (Edward Elgar Publishing 2022), para 10.28.

258 Gascón Inchausti (n.257), para 10.28.

259 As arises from Recital 38 EAPO Regulation, these time limits should be calculated according to Regulation 1182/71.

Where the creditor does not provide proof of having initiated proceedings in due time, 'the preservation order shall be revoked or shall terminate and the parties shall be informed accordingly' (Art. 10 (2) EAPO Regulation). In spite of some doubts on the distinction between revocation and termination[260], what certainly follows is that the EAPO ceases its effects lacking its validity and effectiveness[261]. If enforcement has not started yet, all steps in that regard should stop; on the other hand if the bank account has already been seized, the measure should be revoked and the debtor should recover free disposition of his assets, and this entails that the bank should be immediately informed[262].

bb) Issuing the decision

Art. 18 EAPO Regulation lays down a specific timeframe which must be complied with by courts when deciding on EAPO applications which differs depending on whether the creditor obtained a title on the substance of the matter.

If the creditor has not yet obtained a title on the substance of the matter, the court shall decide on the EAPO application by the end of the tenth working day after the creditor lodged, or eventually completed his application (Art. 18 (1) EAPO Regulation).

On the other hand, if the creditor has already obtained a title on the substance of the matter, the court shall issue its decision by the end of the

260 The Regulation does not define these two concepts. Recital 16 simply states that the EAPO 'should be revoked by a court of its own motion or should terminate automatically'. In this regard, it has reasonably been argued that 'revocation must be ordered by a court, and is thus a judicial remedy, whereas termination occurs without the intervention of a court, by the operation of the law. The Regulation does not explain the respective scopes of revocation and termination. In accordance with the general rule of the Regulation that the effect of preservation orders is governed by the law of the Member State of enforcement, it must be considered that whether the Preservation order should be revoked or will terminate automatically is to be determined by the law of the Member State of enforcement, i.e. the law of the place where the account is maintained'. See Cuniberti and Migliorini (n.256), 149.

261 Marco Farina, 'L'Ordinanza Europea di Sequestro Conservativo su Conti Bancari' (2015) Le nuove leggi civili commentate, 519.

262 Gascón Inchausti (n.257), para 10.32. In particular, revocation or termination may require specific implementation measures to be adopted according to Art. 10 (2).

fifth[263] working day after the creditor lodged, or eventually completed his application (Art. 18 (2) EAPO Regulation).

The wording 'by the end of' suggests that the time limits of 5 and 10 working days are maximum time limits that cannot to be exceeded. Their starting point generally begins when the court seized of the EAPO application has all the elements to take its decision, i.e. the day on which the application is lodged, completed or rectified[264].

However, it is possible to extend the above time limits under certain circumstances, which are not exhaustively listed by Art. 18 EAPO Regulation.

First, Art. 18 (3) EAPO Regulation deals with the case where the court oganizes an oral hearing of either the creditor or any of his witnesses. In such situation, the court shall hold the hearing 'without delay' and issue its decision by the end of the fifth working day (whichever the nature of the preservation order) after the hearing has taken place. The time limit runs from the first working day following the day of the hearing.

Art. 18 (4) EAPO Regulation further addresses the situation in which a security must be provided by the creditor. In this respect, the 5 or 10 days time limit laid down in Art. 18 (1), (2) and (3) are applicable to the decision requiring the creditor to provide a security. Once the creditor has provided the latter security, the court shall decide on the EAPO application 'without delay'.

Finally, Art. 18 (5) EAPO Regulation provides for the possibility that a request for obtaining account information has been made under Art. 14 EAPO Regulation. Collecting information on assets abroad is an operation taking time and requiring flexibile time limits. That is why Art. 18 (5) derogates to the fixed time limits provided for in Art. 18 (1), (2) and (3) by stating that 'in situations referred to in Art. 14 the court shall issue its decision without delay once it has received the information referred to in Art. 14 (6) or (7), provided that any security required has been provided by the creditor by that time'.

---

263 It should be noted that the length of this time limit is twice as long if the creditor has not yet obtained a title. This is justified by the fact that the court when issuing an EAPO without a title on the substance of the matter needs more time as it should check some additional requirements, e.g. the creditor is likely to succeed on the substance of the claim against the debtor. See Guillaume Payan, 'Art. 18' in Elena D'Alessandro and Fernando Gascón Inchausti (eds), *Commentary of Regulation No 655/2014* (Edward Elgar Publishing 2022), para 18.06.

264 As arises from Recital 38 EAPO Regulation, these time limits should be calculated according to Regulation 1182/71.

In addition to these hyphoteses, according to Art. 45 EAPO Regulation time limits can also be extended when, in exceptional circumstances[265], courts cannot comply with the above timeframe for deciding. In such case, the court is required to act as soon as possible.

As no procedural sanction is foreseen if courts do not comply with the time limits under Art. 18 EAPO Regulation, one could wonder about the effectiveness of these time limits[266]. Nevertheless, the possibility of envisaging procedural sanctions according to the law of the Member State in which proceedings are conducted (Art. 46 EAPO Regulation) seems to guarantee the rationale of Art. 18[267]. In theory, it could even be possible for the European Commission to initiate proceedings against the relevant Member State for failure to act, i.e. the lack of compliance with Art. 18 time limits[268].

cc) Appeal against the refusal to issue an EAPO

Art. 21 EAPO Regulation provides the creditor with the right to appeal against any decision of the court rejecting, wholly[269] or in part[270], the EAPO application.

---

265 The meaning of exceptional circumstances is here interpreted very strictly. In particular, it is assumed that the reasons for derogating from a time limit must not be internal to the judiciary, but only specific to the case or the parties. As confirmed by CJEU case law court holidays do not constitute indeed exceptional circumstances. See Case C-555/18 *KHK v BAC abd EEK* (2019) EU:C:2019:937; Payan (n.263), para 18.15.

266 Paolo Biavati, Il Sequestro Conservativo Europeo su Conti Bancari: alla Ricerca di un Difficile Equilibrio' (2015) 79 Riv. trim. dir. e proc. civ., 863.

267 Payan (n.263), para 18.09.

268 An unjustified serious breach of the time limit to issue the decision could indeed entail a violation of EU law which could theoretically be used as ground for initiating an infringement procedure for violation of the TFEU (Art. 258 TFEU) or as a claim for damages by the debtor against the Member State that breached EU law (Art. 340 TFEU). Neverthless, this possibility in practice seems very unrealistic. See Cuniberti and Migliorini (n.256), 208; Burkhard Hess, 'EuKtPVO Arts. 17–19' in Peter Schlosser and Burkhard Hess (eds), *EU-Zivilprozessrecht* (5th edn, C.H.Beck 2021).

269 Where the appeal is lodged against a decision that has fully rejected the EAPO application, appeal proceedings will be conducted *ex parte* according to Art. 21 (3) EAPO Regulation.

270 Art. 21 (3) EAPO Regulation does not refer to the situation where the EAPO application is only partially rejected. In such case it has been argued that it is on

According to Art. 21 (2) EAPO Regulation the creditor may lodge his appeal[271] before the competent national court[272] within 30 days running from the date on which the decision rejecting the EAPO application was brought to his notice pursuant to the law of the Member State of the issuing court[273].

dd) Recognition and enforcement of the EAPO

Once the EAPO is issued, it can automatically be recognised and enforced within the EU without the need for a declaration of enforceability (Art. 22 EAPO Regulation).

As arises from Art. 23 (1) EAPO Regulation, EAPOs shall be enforced in accordance with the procedures applicable to the enforcement of equivalent national measures in the Member State of enforcement[274].

---

national kegislators to decide wheither appeal proceedings should be conducted *ex parte* or the debtor should be heard. See Enrique Vallines Garcia, 'Art. 21' in Elena D'Alessandro and Fernando Gascón Inchausti (eds), *Commentary of Regulation No 655/2014* (Edward Elgar Publishing 2022), para 21.26.

271 The form of the brief of appeal is not regulated at EU level, but it is established by the law of the Member States. The appeal is normally made via submisission of a written brief of appeal, which shall comply with the formalities provided for by national law. See Vallines Garcia (n.270), para 21.23.

272 As arises from Art. 21 (2) EAPO read in conjoction with Art. 50 (1)(d) EAPO Regulation, the competent jurisdiction dealing with appeal proceedings shall be determined by the national law of the Member States. See Vallines Garcia (n.270), para 21.13.

273 As arise from Recital 38 EAPO Regulation, this time limit should be calculated according to Regulation 1182/71.

274 This rule shall be interpreted in accordance with the EU principles of equivalence and effectiveness (see 1) Non-discrimination of national and foreign defendants for further details on the application of these principles). Neverthless, since the EAPO is deemed to be a protective measure *in rem*, the application of the latter principles may prove to be difficult when the Member State of enforcement only deal with protective measures *in personam*, e.g. in common law systems like Cyprus or Ireland. Since protective measures *in personam* – unlike protective measures *in rem* – are effective as soon as they are issued, with no need to take steps to block the debtor's account, such Member States had to adapt their national law to the European preservation order (*in rem*). See Elena D'Alessandro, 'Art. 23' in Elena D'Alessandro and Fernando Gascón Inchausti (eds), *Commentary of Regulation No 655/2014* (Edward Elgar Publishing 2022), para 23.03; Cuniberti and Miglorini (n.256), 224. On a minor opinion, someone argued that the EAPO has *in rem* or *in personam* effects depending on the law of the Member State of enforcement. See

In order to ensure swift enforcement[275], all authorities involved in the enforcement of the EAPO shall act (as required by Art. 23 (2) EAPO Regulation) without delay.

In this respect, it should be noted that when preservation orders shall be enforced in a Member State other than that in which they were issued, the law of the Member State of origin determines under Art 23 (3) EAPO Regulation whether the creditor or the issuing court is under a duty to transmit the proper documentation to the enforcement authority.

In spite of directly dealing with enforcement, the EAPO Regulation does not contain any specific reference to the temporal validity of the enforcement title issued in the context of the EAPO procedure. This makes in principle the duration of the EAPO title unlimited in time. However, this result contrasts with the instrumental function and nature of provisional measures – as it is the EAPO – which are by definition limited in time and incompatible with any other enforcement measure insisting on the same claim[276]. As the EAPO is deemed to be a protective measure *in rem*[277], it does not automatically produce its effects as soon as it is issued – as it is generally the case with protective measures in personam – but it requires steps to be practically enforced within specific time limits[278]. Provided that the EAPO Regulation does not regulate the time limits to enforce the EAPO across the EU, it is questionable if the *lex fori* of the Member State of enforcement (as arises from Art. 23 EAPO Regulation) or the law of the Member State of origin where the EAPO procedure took place (as prescribed in Art. 46 EAPO Regulation) governs the validity of the European enforcement title[279].

Based on the CJEU arguments in *Al Bosco*, the time limit provided for under the law of the Member State of enforcement should apply to the EAPO. Neverthless, one could argue that this interpretation barely finds

---

Nico Ritz, *Vorläufige Kontenpfändung in Europa* (Peter Lang 2019), 177. Neverthless, arguments based on the lack of unifom effects of the EAPO within the EU contrasts this interpretation.

275 See Recital 37 EAPO Regulation.

276 Carmen Senés Motilla, La Orden Europea de Retención de Cuentas: Aplicación en Derecho Español del Reglamento (UE) Núm. 655/2014 de 15 de Mayo de 2014 (Aranzadi 2015), 166.

277 See fn 274.

278 Depending on the applicable national law, it will be up either to the creditor or to the issuing court to proceed to the enforcement of the EAPO within the time limits.

279 The very same question has already been decided by the CJEU under the scope of the Brussels Ibis Regulation in *Al Bosco*. See fn 170.

justification under the EAPO Regulation Where enforcement of the EAPO is sought in more than one Member State, its temporal validity would be *de facto* subject to different regimes depending on the time limits provided for under the law of the various places of enforcement, e.g. an EAPO issued in Italy would have a different duration depending if its enforcement is sought in Italy, France or Germany which undermines the rationale of having a European uniform title and the scope of the EAPO Regulation.

To conclude, the time limits to enforce the EAPO do not pertain to the law of the Member State of enforcement, but are regulated by the law of the Member State of origin. This mechanism makes the temporal validity of the European enforcement title depending on where this has been issued irrespective of where it should actually be enforced. The *dies a quo* of the time limits to enforce the EAPO – calculated according to national law – should run from the day of its issue, as indicated in the specific standard form for issuing it[280]. Under the current legal framework where such procedural issue is not dealt with at EU level, the latter interpretation seems the most valuable. In order to simplify the identification of the time limits to enforce EAPOs across the EU, it would be helpful if Art. 19 EAPO Regulation among the information to fill in the form provided for in Annex 2 of Regulation 2016/1823 indicated – in addition to the date of issue – the expiry date of the preservation order.

Moreover, divergences between the time limits to enforce the EAPO in the Member State of origin lead to fragmentation. This undermines the uniformity of the EAPO enforcement title whose temporal vailidity depends on where it has been issued, instead of being harmonised at EU level. The situation is burdensome for creditors as it decreases their expectations in legal certainty. It would thus be advisable to address the issue in the future EAPO reform by laying down – as it happens for instance with respect to the European Certficate of Succession[281] – an EU uniform rule governing the temporal validity of the EAPO across the Member States.

280 See Annex II of Commission Implementing Regulation (EU) 2016/1823 of 10 October 2016 establishing the forms referred to in Regulation (EU) No 655/2014 of the European Parliament and of the Council establishing a European Account Preservation Order procedure to facilitate cross-border debt recovery in civil and commercial matters (2016) OJ L 283.

281 The validity of the European Certficate of succession is limited to 6 months. See Art. 70 of Regulation (EU) No 650/2012 of the European Parliament and of the Council of 4 July 2012 on jurisdiction, applicable law, recognition and enforcement of decisions and acceptance and enforcement of authentic instruments in matters of

ee) Implementation of the EAPO

Once notified of the preservation order, the bank should proceed to its Implementation 'without delay' (Art. 24 (1) EAPO Regulation). The swiftness of the implementation therefore depends on the law of the Member State addressed which will concretely assess the timing of the implementation of the preservation order by the bank[282]. If the implementation of the EAPO happens to be delayed, the bank will be liable towards the creditor in accordance to the applicable national law[283].

The formulation of Art. 24 (1) replaces the one suggested by the Commission in its proposal of Art. 26 which required the bank to implement the EAPO 'immediately upon receipt'. While the proposed version insisted on an instantaneous reaction from the bank on the day of receipt, the final wording of Art. 24 (1) is more flexible and seems to lay down 'a wider timeframe to accomodate existing national differences as well as additional steps a bank would need to take to be able to implement the order'[284].

Notwithstanding some open questions regarding the moment in time at which the preservation order becomes effective, the bank given the urgency of the situation at hand must in any event react quickly by implementing the EAPO as soon as possible. Notably, implementation should be structured as to prevent the debtor from withdrawing and/or transfering amounts contained in the preserved account from the day the EAPO is received by the bank[285]. In spite of the lack of fixed time limits to implement the EAPO, one could argue that the structure of the implementation process implicitly calls for a uniform rule as to the date or moment in time

succession and on the creation of a European Certificate of Succession (2012) OJ L 201.

282 As arises from Art. 26 EAPO Regulation, if the implementation of the EAPO happens to be delayed, the bank will be liable towards the creditor in accordance to the applicable national law. See Antonio Leandro, 'La circolazione dell'Ordinanza Europea di Sequestro Conservativo dei Conti Bancari' in Pietro Franzina and Antonio Leandro (eds), *Il Sequestro Europeo di Conti Bancari* (Giuffrè Editore 2015), 139, 140; Elena Alina Ontanu, 'Art. 24' in Elena D'Alessandro and Fernando Gascón Inchausti (eds), *Commentary of Regulation No 655/2014* (Edward Elgar Publishing 2022), para 24.06.

283 Ontanu (n.282), para 24.07.

284 Ontanu (n.282), para 24.06.

285 Biavati (n.266), 864.

when the EAPO begins producing its effects, which should be the date of receipt of the preservation order by the bank[286].

In this respect, the bank must issue a specific declaration concerning the preservation of debtors' funds (Art. 25 (1) EAPO Regulation) by the end of the third working day[287] following the implementation of the EAPO. If under exceptional circumstances[288] it is not possible for the bank to comply with the 3 days time limit, the requested act must be taken as soon as possible, but no later than the end of the 8 working day following the implementation of the order.

ff) Need to regulate the time limits to enforce the EAPO

What emerges is that the setting of these time limits requires courts, creditors and banks to act speedily and without delay in order to ensure that the issue, recognition, enforcement and implementation of an EAPO do not excessively undermine debtors' rights in *ex parte* proceedings. Except for not addressing the issue of the duration of the EAPO, the latter timeline set out by the EAPO Regulation seems to be detailed and comprehensive.

Without intervening on other aspects of the procedure, it would be desirable to address in future legislative reforms the question of the time limits to enforce EAPOs, whose lack of regulation within the EAPO procedure raise practical issues. To facilitate the identification of these time limits under the law of the Member State of origin, reference to the expiry date of the preservation order should be included among the information required by Art. 19 EAPO Regulation to fill in the form attached to Annex II of Regulation 2016/1823.

Furthermore, the fact that the temporal validity of preservation orders is governed by national law contradicts the uniform character of the EAPO as a European enforcement title. Providing for the same time limits to enforce EAPOs across the Member States would avoid this fragmentation and ensure a smoother functioning of the EAPO procedure.

---

286 Cuniberti and Migliorini (n.256), 244.

287 As arises from Recital 38 EAPO Regulation, this time period should be calculated according to Regulation 1182/71.

288 The definition of xceptional circumstances is interpreted very narrowly. See fn 265; Katharina Lugani, 'Art. 25' in Elena D'Alessandro and Fernando Gascón Inchausti (eds), *Commentary of Regulation No 655/2014* (Edward Elgar Publishing 2022), para 25.05; Case C-555/18 *KHK v BAC abd EEK* (2019) EU:C:2019:937, para 11.

b) Lodging remedies[289] against the EAPO

Once the preservation orders have been issued, enforced and implemented, the debtors are served with them according to Art. 28 EAPO Regulation and can challenge their issuance and enforcement.

As EAPOs are adopted in *ex parte* proceedings, the need to provide debtors with an effective mechanism to contest the EAPO is crucial to ensure their rights to a fair trail, as embedeed in Art. 6 ECHR and Art. 47 CFR.

The EAPO Regulation in Arts. 33 and 34 provides the means by which debtors can oppose under general circumstances[290] the issue or enforcement of preservation orders in the context of a specific autonoumous procedure (Art. 36) which is subject to appeal (Art. 37). In particular, the grounds and procedures for challenging preservation orders will be analysed by mainly focusing on the interplay between time limits and national law.

aa) Time limits as grounds for challenging the issue or enforcement of the EAPO

i) Insufficient time for challenging the EAPO

Among the different grounds to challenge the issue of EAPOs, the debtor pursuant to Art. 33 (1)(b) EAPO Regulation[291] could challenge failures in the service of the EAPO as not having allowed him an effective possibility

289 One could argue that 'the terminology of remedies is imprecise because what is being established is not true remedies, but rather 'autnomous mechanisms to challenge or react against European preservation measures'. María Luisa Villamarín López, 'Art. 33' in Elena D'Alessandro and Fernando Gascón Inchausti (eds), *Commentary of Regulation No 655/2014* (Edward Elgar Publishing 2022), para 33.01.

290 In case of exceptional circumstances there is a specific remedy provided for in Art. 35 EAPO Regulation which is opened both to debtors and creditors.

291 It should be noted that the same ground regarding defects in the service of the EAPO can also be raised at the enforcement stage in accordance with Art. 34 EAPO Regulation. See María Luisa Villamarín López. 'Art. 34' in Elena D'Alessandro and Fernando Gascón Inchausti (eds), *Commentary of Regulation No 655/2014* (Edward Elgar Publishing 2022), para 34.12.

to defend himself against it, e.g. the EAPO has not been served, it has been served incorrectly or in an ill-timed fashion[292].

As arises from Art. 33 (1)(b), the EAPO[293] must be served[294] on the debtor within a maximum period of time of 14 days. This time limit starts to run from the preservation of the bank account, which in spite of not being clearly identifed within the EAPO Regulation, seems to coincide with the moment of implementation of the preservation order[295].

What follows is that a period of 14 days is therefore considered to be acceptable for not excessively undermining debtors' rights while the EAPO is implemented *ex parte.* Save where defects in service are cured[296] within 14 days from the moment the creditor received information of the debtor's application for a remedy, the lack of service in sufficient time justifies the granting of the remedy pursuant to Art. 33 (1)(b) which lead to the revocation or modification of the EAPO.

ii) Expiry of the time limits to enforce the judgment underlying the EAPO

According to Art. 34 (1)(b)(iii) EAPO Regulation one of the grounds allowing debtors to challenge the enforcement of preservation orders in the Member State of enforcement is linked to the suspension of the enforceable

292 Villamarín López (n.289), para 33.11.

293 In this respect, see Art. 28 EAPO Regulation which deals with service of the preservation order on the debtor and other documents that are necessary for ensuring defendants' rights.

294 Contrary to Art. 28 EAPO Regulation which requires that service must have been initiated by the end of the third working day following the day of receipt of the declaration of preservation, Art. 33 (1) EAPO Regulation requires that service on the debtor must have been completed and not simply initated. See Fernando Gascón Inchausti, 'Art. 28' in Elena D'Alessandro and Fernando Gascón Inchausti (eds), *Commentary of Regulation No 655/2014* (Edward Elgar Publishing 2022), para 28.11.

295 Cuniberti and Migliorini (n.256), 280.

296 Unless the lack of service is cured by other means, Art. 33 (3) EAPO Regulation considers the lack of service to be cured in the following cases: a) if the creditor requests the body responsible for service under the law of the Member State of origin to serve the documents on the debtor; or (b) where the debtor has indicated in his application for a remedy that he agrees to collect the documents at the court of the Member State of origin.
In case, the creditor must prove that he had taken all the steps he was required to take to have the initial service of the documents effected.

character of the judgment[297] on the basis of which the EAPO has been issued in the Member State of origin. This could happen, for instance if the time limits to enforce the judgment supporting the EAPO expire leading to the suspension of enforceability of that judgment in the Member State of origin. As arises from Art. 34, under these circumstances enforcement proceedings must be terminated[298].

iii) Public policy in the Member State of enforcement

Under execptional circumstances, time limits could fall within the definition of procedural public policy[299] laid down in Art. 34 (2) EAPO Regulation and justify the termination of enforcement proceedings.

bb) Time limits within the procedures to contest the EAPO

i) Absence of uniform time limits for lodging the remedies

No specific time limit for contesting the EAPO has been envisaged within the uniform procedure laid down in Art. 36 EAPO Regulation. Contrary to the Commission proposal[300] which required that the application for

297 It should be noted that the wording of Art. 34 (1)(b)(iii) EAPO Regulation only refers to judgments without including court settlements and authentic instruments. It seems difficult to justify this exclusion. It has been argued in the literature that 'the only logical rationale for this exclusion 'would be to consider that where preservation orders are used for the purpose of securing payment of judgments, they are the first step to the enforcement of such judgments, and should thus only be available if enforcement is permissible in the relevant Member State'. Cuniberti and Migliorini (n.256), 289; Villamarín López (n.291), para 34.11; Senés Motilla (n.276), 238.

298 As Art. 34 (1)(b)(iii) EAPO Regulation addresses the case of suspension of enforceability in the Member State of origin, it would have probably been more appropriate – as it was the case in the Commission proposal to the EAPO Regulation – to provide the suspension of enforcement proceedings instead of their termination. See Cuniberti and Migliorini (n.256), 290; Commission Proposal, Art. 35 (3). See Proposal for a Regulation of the European Parliament and of the Council Creating a European Account Preservation Order to facilitate cross-border debt recovery in civil and commercial matters COM/2011/0445 final.

299 For further details on the definition of procedural public policy and its possible interaction with time limits see II) Time limits and public policy under Art. 45 (1)(a) .

300 See fn 298.

the remedies had to 'be made promptly and in any event within 45 days from the day the defendant was effectively acquainted with the contents of the order and was able to react', the EU legislator excluded in Art. 36 any reference to fixed time limits. Art. 36 (1) simply states that the application can be submitted 'at any time'.

The absence of any clear time limit is justified by the fact that the EAPO can be challenged not only on grounds linked to the issuance of the preservation order itself, but also supervening circumstances, which could occur at any time. A uniform time limit for applying for the remedies would therefore not be beneficial[301].

In principle, such procedural issue should be regulated by the law of the Member State which issued the EAPO pursuant to Art. 46. Nevertheless, time limits for lodging the remedies indicated by the different national laws should be considered inadmissible as this would create the very differences from Member State to Member State which the EU legislator wanted to avoid in the first place.

Moreover, 'the conscious decision of the EU legislator not to provide any time limits for applying for the remedies ... is proven by the fact that Art. 50 (1)(m) of the EAPO Regulation does not require Member States to notify the Commission of a time limit, but only requires them to indicate the competent authorities to decide on the remedy'[302].

This interpretation is further confirmed by the law of some Member States, e.g. Italy which does not provide any final time limits for lodging remedies against domestic preservation orders[303].

301 Silvana Dalla Bontà, 'Art. 36' in Elena D'Alessandro and Fernando Gascón Inchausti (eds), *Commentary of Regulation No 655/2014* (Edward Elgar Publishing 2022), para 36.10. On the contrary, some authors argued that the absence of a uniform time limit introduces an obvious loss of legal certainty and fragmentation, see Burkhard Hess and Katharina Raffelsieper, 'Eckpunkte der Kontenpfändungsverordnung' in Burkhard Hess (ed), Die Anerkennung im Internationalen Zivilprozessrecht: Europäisches Vollstreckungsrecht (Gieseking 2014), 218.

302 Dalla Bontà (n.301), para 36.10.

303 Elena D'Alessandro, 'I Mezzi di Ricorso e la Protezione dei Terzi' in Pietro Franzina and Antonio Leandro (eds), *Il Sequestro Europeo di Conti Bancari* (Giuffrè Editore 2015), 94.

ii) Time limits for deciding on the remedies

In addition, the EU legislator laid down in Art. 36 (4) EAPO Regulation a precise timeframe which shall be complied with by the competent authority (either a court or an enforcement authority) when issuing its decision on the EAPO remedies[304].

In particular, the authority shall act without delay, but no later than 21 days after it received all necessary information for deciding[305]. The time limit is rather short in order to compensate the *ex parte* nature of the EAPO proceedings which led to the actual preservation of debtors' bank accounts without hearing him.

The competent authority is thus required to decide speedily to prevent delays which may derive from the possible cross-border service of the application lodged against the EAPO[306]. However, the current wording is not sufficiently clear when it comes to the *dies a quo* of the time limit which starts to run on the day the competent authority is provided with all the necessary information to reach its decision. This vagueness leaves much discretion to the competent authority and entails the risk that the decision is delayed.

As no procedural sanction is expressly established by the EU legislator for not complying with the above time limits, sanctions should be determined according to the law of the Member State in which appeal proceedings took place (Art. 46 EAPO Regulation)[307].

304 As it is the case under Art. 18 EAPO Regulation (see bb) Issuing the decision), this timeframe could eventually be derogated under exceptional circumstances.

305 As arises from Recital 38 EAPO Regulation, this time limits should be calculated according to Regulation 1182/71.

306 E.g. service is effected in a Member State other than the one of the competent authority to decide or in a third State. See Dalla Bontà (n.301), para 36.20.

307 As it is the case under Art. 18 EAPO Regulation (see bb) Issuing the decision), It is possible that an unjustified serious breach of the time limit to issue the decision would entail a violation of EU law which could theoretically be used for initiating an infringement procedure. Dalla Bontà (n.301), para 36.22.

iii) Time limits to appeal decisions on the remedies

Against the latter decision both parties have the right to appeal[308] which must be exercised in accordance with the law of the Member State in which appeal proceedings will be carried out, as required by Art. 46 (1) EAPO Regulation.

It follows that the duration and *dies a quo* of the time limits to appeal depend on national law[309].

cc) No need to address any specific deficiency

What emerges from the above is that debtors can eventually invoke time limits as means of defence for challenging the issue or enforcement of EAPOs. However, under the current scenario no recurrent deficiency regarding time limits should be underlined as generally falling within the EAPOs grounds of defence.

The issue or enforcement of EAPOs should be challenged in the context of a uniform procedure provided for in the EAPO Regulation. This procedure does not include harmonised time limits for lodging the remedies which are regulated at national level. In spite of some criticism, the interfaces between the uniform procedure and national time limits do not seem to highlight any specific issue to be addressed in the future.

Against this decision, parties can lodge an appeal according to the rules provided for under the law in which appeal proceedings will take place. It logically follows that the respective time limits to appeal are determined by national law.

308 The term appeal is here interpreted in a very wide sense as to include in its meaning any form of recourse against a decision issued on the EAPO remedies, regardless of how this recourse is named under national law. See Silvana Dalla Bontà, 'Art. 37' in Elena D'Alessandro and Fernando Gascón Inchausti (eds), *Commentary of Regulation No 655/2014* (Edward Elgar Publishing 2022), para 37.03.

309 See in this regard the information communicated by the Member States to the Commission pursuant to Art. 50 (1)(m) EAPO Regulation.

II) Time limits and review proceedings under the EEO, EPO and ESCP Regulations

1) Review proceedings under the EEO, EPO and ESCP Regulations

Under the scope of the EEO, EPO and ESCP Regulations, judgments are directly enforceable within the EU without any general possibility granted to defendants – contrary to what happens under the Brussels Ibis Regulation – to apply for refusal grounds in the Member State of enforcement. However, under exceptional circumstances defendants could be entitled to apply for review before the court of origin.

The review is an exceptional remedy that is meant to safeguard defendants' procedural rights and to secure compliance with the requirement of a fair trial in accordance with Art. 6 ECHR and Art. 47 CFR[310]. The possibility of applying for review is interpreted very restrictively in order to prevent possible abuses that would break the balance between the applicant's access to justice and the defendant's right of defence.

These remedies are established for cases in which the system did not produce the outcome as it should have, e.g. either defendants have not been granted sufficient time to defend themselves or proceedings took place without defendants being aware of their existence without any fault on their part.

Under the scope of the EEO Regulation, review proceedings are required as a minimum procedural standard for certifying a judgment as a European enforcement order. Providing for review proceedings is optional under the scope of the EEO Regulation[311]; where the law of the Member State of origin lacks any review procedure, judgments cannot simply be certified as European Enforcement Orders.

On the other hand, the EPO and ESCP Regulations deal with review proceedings as an autonomous remedy which aims at ensuring the right of defence within the scope of the Regulations themselves. The review is then a mandatory recourse provided in the jurisdiction of origin[312].

The following analysis of Arts 19 EEO, 20 EPO and 18 ESCP will show that, in spite of generally pursuing the same rationale, review proceedings are not dealt with uniformly under the EEO, EPO and ESCP Regulations.

---

310 Ontanu (n.220), 51.

311 Hess (n.235), 400.

312 Hess (n.235), 400.

The conditions for applying for review are indeed not the same, but practically retain some differences.

a) Art. 19 EEO

The EEO Regulation sets certain 'minimum standards' that must be fulfilled by the procedural rules of the Member States for certifying judgments on uncontested claims as EEO[313].

In particular, the EEO Regulation provides for a double check system to certify claims as uncontested.

First, generally under Art. 6 EEO Regulation the court, when issuing the certificate, shall verify the following requirements: enforceability of the judgment in the Member State of origin (Art. 6 (1)(a)), respect of the jurisdictional system of the Brussels Ibis Regulation (Art. 6 (1)(b)), compliance with the minimum procedural standards regarding service and the information which shall be contained in the document instituting the proceedings (Art. 6 (1)(c)). Furthermore, the judgment must be given in the Member State of the debtor's domicile in cases 'where a claim is uncontested within

313 Art. 3 EEO Regulation distinguishes the four following cases that could constitute an 'uncontested' claim: (a) the debtor has expressly agreed to it by admission or by means of a settlement which has been approved by a court or concluded before a court in the course of proceedings; or (b) the debtor has never objected to it, in compliance with the relevant procedural requirements under the law of the Member State of origin, in the course of the court proceedings; or (c) the debtor has not appeared or been represented at a court hearing regarding that claim after having initially objected to the claim in the course of the court proceedings, provided that such conduct amounts to a tacit admission of the claim or of the facts alleged by the creditor under the law of the Member State of origin; or (d) the debtor has expressly agreed to it in an authentic instrument. With respect to Art. 3 (b) read in conjunction with recital 6, the question of whether or not default judgments could be certified as uncontested became controversial and raised some interpretative issues which were brought before the CJEU in the *Pebros Servizi* case. In that case, some doubts arose because under Italian law failing to attend proceedings does not amount to acquiescence to the claim. The CJEU, in line with Recital 6 EEO, decided that a defendant's default in appearing, if he was duly informed of the proceedings, could constitute an 'uncontested claim' in the sense intended by the EEO. The nature of the claim under domestic law does not matter as the Regulation is autonomously interpreted. See Case C-511/14 *Pebros Servizi Srl v Aston Martin Lagonda Ltd* (2016) EU:C:2016:448. See also Giovanni Chiapponi, 'Time Limits to React under the Brussels Ibis and EEO Regulations: Need for Harmonisation?' in Katalin Ligeti and Kei Hannah Brodersen (eds), *Studies on Enforcement in Multi-Regulatory Systems* (Nomos 2022), 146–149.

the meaning of Art. 3(1)(b) or (c); it relates to a contract concluded by a person, the consumer, for a purpose which can be regarded as being outside his or her trade or profession; and the debtor is the consumer' (Art. 6 (1)(d)).

Second, Art. 19 EEO Regulation provides for specific additional safeguards. According to this provision, judgments can only be certified under the EEO Regulation when the law of the Member State of origin provides for a review procedure in the two following cases: a) where the defendant was served with the document instituting the proceedings without proof of receipt and not in sufficient time to arrange for his defence without any fault on his side; or b) where the defendant could not object to the claim due to force majeure or extraordinary circumstances without any fault on his side. In both cases, the defendant is required to act 'promptly'[314].

Under the EEO regime, review represents a minimum standard of certification which aims at balancing the abolition of any check on the foreign judgment at the enforcement stage. Namely, the review mechanism aims at ensuring that the defendant's inactivity stems from his own personal choice, and it is not due to the lack of sufficient time to organize defences or to other exceptional circumstances[315].

It should be noted that these are minimum standards of review as Member States could provide for a review mechanism under more generous conditions (Art. 19 (2)).

The Regulation does not imply any obligation for the Member States either to adapt their national legislation to the minimum procedural standards of review or to establish a specific review procedure within the meaning of Art. 19. The EEO Regulation provides for an optional regime. If EU Member States do not adapt their national laws to the minimum standards of the Regulation, its regime simply does not apply[316].

Since the EEO Regulation only sets some minimum standards of review, it is the law of the Member State of origin that concretely regulates review procedures. Member States could adopt various types of remedies dealing with the hypotheses referred to in Art. 19 (1)(a) and (b): either they put in place a specific review procedure or they adapt procedures already existing under their domestic law.

---

314 See below bb) Lack of uniform time limits for review.

315 Gascón Inchausti (n.125), 505.

316 Thalia Kruger and Fieke Van Overbeeke, 'European Enforcement Order' in Jan Von Hein and Thalia Kruger (eds), *Informed Choices in Cross-Border Enforcement. The European State of the Art and Future Perspectives* (Intersentia 2021), 61.

What matters is that these remedies fully ensure the adequate protection of the right to a fair trial[317]. This requires, as the CJEU specified in *Imtech Marine Belgium*[318], that the review mechanism shall guarantee a full review, in law and in fact, of the judgment. Furthermore, it must allow a debtor to request such a review outside the ordinary periods laid down by national law for bringing a challenge or an appeal against the judgment.

b) Art. 20 EPO

Once the general time limits of 30 days for opposing the issuance of the payment order expire, Art. 20 EPO Regulation provides for the possibility to exceptionally apply for review.

According to Art. 20 (1), the defendant – after the expiry of the general opposition period – is entitled to apply for review against the payment order issued against him before the competent court in the Member State of origin where: (a) the order was served by one of the methods without proof of receipt by the addressee, and service was not effected in sufficient time to enable him to arrange for his defence, without any fault on his part, or (b) the defendant, even if service of the payment order was validly effected, was prevented from objecting to the claim by reason of force majeure or due to extraordinary circumstances without any fault on his part. In both situations, the applicant shall act 'promptly'[319].

In addition, Art. 20 (2) affirms that review is possible where the order for payment was clearly wrongly issued, having regard to the requirements laid down in the Regulation, or due to other exceptional circumstances[320].

---

317 Frédérique Ferrand, 'Titre Exécutoire Européen' (2019) *Répertoire de procédure civile*, para 128; Maria López de Tejada, 'Titre Exécutoire Européen. Règlement (CE) n. 805/2004 Portant Création d'un Titre Exécutoire Européen pour les Créances Incontestées' (2020) J-CL Europe Traité, para 39.

318 Case C-300/14 *Imtech Marine Belgium NV v Radio Hellenic SA* (2015) EU:C:2015:825.

319 See below bb) Lack of uniform time limits for review.

320 Art. 20 (2) is to be read in conjunction with Recital 25 which insists on a limited application of review proceedings. It follows that 'during the review procedure the merits of the claim should not be assessed beyond the grounds resulting from the exceptional circumstances invoked by the defendant'; and the reference to other 'exceptional circumstances could include a situation where the European order for payment was based on false information provided in the application form'.

The EPO Regulation thus establishes in Art. 20 uniform conditions which must be fulfilled when applying for review. Review proceedings are then practically implemented by the law of the Member State of origin.

The CJEU in its case law has repeatedly underlined the exceptional character of review proceedings, insisting on their limited application as they are not intended to grant the defendant a second opportunity to oppose the claim.

In this respect, the CJEU specified that non-compliance with 'the time limit for lodging a statement of opposition to a EPO, by reason of the negligence of the defendant's representative, does not justify a review of that order for payment, since such a failure to observe the time limit does not constitute extraordinary circumstances within the meaning of Art. 20 (1)(b) or exceptional circumstances within the meaning of Art. 20 (2)'. Failure by the defendant's representative to comply with the time limit is thus not considered neither exceptional nor extraordinary as it depends on the representative's fault and could have been assessed differently and avoided[321].

Moreover, as interpreted by the CJEU[322], Art. 20 (2) prevents a defendant who has validly been served with an EPO in a case where parties agreed on a jurisdiction clause, from applying for review 'by claiming that the court of origin incorrectly held that it had jurisdiction on the basis of allegedly false information provided by the claimant in the application form'. It follows that the defendant who does not lodge his opposition on time cannot later apply for review to contest the jurisdiction of the judge who originally issued the payment order as he could have lodged his ordinary remedy within the general time limits of Art. 16[323].

As further analysed below[324], according to CJEU case law[325] the application of Art. 20 is also excluded if service of the EPO is not consistent with the minimum standards laid down in the EPO Regulation (Arts 13 to 15).

---

321 Frédérique Ferrand, 'Injonction de Payer Européenne' in Serge Guinchard, *Droit et Pratique de la Procedure Civile* (10th edn, Dalloz 2021), para 146.

322 CJEU Case C- 245/14 *Thomas Cook Belgium NV v Thurner Hotel GmbH (2015)* EU:C:2015:715.

323 Ferrand (n.321), para 146; Burkhard Hess and Katharina Raffelsieper, 'Shuldnerschutz bei Fehlender Zustellung eines EU-Mahnbescheids: Regelungslucken der EUMahnVO' (2015) 35 IPRax; Hess (n.235), 401.

324 See aa) Absolute lack of service of the documents instituting the proceedings.

325 *Eco cosmetics* (n.223); *Catlin Europe* (n.222).

c) Art. 18 ESCP

The structure of review proceedings under the scope of the ESCP procedure was in the original version of the Regulation practically identical to that laid down in the EPO Regulation[326]. Against this backdrop, Regulation 2015/2421[327] has amended ESCP review proceedings in order to harmonise some of the aspects which were seen as problematic within the EPO system[328], making use of the improvements that had already been put into place by the Maintenance Regulation[329].

Art. 18 ESCP Regulation, as amended, thus exceptionally provides for review proceedings. In particular, the defendant who did not enter an appearance, can apply for review before the competent court of the Member State in which the judgment was given in the two following situations: (a) if he was not served with the claim form, or, in the event of an oral hearing, was not summoned to appear to that hearing, in sufficient time and in such a way as to enable him to arrange for his defence[330]; or (b) if he was prevented from contesting the claim by reason of force majeure or due to extraordinary circumstances without any fault on his part.

Review proceedings are meant to be exceptional and cannot be admitted if the defendant failed to challenge the judgment when it was possible for

---

326 The previous version of art. 18 ESCP Regulation reads as follows: 'The defendant shall be entitled to apply for a review of the judgment given in the European Small Claims Procedure before the court or tribunal with jurisdiction of the Member State where the judgment was given where: a)(i) the claim form or the summons to an oral hearing were served by a method without proof of receipt by him personally, as provided for in Art. 14 of Regulation (EC) No 805/2004; and (ii) service was not effected in sufficient time to enable him to arrange for his defence without any fault on his part, or (b) the defendant was prevented from objecting to the claim by reason of force majeure, or due to extraordinary circumstances without any fault on his part, provided in either case that he acts promptly'.

327 Regulation (EU) 2015/2421 of the European Parliament and of the Council of 16 December 2015 amending Regulation (EC) No 861/2007 establishing a European Small Claims Procedure and Regulation (EC) No 1896/2006 creating a European order for payment procedure (2015) OJ L 341.

328 See below a) The lack of EU standards of review.

329 See Commission ESCP Report, COM (2013) 795 final.

330 The 2015 ESCP reform abolished in such situations the reference to the method of service of the claim form without proof of receipt by the defendant personally. This made the scope of Art. 18 (1) broader.

him to do so, e.g. he was served with the judgment but he did not challenge it according to the general appeal procedure[331].

The 2015 ESCP reform further replaced the wording 'promptly' by adding a specific time requirement to the right to apply for review which aimed both at establishing a speedier procedure for small claims in cross-border cases and at securing a balance between the parties' procedural rights. In particular, Art. 18 (2) provides for a time limit of 30 days, with no extensions, which shall run from the day the defendant was effectively acquainted with the contents of the judgment and was able to react. The latest date for calculating this time limit is the date of the first enforcement measure having the effect of making the assets of the defendant non-disposable in whole or in part[332].

Art. 18 (3) finally provides that if the judge admits the review, the judgment given within the ESCP shall be declared null and void. However, the claimant shall not lose the benefit of any interruption of prescription or limitation periods where such an interruption applies under national law[333].

The Regulation thus establishes uniform conditions for applying for review. Their practical implementation then depends on the choice of each national system.

2) The role of time limits in review proceedings

What emerges from the above is that Arts 19 EEO, 20 EPO and 18 ESCP set out under exceptional circumstances common standards of review generally requiring courts to check in the Member State of origin, 1) whether the defendant was granted effective and adequate time limits to arrange for his defence and 2) whether the defendant was in a position to challenge the judgment but did not do so due to his own fault.

---

331 Gascón Inchausti (n.125), 494.

332 In this regard, it has been argued that in order to protect the right of defense the *dies a quo* of the time limit for review shall run only when the defendant becomes aware of the first enforcement measure provided that if the original service of the claim on the defendant is ineffective, this could also lead to the ineffectiveness of service on him of the first enforcement measure. See Gascón Inchausti (n.125), 494.

333 In this respect, it is highly unlikely that a lay user will be aware of this arrangement, especially with regard to the legislation of a different Member State. Ontanu (n.220), 52.

However, review proceedings are not fully regulated at the EU level; all procedural issues not explicitly dealt with by Arts 19 EEO, 20 EPO and 18 ESCP are governed by national law.

Against this background, issues on time limits might stem, on the one hand, from some deficient legislation at EU level (in particular within the EEO and EPO Regulations) and, on the other hand, from national rules of implementation which might overshadow the uniform interpretation laid down in the Regulations.

a) The lack of EU standards of review

When comparing Arts 19 EEO, 20 EPO, on the one hand, and Art. 18 ESCP, on the other hand, it should be noted, as a preliminary observation, that the ESCP review proceedings are only available for defendants who did not appear in the proceedings; however, the EEO and EPO review proceedings do not contain such limitation, even if in practice they generally concern default defendants[334].

The rules for applying for review under Arts 19 EEO, 20 EPO and 18 ESCP are fragmented. The ESCP Regulation, recently amended, seems to provide the best model of review proceedings; on the contrary, the following deficiencies arise within the EEO and EPO review proceedings.

aa) Absolute lack of service of the documents instituting the proceedings

First, it should be noted that, review proceedings under the EEO and EPO, contrary to the ESCP[335], are available only if the document instituting the proceedings was served by a method without proof of receipt by the defendant.

Notably, requiring service without proof of receipt by the defendant under Arts 19 EEO and 20 EPO triggers the question whether review proceedings are available in a case in which the order or the document instituting the proceedings was not served in a manner which complies

334 Theoretically it is possible that a defendant who partially appeared in the proceedings apply for review under the EEO Regulation. See Richard (n.60), 485.

335 Art. 18 ESCP Regulation explicitly includes the case of lack of service – 'he was not served' – within its scope.

with the minimum standards laid down in the EEO (Arts 13–15) and EPO (Arts 13–15) Regulations, e.g. there is an absolute lack of service.

Such issue has been decided by the CJEU in *Eco cosmetics*[336] under the scope of the EPO Regulation. In particular, the CJEU held that the case of total absence of service is not covered by Art. 20 EPO Regulation, but is governed in accordance with the possible remedies available under national law.

Further, where the irregular service of the order is discovered only after the declaration of enforceability of the EPO, the defendant could still raise such irregularity[337], which, if it is duly established, will invalidate the declaration of enforceability[338].

In addition, the minimum standards of service laid down in the EPO Regulation shall be interpreted in accordance with the Service Regulation. Based on the *Eco cosmetics* principle, the CJEU in *Catlin Europe* excluded the application of the Art. 20 review procedure when the service of the payment order was irregular because it did not inform the defendant of his right to refuse service of an untranslated document, as required by Art. 8 (1) (now Art. 12 of the Service Regulation Recast). The defendant indeed could not apply for review because the payment order never acquired an enforceable character.

If service is regularised, it could be argued that the general time limits for opposing the payment order start to run, granting the defendant the possibility to lodge his regular opposition according to Art. 16 EPO Regulation[339].

Under these premises, someone may wonder if the review mechanism provided for in Art. 19 EEO also does not apply if the document instituting the proceedings was not served in a manner which complies with the minimum standards laid down in the EEO Regulation for absolute lack of service. Provided that Art. 20 EPO contains a provision almost identical to Art. 19 EEO, one could argue that the same conclusions of *Eco Cosmetics* apply within the EEO regime[340].

This case law thus suggests that the interpretation of Arts 19 EEO and 20 EPO will be very narrow, in order to exclude any application by analogy of these provisions. If the document instituting the proceedings is not served properly, the time to react does not start running. This situation does not

336 *Eco cosmetics* (n.223).
337 The procedure to raise this irregularity is governed by national law.
338 *Eco cosmetics* (n.223); Gascón Inchausti (n.125), 493.
339 Ferrand, (n.317), para 448.34.
340 Hess (n.235), 401.

fall within the list of cases referred to in Arts 19 EEO and 20 EPO, whose application is literally possible only when 'service was effected by a method without proof of receipt by the defendant'.

It follows that where service is not performed in a manner consistent with the minimum standards laid down in the EEO and EPO Regulations, the application of the Arts 19 EEO and 20 EPO review procedure shall be excluded. The defendant shall therefore proceed according to the domestic law of the issuing court[341].

bb) Lack of uniform time limits for review

Another inconsistency regarding the conditions to apply for review relates to the length and *dies a quo* of the time limits for filing the review which are subject to fragmentary rules under the scope of the EEO, EPO and ESCP Regulations.

On the one hand, under the scope of the ESCP Regulation, Art. 18 provides for a fixed uniform time limit for review which amounts to 30 days. Its *dies a quo* starts either when the defendant becomes aware of the judgment or when the first enforcement measure is issued. Notably, the introduction of this specific time frame facilitated the task of the reviewing courts in appreciating 'the prompt reaction of the defendant, and establishing objective criteria for the calculation of the 30-days period'[342]. This further reinforced legal certainty by granting the creditor a certain date after which the already enforceable title could not be contested anymore[343].

On the other hand, Arts 19 EEO and 20 EPO do not provide for any fixed uniform time limit for applying for review, but they simply require the defendant to act 'promptly'. This flexible time requirement – deemed to be too vague[344] – is concretely assessed by legislators and courts at national level. The length and *dies a quo* of the time limits for review are therefore governed by national law.

Against this backdrop, defendants, as review proceedings are implemented differently by each specific Member State, will examine under the system at hand the remedies and time limits (only within the EEO and EPO Regulations where there are no uniform time limit to apply for review)

341 Hess (n.235), 401.
342 Ontanu (n.220), 52.
343 Richard (n.60), 491, 492.
344 Gascón Inchausti (n.125), 492; Lupoi (n.55), 191.

within which to file their review. Such assessment which defendants shall make prior than filing their challenges reduces *de facto* the length of the general time limits for applying for review within the EEO, EPO (and partially also within the ESCP) Regulations.

Under these circumstances, it follows that either domestic time limits within the EEO or EPO review procedure or the 30 days time limit within the ESCP review procedure might be *de facto* abbreviated having negative effects on the protection of defendants' rights at cross-border level.

b) Different national pre-understandings of time limits when checking the grounds for review *in concreto*

The grounds for review under Arts 19 EEO, 20 EPO and 18 ESCP are *in concreto* assessed by domestic courts as follows:

aa) Assessment by national courts under Art. 19 EEO

Under the EEO Regulation, the court reviewing the judgments exercises its check on the sufficiency of time and on the involuntary expiry of time limits in light of the requirements set out in the national procedure implementing Arts 6 and 19 (1)(a) and (b). In particular, the court must check if these conditions ensuring the right of defence have been complied with in the national procedure which led to the judgment recognised as EEO.

It all depends then on how the Member State of origin shapes the review procedure under its national law defining the criteria of sufficient time, force majeure or extraordinary circumstances.

In this regard, Member States have notified the Commission of their choice as to how they have implemented the Art. 19 (1)(a) and (b) EEO review procedure under their national law.

For instance, France in its declaration to the Commission indicated that the Art. 19 EEO review procedure 'is the ordinary procedure applicable to decisions taken by the court that issued the original enforcement order'. This concretely means that the general rules laid down in Arts 527 to 639–4 CPC apply. In particular, where the judgment has been issued without the defendant entering an appearance the procedure for relief (Art. 540 CPC) applies to the decision taken by the court that issued the original enforcement order. This procedure allows the judge to relieve the defendant from the expiry of time limits if he shows that without any fault on his part he was not informed of the judgment in sufficient time ('temps utile') to exercise his recourse, or if he found it impossible to act.

What follows is that the assessment of French courts on the requirements of Art. 19 (1)(a) and (1)(b) EEO Regulation is based on the flexible rules – e.g. 'temps utile' – provided for in Art. 540 CPC[345].

Further, Italy stated that the Art. 19 (1)(a) and (b) EEO review procedure is governed by the general ordinary rules for challenging judgments. This concretely means, that depending on the sort of service of the judgment, the requirements of Art. 19 (1)(a) will be assessed by national courts as follows:

- If service is null, according to Art. 327 c.p.c., parties can challenge default judgments even after the *res judicata* is formally achieved.
- If service is irregular, parties in default can challenge judgments in compliance with the general ordinary time limits provided for in Art. 325 c.p.c.
- If service is 'regular' under Italian law, but it does not enable the defendant to prepare his defence in a timely manner as required by Art. 19 (1)(a), parties shall in principle be entitled to apply for review. However, there is no case law on this assumption[346].

On the other hand, with respect to Art. 19 (1)(b) relief proceedings (Art. 153 c.p.c.) will generally[347] be applicable. Defendants will be relieved from the expiry of final time limits where they show that they have been prevented from raising their objections by reason of force majeure or due to extraordinary circumstances.

345 Marco Buzzoni, *Collection of French Implementation Rules in Towards More Effective EnFORcemenT of ClaimS in Civil and Commercial Matters within the EU EFFORTS (Project JUST-JCOO-AG-2019–881802),* 32; Richard (n.60), 493.

346 Francesca Villata, Lidia Sandrini, Marco Farina, Gabriele Molinaro, Valeria Giugliano, Michele Casi and Denisa Docaj, *Collection of Italian Implementation Rules in* Efforts' *in Towards More Effective EnFORcemenT of ClaimS in Civil and Commercial Matters within the EU EFFORTS (Project JUST-JCOO-AG-2019–881802),* 30.

347 Exceptionally, where the EEO is granted for a payment order, review proceedings will be governed by the specific rules on late oppositions (Art. 650 c.p.c.). In particular, late challenges will be admitted if parties prove that they had not been informed in time of the payment order because of a fortuitous or force majeure event. See Villata, Sandrini, Farina, Molinaro, Giugliano, Casi and Docaj (n.346), 30.

What emerges from the above is that the review procedure is a domestic one, but the standards of review – ensuring that the right of defence has been respected within the national procedure which led to the title recognised as EEO – are defined at the European level. Nevertheless, these common standards might be overshadowed by different pre-understandings of national rules (including time limits) which impact on the actual interpretation of the notions of sufficient time, extraordinary circumstances or force majeure under Art. 19 (1)(a) and (b) EEO Regulation,

Where the judgment is reviewed, the defendant will be restored to his original position and granted a new time limit identical to the original one to contest the decision rendered in the Member State of origin. If the decision is declared null, the EEO will also lose its validity as one of the requirements for issuing an EEO will be absent[348].

bb) Assessment by national courts under Arts 20 EPO and 18 ESCP

Under the EPO and ESCP Regulations, the courts reviewing the judgment exercise their check on the sufficiency of time and on the involuntary expiry of time limits based on the national procedural rules implementing Arts 20 EPO and 18 ESCP. Notably, the adjudicating court will interpret on a case-by-case basis the legal and factual circumstances which might have prevented the respect of the right of defence within the EPO or ESCP procedure. The assessment is here made with respect to a fully harmonised European procedure – not a national one as happens within the EEO – which led to the issuance of a European title.

In this regard, Member States have notified the Commission of their choice as to how they have implemented the Art. 20 EPO and Art. 18 ESCP review procedures under their national law.

For instance, the Art. 20 EPO review procedure has been implemented as follows by France and Italy.

France has indicated that the Art. 20 EPO review procedure is governed by exactly the same rules applicable to the opposition procedure against the European payment order (Arts 1424–15 CPC)[349]. The applicant must thus submit – 'promptly' – his late opposition before the same court which originally issued the European payment order.

348 It should be noted that depending on the type of proceedings at hand, conclusions which will emerge might also refer to time limits to challenge judgments.

349 See Arts. 1424–8 – 1424–13 CPC.

According to the communication issued by the Italian government, as far as EPO review proceedings are concerned, the judge competent under Art. 20 (1) EPO Regulation is the same judge that issued the payment order pursuant to Art. 650 c.p.c. In this regard, the reference to late oppositions is clear. Such interpretation has recently been confirmed by the Italian Supreme Court in its case law[350]. The Court clarified that 'as far as the European payment order is concerned, the time limit for the submission of the review, in cases referred to in Art. 20 (1) EPO Regulation, is identified in those inferable from Art. 650 c.p.c., intended as the provision governing the relevant procedure in Italy'[351].

What follows is that if enforcement has not started yet, the applicant can submit his challenge within the general time limits for opposing national payment orders (Art. 641 c.p.c.), i.e. 40 days from the moment when the party is in a position to oppose the order. On the contrary, if enforcement has begun late opposition will not be admissible after 10 days from the first enforcement measure (Art. 350 (3) c.p.c.)[352].

In addition, Italy has indicated that the court competent for reviewing proceedings under Art. 20 (2) EPO Regulation is the ordinary court which has jurisdiction over the order in accordance with the commonly applicable rules, i.e. in practice the solution is that of the summons to appear[353].

Further, the following rules have been decided with regard to the Art. 18 ESCP review procedure by France and Italy.

France has indicated that the Art. 18 ESCP review procedure is generally governed by the rules applicable to opposition proceedings against default judgments[354], or if these are not available, according to similar procedural

350 Italian Supreme Court (Sezioni Unite) 20–03–2017, n. 7075.

351 Villata, Sandrini, Farina, Molinaro, Giugliano, Casi and Docaj (n.346). On a different note, in academia it has been argued that the Art. 20 (1) application for review cannot be subject to any absolute time limit. Even if such a barrier would be desirable in the interests of the creditor and legal certainty, Member States shall not provide for any absolute time limit for review because this would contradict a wider interpretation – based on the wording 'promptly' – of the Regulation. Bernhard Ulrici, 'Art. 20 EG-MahnVO' in Von Wolfgang Krüger and Thomas Rauscher (eds.), *Münchener Kommentar zur Zivilprozessordnung: mit Gerichtsverfassungsgesetz und Nebengesetzen*, vol. 3 (5th edn, C.H. Beck 2022), 18, 19; Luiz Gomez Amigo, *El Proceso Monitorio Europeo* (Thomson Thomson Reuters Aranzadi 2008), 119.

352 Villata, Sandrini, Farina, Molinaro, Giugliano, Casi and Docaj (n.346), 42.

353 Villata, Sandrini, Farina, Molinaro, Giugliano, Casi and Docaj (n.346), 42.

354 Art. 571 French CPC and f.

modalities (Art. 1391 CPC)[355]. Opposition must thus be brought - within the 30 days time limit provided for in Art. 18 ESCP Regulation[356] - before the same court which originally rendered the judgment.

According to the declaration of the Italian government, Art. 18 ESCP review proceedings are governed by the same general rules applicable for filing national challenges (Art. 323 and f. c.p.c.)[357]. Requests for review must therefore be submitted - within the 30 days time limit as provided for in Art. 18 ESCP Regulation[358] - before the competent judge, i.e. the tribunal for decisions taken by the justice of the peace or the court of appeal for decisions taken by the tribunal.

What follows is that both under the EPO and ESCP regime the review procedure is a domestic one, but the standards of review - ensuring that the right of defence have been respected within the European procedures which led to the EPO or ESCP - are set at the European level. Nevertheless, these common standards might be overshadowed by different pre-understandings of national rules (e.g. time limits within the EPO review procedure[359]) which impact on the actual interpretation of the notions of sufficient time, extraordinary circumstances or force majeure under Arts 20 EPO and 18 ESCP Regulations.

Where the court finds that the review is justified, either the European payment order or the judgment given in the ESCP, will be declared null and void losing as such any validity.

c) Need for reform?

What emerges from the above-mentioned situations is that time limits raise practical issues for the cross-border enforcement of civil claims with respect

355 In this respect, it should be noted that appeal proceedings are in principle excluded because under French law the value of the small claims is lower than the cost of appeal. The availability of cassation proceedings is debatable as they do not ensure a full review of the decision in fact and in law. This need to require a full review in fact and in law seems indeed to arise also with regard to the ESCP. See CJEU Case *Imtech Marine* (n.318) para 38; Richard (n.60), 496.

356 The time limit is indeed provided for at the EU level.

357 Appeal proceedings will generally apply. The availability of appeal on legal grounds is debatable, see fn 355.

358 The time limit is indeed provided for at the EU level.

359 On the contrary, time limits for applying for review under the ESCP Regulation are uniform and their interpretation is harmonised within national implementing procedures.

both to some deficiencies regarding the regulation of review proceedings at EU level (e.g. the absolute lack of service of the document instituting the proceedings or the lack of uniform time limits for review) and to a different pre-understanding of national rules (e.g. time limits).

Under these circumstances, it has been argued that the referral to national law leads to fragmentation, instead of harmonisation, as solutions diverge between the Member States[360]. This weakens the position of the debtor who is 'obliged to seek for information about the redress in the court of origin – at present, this information is not (fully) available at the e-Justice Portal of the European Union'[361].

Against this fragmented scenario, there seems to be awareness at EU law level that, first, Art. 19 EEO and Art. 20 EPO need to be reformed in order to achieve more coherence and uniformity[362].

The Commission (also supported by academics[363]), in its proposal to reform the ESCP Regulation has explicitly indicated the need to rephrase these provisions. It stated that 'there is no reason why these provisions on review, which pursue exactly the same objective, are formulated differently in the various European regulations'.

One could then argue that the model to follow should be that laid down in the ESCP Regulation, as reformed in 2015[364], which explicitly includes in the meaning of review procedure the lack of service of the document instituting the proceedings and lays down fixed uniform time limits for review[365].

360 Ferrand, (n.317), para 448.34.

361 Hess (n.235), 401.

362 Hess (n.235), 410; Marco Buzzoni, Cristina M. Mariottini, Michele Casi and Carlos Santaló Goris, *Report on EU Policy Guidelines in Towards More Effective EnFORcemenT of ClaimS in Civil and Commercial Matters within the EU EFFORTS (Project JUST-JCOO-AG-2019–881802)*, 24, 25.

363 See Xandra Kramer, 'Specific Instruments' in Burkhard Hess and Pietro Ortolani (eds), *Impediments of National Procedural Law to the Free Movement of Judgments* (Beck-Hart-Nomos, 2019), para 65.

364 This reform found its reference in Art. 19 of Council Regulation (EC) 4/2009 of 18 December 2008 on jurisdiction, applicable law, recognition and enforcement of decisions and cooperation in matters relating to maintenance obligations (2009) OJ L 7.

365 Fernando Gascón Inchausti, 'Ensuring Adequate Protection in Cross-Border Enforcement for Debtors' in Jan Von Hein and Thalia Kruger (eds), *Informed Choices in Cross-Border Enforcement. The European State of the Art and Future Perspectives* (Intersentia 2021), 433, 434.

Going a step further, it could also be advisable to establish review proceedings fully regulated by EU law within the EPO and ESCP Regulations[366]. This would create a more coherent framework on review proceedings addressing issues (*inter alia* time limits) on the interfaces between national and EU law.

366 Richard (n.60), 496; Hess (n.235), 406. On a different note, such harmonisation of procedures will not be envisaged under the EEO as long as the existence of a review procedure is a standard of certification which shall be provided for under the law of the Member State of origin against judgments issued within national proceedings.

Chapter 3: Time limits from the perspective of the EU lawmaker

What arises from the above is that setting and defining time limits in cross-border litigation has become a sensitive issue. It is clear that litigants (especially non-experienced ones) in cross-border cases face specific difficulties, e.g. they are confronted with an unfamiliar, foreign procedure applying foreign law and they often face language barriers. Foreign defendants thus stand in a weaker procedural position than national ones. These impediments, as proved by the cases described above arising under the scope of the Brussels Ibis Regulation and second generation instruments, might be obstacles to judicial cooperation in civil matters and should be addressed by the EU in future legislative reforms. There is therefore a compelling need for more coherent rules on the regulation of time limits in cross-border cases, which would allow more uniformity, thus probably decreasing cases of refusal of recognition and enforcement of judgments in civil and commercial matters.

Against this backdrop, harmonising time limits in EU civil procedure would address several problems connected with the current fragmented scenario in which each Member State lays down its own procedural rules on time limits. In light of its deep attachment to national history and cultural traditions, 'harmonisation should walk on a path through the mountains' of such legal cultures'[367].

is means that the feasibility and desirability of achieving common fixed time limits within EU civil procedure must be assessed and balanced with Member States' procedural autonomies[368].

The question on feasibility and desirability will deal with those time limits regulated at national level raising issues under the scope of the Brussels Ibis Regulation, i.e. time limits to react in general first instance proceedings,

367 Paolo Biavati, 'Is Flexibility a Way to the Harmonization of Civil Procedural Law in Europe?' in Federico Carpi and Michele Angelo Lupoi (eds), *Essays on Transnational and Comparative Civil Procedure* (Giappichelli Editore 2001), 91.

368 Gilles Cuniberti, 'The Promotion of Best Practices in European Civil Procedure: Some Introductory Remarks' in Burkhard Hess and Xandra Kramer (eds), *From Common Rules to Best Practices in European Civil Procedure* (Nomos-Hart Publishing 2017), 439–450.

time limits for opposing the issuance of payment orders, time limits to appeal on factual and legal grounds[369].

On the other hand, the feasibility and desirability question of EU action on time limits will not be analysed under the EEO, EPO, ESCP and EAPO Regulations. There is indeed no need to address the issue of the competence of the EU under the second generation instruments as it is certainly possible to enact legislation on time limits within these European uniform Regulations. In this respect, some concrete policy proposals will simply be considered.

A) Feasibility of EU action on time limits

First, determining if EU action on time limits is feasible under the Lisbon Treaty regime raises questions on the competence of the EU in the field of civil procedure[370].

Within the current institutional framework, developments in EU procedural law insist on two dimensions: a horizontal one based on Art. 81 TFEU and a vertical one based on Art. 114 TFEU.

Under these premises, an assessment will be made as to which is the most appropriate legal basis for enacting EU action on time limits.

I) Art. 81 TFEU

Art. 81 TFEU grants the EU general competence in the policy area of judicial cooperation in civil matters, empowering the EU to enact legislation in order to improve and guarantee effective access to justice and eliminate obstacles to the proper functioning of civil proceedings.

369 It should be noted that the question on desirability and feasibility will not deal with the time limits to enforce judgments as their harmonisation wil not be envisaged under the scope of the Brussels Ibis Regulation. The issues which arise from the application of the time limits to enforce judgments in cross-border proceedings will be addreseesd by arguing that these time limits should be governed by the law of the Member State of origin and not by the one of the Member State of enforcement. See b) Overruling the *Al Bosco* solution?

370 As a preliminary condition, the EU competence to enact legislation on time limits shall comply with EU general principles of subsidiarity and proportionality.

Civil justice is thus a distinct and separate field of EU competence - included in a separate chapter within Title V regarding the creation of an 'area of Freedom, Security and Justice'[371] - where Art. 81 TFEU is the specific legal basis for regulating cross-border civil proceedings at the EU level.

371 The EU competence within the policy area 'judicial cooperation in civil matters' finds its origin in Art. 220 EEC of the Treaty of Rome of 1957, which initially insisted on cooperation at intergovernmental level. Art. K.1 (6) of the Maastricht Treaty of 1993 included within the scope of the third pillar ('justice and home affairs') judicial cooperation in civil matters which so became a matter of 'common interest' of the Member States. Art. 65 of the Amsterdam Treaty of 1999 transferred the issue of judicial cooperation in civil matters from the third pillar to the first one ('visas asylum, immigration and other policies related to the free movement of persons') which communitarized such policy area. The Lisbon Treaty by including the policy area judicial cooperation in a separate chapter within Title V finally moved the process of strengthening and emancipation of EU competence in civil procedure to a yet higher level. On these historical developments which led to the current version of Art. 81 TFEU see *inter alia* Berthold Goldman, 'Un Traité Fédérateur. La Convention entre États Membres de la CEE sur la Reconnaissance et l'Exécution des Décisions en Matière Civile et Commerciale' (1971) 7 RTD eur, 1–39; Jörn Pipkorn, 'Les Méthodes de Rapprochement des Législations à l'Intérieur de la CEE', in Pierre Bourel, Ulrich Drobnig and Georges Droz (eds), *L'Influence des Communautés Européennes sur le Droit International Privé des États Membres* (Larcier 1981), 13–48; Deirdre Curtin, 'The Constitutional Structure of the Union: a Europe of Bits and Pieces' (1993) 30 CMLR, 17–71; Anne-Marie Rouchaud, 'Le Renforcement de la Coopération Judiciaire' in Marcel Storme (ed), *Approximation of Judiciary Law in the European Union* (Maklu 2003), 450; Peter-Christian Muller-Graff, 'The Legal Bases of the Third Pillar and its Position in the Framework of the Union Treaty' in Roger Morgan and Jörg Monar (eds), *The Third Pillar of the European Union: Cooperation in the Fields of Justice and Home Affairs* (European Interuniversity Press 1995), 21–37; Gavin Barrett, 'Cooperation in Justice and Home Afffairs in the European Union - An Overview and a Critique' in Gavin Barrett (ed), *Justice Cooperation in the European Union* (Institute of European Affairs 1997), 3–48; James O'Keefe, 'A Critical View of the Third Pillar' in Alexis Pauly (ed.), *De Schengen à Maastricht: Voie Royale et Course d'Obstacles* (European Institute of Public Administration 1996), 1–16; John Adrian Fortescue, 'First Experiences with the Implementation of Third Pillar Provisions' in Roland Bieber and Jörg Monar (eds), *Justice and Home Affairs in the European Union: The Development of the Third Pillar* (European Interuniversity Press 1995), 26; Jörg Monar, 'European Union - Justice and Home Affairs: a Balance Sheet and an Agenda for Reform' in Geoffrey Edwards and Alfred Pjpers (eds), *The Politics of European Treaty Reform. The 1996 Intergovernmental Conference and Beyond* (Pinter 1997), 328–331; Alberto Achermann, 'Asylum and Immigration Policies: from Cooperation to Harmonization' in Roland Bieber and Jörg Monar (eds), *Justice and Home Affairs in the European Union: The Development of the Third Pillar* (European Interuniversity Press 1995), 129, 130; Kay Hailbronner, 'Migration Law and Policy within the Third Pillar of the Union Treaty' in Roland Bieber and Jörg Monar (eds), *Justice and*

The legislative activity of the EU under Art. 81 TFEU operates in a

Home Affairs in the European Union: The Development of the Third Pillar (European Interuniversity Press 1995), 102, 103; Elke Esders, 'The European Parliament's Committee on Civil Liberties and Internal Affairs – the Committee Responsible for Justice and Home Affairs', in Roland Bieber and Jörg Monar (eds), *Justice and Home Affairs in the European Union: The Development of the Third Pillar* (European Interuniversity Press 1995), 259–275; Jörg Monar, 'Democratic Control of Justice and Home Affairs: the European Parliament and the National Parliaments', in Roland Bieber and Jörg Monar (eds), *Justice and Home Affairs in the European Union: The Development of the Third Pillar* (European Interuniversity Press 1995), 243 - 258; Jörg Monar, 'The Evolving Role of the Union institutions in the Framework of the Third Pillar' in Roland Bieber and Jörg Monar (eds), *Justice and Home Affairs in the European Union: The Development of the Third Pillar* (European Interuniversity Press 1995), 75–80; Gráinne De Burca, 'The Quest for Legitimacy in the European Union' (1996) 59 MLR, 361; Jürgen Basedow, 'EC Regulations in European Private Law' in Jürgen Basedow, Isaak Meier, Daniel Girsberger Talia Einhorn and Anton K. Schnyder (eds), *Private Law in the International Arena: from National Conflict Rules Towards Harmonization and Unification. Liber Amicorum Kurt Siehr* (T.M.C. Asser Press 2000), 20; Christian Kohler, 'Interrogations sur les Sources du Droit International Privé Européen après le Traité d'Amsterdam' (1999) 89 RCDIP, 198; Jürgen Basedow, 'The Communitarization of the Conflict of Laws under the Treaty of Amsterdam' (2000) 37 CMLR, 697; Pedro Alberto De Miguel Asensio, 'La Evolución del Derecho Internacional Privado Comunitario en el Tratado de Ámsterdam' (1998) 58 REDI 376; Roberto Adam, 'La Cooperazione in Materia di Giustizia e Affari Interni tra Comunitarizzazione e Metodo Intergovernativo' (1994) Riv. dir. eu., 504; Philippe Emmanuel Partsch, *Le Droit International Privé Européen: De Rome a Nice* (Larcier 2003); Luigi Moccia, 'Du 'Marché' à la 'Citoyenneté' : à la Recherche d'un Droit Privé Européen Durable et de sa Base Juridique' (2004) 56 RIDC 291 - 327; Lucia Serena Rossi, 'L'Incidenza dei Principi di Diritto Comunitario sul Diritto Internazionale Privato: dalla "Comunitarizzazione" alla "Costituzionalizzazione"' (2004) 40 RIDPP, 65; Eva Storskrubb, *Civil Procedure and EU law. A Policy Area Uncovered* (Oxford University Press 2008), 42; Andrea Bonomi, 'Il Diritto Internazionale Privato dell'Unione Europea: Considerazioni Generali' in Andrea Bonomi, *Diritto Internazionale Privato e Cooperazione Giudiziaria in Materia Civile* (Giappichelli Editore 2009), 21; Burkhard Hess, 'Procedural Harmonization in a European Context' in Xandra Kramer and Remco Van Rhee (eds), *Civil Litigation in Globalising World* (Springer 2012), 161–163; Remco Van Rhee, 'Harmonization of Civil Procedure: An Historical and Comparative Perspective', in Xandra Kramer and Remco Van Rhee (eds), *Civil Litigation in Globalising World* (Springer 2012), 54; Rafal Manko, *Europeanisation of Civil Procedure: Towards Common Minimum Standards?* (European Parliamentary Research Service 2015), 10; Steve Peers, 'Civil Cooperation' in Steve Peers, *EU Justice and Home Affairs Law – EU Criminal Law, Policing, and Civil Law,* vol 2 (Oxford University Press 2016), 345–347; Hess (n.51), 2–5; Magdalena Tulibacka, Margarita Sanz and Roland Blomeyer, *Common Minimum Standards of Civil Procedure* (European Added Value Assessment Annex I 2016), 57, 58; Jan Von Hein, 'EU Competence to Legislate in the Area of Private International Law and Law Reforms at the EU level' in Paul Beaumont, Mihail Danov, Katarina Trimmings and Burku Yuksel (eds), *Cross-Border* 'horizontal' way: it aims at overcoming impediments in national procedural laws to the free circulation of judgments in the civil justice area[372].

The CJEU contributes to the general development of EU procedural law by ensuring the uniform interpretation of the preliminary questions – whose regime is subject to Art. 267 TFEU – referred to it with regard to the policy area of judicial cooperation in civil matters[373].

Litigation in Europe (Bloomsbury 2017), 23; Xandra Kramer, Judicial Cooperation in Civil Matters in Pieter Jan Kuijper, Fabian Amtenbrink, Deirdre Curtin, Bruno De Witte, Alison McDonnell and Stefaan Van den Bogaert (eds), *The Law of the European Union* (Kluwer Law International 2018) 673–691; Fausto Pocar, 'The Brussels Convention: 50 Years of Contribution to European Integration' in Burkhard Hess and Koen Lenaerts (eds), *The 50th Anniversary of the European Law of Civil Procedure* (Nomos-Hart Publishing 2020), 251; Burkhard Hess, 'Seminal Judgments (les Grands Arrets) in the Case Law of the European Court of Justice' in Burkhard Hess and Koen Lenaerts (eds), *The 50th Anniversary of the European Law of Civil Procedure* (Nomos-Hart Publishing 2020), 11,

372 Burkhard Hess, *Harmonized rules and Minimum Standards in the European Law of Civil Procedure* (Policy Department C: Citizens' Rights and Constitutional Affairs 2016), 5.

373 The CJEU was initially conferred jurisdiction to interpret preliminary questions referred by national courts on the interpretation of the 1968 Brussels Convention (see the Protocol concerning the interpretation by the CJEU of the Brussels Convention, signed in Luxembourg on 3 June 1971). With the entry into force of the Amsterdam Treaty of 1999 (Art. 68 EC) the CJEU was given the function of ensuring the uniform interpretation of all preliminary questions related to the policy area of judicial cooperation in civil matters. However, the scope of Art. 68 EC was limited by the fact that only courts of last resort were allowed to submit preliminary references to the CJEU. The Lisbon Treaty finally extended this possibility to all national courts by referring to Art. 267 TFEU. See Nanette Neuwahl, 'Judicial Control in Matters of Justice and Home Affairs: What Role for the Court of Justice?' in Roland Bieber and Jörg Monar (eds), *Justice and Home Affairs in the European Union: The Development of the Third Pillar* (European Interuniversity Press 1995), 301–320; Damian Chalmers, 'The Court of Justice and the Third Pillar' (2004) E.L. Rev., 773–774; Camelia Toader, 'La Confiance Mutuelle, Fondement et Temoignage de la Valeur de l'Union europeenne' in Burkhard Hess and Koen Lenaerts (eds), *The 50th Anniversary of the European Law of Civil Procedure* (Nomos-Hart Publishing 2020), 49; Hess (n.371), 12; Kramer Xandra and Jos Hoevenaars, 'European Civil Procedure and the Dialogue between National Courts and the European Court of Justice', in Burkhard Hess and Koen Lenaerts (eds), *The 50th Anniversary of the European Law of Civil Procedure* (Nomos-Hart Publishing 2020), 186.

Matters falling within the policy area of judicial cooperation in civil matters are subject to the territorial exclusions provided for by the Protocols of accession of Ireland[374] and Denmark[375] to the Treaty of Lisbon[376].

The following conditions must be complied with when using Art. 81 TFEU as a legal basis for enacting legislation in civil procedural matters (e.g. time limits).

1) Possible measures

Art. 81 (2) TFEU provides for the following list of measures to be adopted under its scope aimed at ensuring: '(a) the mutual recognition and enforcement between Member States of judgments and of decisions in extrajudicial cases; (b) the cross-border service of judicial and extrajudicial documents; (c) the compatibility of the rules applicable in the Member States concerning conflict of laws and of jurisdiction; (d) cooperation in the taking of evidence; (e) effective access to justice; (f) the elimination of obstacles to the proper functioning of civil proceedings, if necessary by promoting the compatibility of the rules on civil procedure applicable in the Member States; (g) the development of alternative methods of dispute settlement; (h) support for the training of the judiciary and judicial staff'.

The latter list of measures is meant to cover 'the full ambit of private law topics and private international law questions'[377]. EU competence to regulate private international and procedural law under the scope of Art. 81 TFEU can arguably be treated as unlimited by subject matter.

---

374 See Protocol n. 21 on the position of the United Kingdom and Ireland in respect of the area of freedom, security and justice OJ C 202, 7.6.2016.

375 See Protocol n. 22 on the position of Denmark OJ C 326, 26.10.2012.

376 It should be noted that the United Kingdom is no longer bound by any instrument following its departure from the EU. See Council Decision (EU) 2020/135 of 30 January 2020 on the conclusion of the Agreement on the withdrawal of the United Kingdom of Great Britain and Northern Ireland from the European Union and the European Atomic Energy Community.

377 Xandra Kramer, *Current Gaps and Future Perspectives in European Private International Law: Towards a Code on Private international law?* (Policy Department C: Citizens' Rights and Constitutional Affairs 2012), 13–15; Manko (n.371), 11; Peers (n.371), 345.

2) Beyond the internal market

According to Art. 81 (2) TFEU, the EU legislative mandate in judicial cooperation in civil matters can be exercised 'particularly when necessary for the proper functioning of the internal market'.

This makes the internal market requirement an optional condition – and not anymore, a mandatory one as was the case under Art. 65 EC[378] – for adopting civil justice measures.

Art. 81 TFEU thus extends judicial cooperation in civil matters beyond the internal market requirement promoting a certain level of emancipation of civil procedure from the internal market function[379]. The new approach shifts towards a European citizenship paradigm where the need to contribute to the development of an area of freedom, security and justice could also be inspired by premises rather different than the internal market ones[380].

3) Limitation to cases with cross-border implications

Art. 81 TFEU grants the EU competence to deal with national procedural matters 'with cross-border implications'[381].

378 Under Art. 65 EC measures in the field of judicial cooperation in civil matters might be adopted 'insofar as necessary for the proper functioning of the internal market'. The interpretation of this requirement has been much debated in academic circles and raised doubts on the competence of the EC to adopt the Rome II Regulation and the private international law Regulations in family matters. For an overview on these debates see Andrew Dickinson, 'European Private International Law: Embracing New Horizons or Mourning the Past' (2005) 1 JPIL, 211–215; Peter Herzog, 'Art 65' in Dennis Campbell and Susan Cotter (eds), *The Law of the European Community: a Commentary on the EC Treaty* (Matthew Bender NexisLexis 1976), para 65.02; Basedow (n.371), 703; Michael Wilderspin, 'The Rome II Regulation: Some Policy Observations' (2008) NIPR, 412, 413; Xandra Kramer, 'The Rome II Regulation on the Law Applicable to Non-Contractual Obligations: The European Private International Law Tradition Continued' (2008) NIPR. 415; Kramer (n.371), 728; Von Hein (n.371). 23; Andrea *Bonomi, Diritto Internazionale Privato e Cooperazione Giudiziaria in Materia Civile* (Giappichelli Editore 2008), 21.

379 Magdalena Tulibacka, 'Europeanisation of Civil Procedure: in Search of a Coherent Approach' (2009) 46 CMLR, 1562.

380 Luigi Moccia, 'European Law: from "Market" to "Citizenship"' in Luigi Moccia (ed), *The Making of European Private Law: Why, How, What, Who* (Sellier European Law Publishers 2017), 51.

381 In spite of an intense discussion on the possibility to extend the scope of Art. 81 TFEU to national cases, the EU legislator finally maintained the limitation to cases

The interpretation of this criterion has been source of debate in academia and a focal point of struggle between EU institutions during the legislative process for adopting certain procedural law instruments. The question reflecting a perpetual tension between the expansion of EU civil justice and the protection of national law was whether an extensive (including also national litigation) or restrictive (limited to cross-border cases) approach of the wording 'cross-border implications' should be retained.

In this respect, it has been argued that constraining the scope of application of judicial cooperation in civil matters to cross-border cases was inappropriate and counterproductive to the proper functioning of the internal market[382]. Differentiating between national and cross-border cases would

---

with cross-border implications. In light of the interdependence between the internal market and the cross-border requirements, some authors argued that as long as the internal market requirement became optional under the Lisbon Treaty regime, there was no need anymore to limit the scope of Art. 81 TFEU to cross-border issues. Authors insisted indeed on the fact that measures based on the internal market have automatically some relationship to cross-border issues because the internal market is not a purely domestic concept: if the subject matter has a disruptive effect on the internal market, it also unavoidably has cross-border implications. It follows that if the need to ensure the proper functioning of the internal market was lacking, there would be no reason to limit the scope of Art. 81 TFEU to matters with cross-border implications. See Tulibacka (n.379), 1562; Peers (n.371), 350.

382 The Commission in subsequent legislative proposals has endorsed this approach. In particular, in its proposals on the Legal Aid Directive, EPO Regulation, Mediation Directive and ESCP Regulation the Commission insisted on an extensive interpretation of Art. 65 EC which should cover both cross-border and domestic disputes. Under the same premises, the Commission in the EAPO and ESCP reform proposals reiterated the latter approach under the scope of Art. 81 TFEU insisting on a negative definition of cross-border cases rather than on a positive one. See Green Paper from the Commission – Legal aid in civil matters: the problems confronting the cross-border litigant COM/2000/0051; Proposal for a Regulation of the European Parliament and of the Council creating a European order for payment procedure COM/2004/0173; Proposal for a Directive of the European Parliament and of the Council on certain aspects of mediation in civil and commercial matters COM/2004/0251; Proposal for a Regulation of the European Parliament and of the Council establishing a European Small Claims Procedure COM/2005/0087; Proposal for a Regulation of the European Parliament and of the Council creating a European Account Preservation Order to facilitate cross-border debt recovery in civil and commercial matter COM/2011/0445; Proposal for a Regulation of the European Parliament and of the Council amending Regulation (EC) No 861/2007 of the European Parliament and the Council of 11 July 2007 establishing a European Small Claims Procedure and Regulation (EC) No 1896/2006 of the European Parliament and of the Council of 12 December 2006 creating a European order for payment procedure COM/2013/0794.

'devise a more efficient set of procedures for cross-border disputes, thus ignoring the various domestic civil procedures'[383]. In particular, if parties when exercising their rights were to have access to diverging mechanisms of protection depending upon the cross-border or domestic nature of the case, this would distort competition in the internal market and have discriminatory effects on parties' access to justice[384].

What follows from this view is that divergences between national procedural laws will constitute *per se* an obstacle to judicial cooperation in civil matters, which would automatically grant cross-border implications to any measure of harmonisation, at least indirectly, e.g. businesses could be affected by national differences when deciding where to produce and market their products[385]. Restricting judicial cooperation in civil matters only to cross-border cases would therefore be inconsistent with the idea of a single area of justice for all and could lead to lack of transparency and clarity[386].

In spite of the latter arguments calling into question the distinction between national and cross-border matters, current EU law-making[387] practically showed that a broad interpretation of the wording cross-border implications was not possible. Member States in the Council, supported by the European Parliament, reacted to the potential extension of judicial cooperation in civil matters to purely domestic litigation by vigorously defending 'the wall of national exceptionalism'[388]. A narrow interpretation of the wording 'cross-border implications' then prevailed in all the discussed legislative instruments. This means that EU action in the area of civil justice

383 Marcel Storme, 'Closing Comments: Harmonisation or Globalisation of Civil Procedure' in Xandra Kramer and Remco Van Rhee (eds), *Civil Litigation in Globalising World* (Springer 2012), 379–387.

384 Kramer (n.371), 727.

385 Van Rhee (n.371), 54; Rossi (n.371), 65.

386 Tulibacka (n.379), 1545.

387 See Council Directive 2002/8/EC of 27 January 2003 to improve access to justice in cross-border disputes by establishing minimum common rules relating to legal aid for such disputes OJ L 26; EPO Regulation, ESCP Regulation, Directive 2008/52/EC of the European Parliament and of the Council of 21 May 2008 on certain aspects of mediation in civil and commercial matters OJ L 136, EAPO Regulation.

388 Carla Crifo, 'Trusted with a Muzzle and Enfranchised with a Clog: The British Approach to European Civil Procedure' in Burkhard Hess, Maria Bergström and Eva Storskrubb (eds), *EU Civil Justice Current Issues and Future Outlook* (Bloomsbury 2016), 94.

is only possible if there are connecting factors in a case (e.g. residence, place of performance) pointing to at least two different Member States[389].

4) Legislative procedure

The co-decision procedure (Art. 294 TFEU) – already introduced as a general rule by the Treaty of Nice – is the ordinary legislative procedure to deal with when adopting measures in the policy area of judicial cooperation in civil matters (Art. 81 (2) TFEU).

Such procedure is based on a proposal of the Commission and requires the joint agreement of the European Parliament and Council to proceed. Neither of them can adopt legislation without the agreement of the other, and both co-legislators must simultaneously consent on the same text (principle of parity). The procedure is built on a three readings system during which the Parliament and the Council can reach a compromise at any stage[390].

However, an exception from the general ordinary regime concerns family law matters[391] (Art. 81 (3) TFEU), where a special legislative procedure requiring a unanimous decision of the Council, with the Parliament only being consulted, applies. This shows 'the difficult balance between the political desire to move forward and the politically sensitive nature of this specific sub-area of civil justice'[392]

Regarding the above special procedure, the Council, upon the Commission's proposal and after having consulted the Parliament, has the right to 'switch' from the special legislative procedure to the ordinary one with

389 Manko (n.371), 11.

390 For further details on the legislative procedure see Art. 294 TFEU.

391 Most of the instruments adopted in the policy area of judicial cooperation in civil matters have a mixed character and are at the crossroad between family matters and other matters. Some issues might then arise on the interpretation of family law matters. Namely, It has been argued that there are two possible interpretations of the family law exception: 'either it applies only where the EU adopt legislation essentially solely related to family law proceedings, or it applies to general rules which govern both family law and non-family law proceedings. In the latter case the exception would mean that such measures would have to be adopted on a dual legal basis, which would entail adopting separate measures, since the two decision making procedures would be incompatible', see Steve Peers, 395. Nevertheless, the scope of this research does not cover family law proceedings.

392 Storskrubb (n.371), 204.

respect to some aspects of family law. Against the decision of changing decision-making rules, national parliaments have a right of veto.

5) Choice of instruments

Regarding the choice of the legal instrument, Art. 81 (2) TFEU has a very general formulation referring indiscriminately to 'measures' for approximating Member States' laws'.

The reference is therefore to those general acts provided for in Art. 288 TFEU. Within this list, the main instruments used for achieving the goals set out in the policy area of judicial cooperation in civil matters are respectively regulations and directives[393].

In such a framework, Art. 296 (1) TFEU, provides that in situations where the Treaties 'do not specify the type of act to be adopted'– as it is the case in Art. 81 TFEU – 'the institutions shall select it on a case-by-case basis, in compliance with the applicable procedures and with the principle of proportionality'.

EU institutions are therefore generally bound by the EU principles of subsidiarity and proportionality when deciding whether to issue a regulation or a directive[394]. Opting either for regulation or directive when adopting a measure in judicial cooperation in civil matters is a difficult choice which EU institutions assess on a case by case basis in light of the objectives pursued by each specific measure.

Contrary to regulations, directives do not apply directly to horizontal relations governed by procedural law; rather, EU citizens are bound by the national implementing provisions which could differ widely in form and method from State to State. The variety of national implementation rules might entail fragmentation and prevent a full harmonisation of EU procedural law.

393 Partsch (n.371), 312.

394 However, what practically happens is that 'the Commission often makes an autonomous decision over what it considers to be in line with these principles when issuing its policy proposals. As a result, there is a range of policy topics in which the Commission enjoys discretion over the choice of the legal instrument, and by implication, the amount of discretion it grants to Member States to decide on the ways and means to reach a certain policy goal', see Steffen Hurka and Yves Steinebach, 'Legal Instrument Choice in the European Union' (2021) 59 JCMS, 278–296.

Because regulations must be enacted in national legislation directly, regulations are deemed to ensure greater uniformity of application and might be proposed as the most favourable regulatory option to achieve general harmonisation of EU procedural law[395]. On the other hand, a regulation probably would not be the right instrument to address selective issues in a broader area of private international law as it would tend to carve out the law applicable in a national court making its interpretation in a harmonious way difficult. 'The risk is particularly pressing in codified legal systems where lawyers expect the relevant provisions to be part of the codification; while a Directive can be implemented in a codification, a Regulation cannot'[396].

Against such an uncertain backdrop where regulations and directives retain both advantages and disadvantages, the tendency indicated by the current EU law-making in the policy area of judicial cooperation in civil matters seems to show preference for regulations[397].

6) Horizontal harmonisation of time limits

As pointed out above, impediments in national procedural laws to the free circulation of judgments in the civil justice area depend also on the differences of time limits (e.g. time to react, time to appeal) in the proceedings, which is certainly a core procedural matter. It is therefore clearly possible to enact legislation on time limits based on Art. 81 TFEU.

Based on the mentioned criteria, harmonised rules on time limits would be limited to cross-border civil proceedings; would remove obstacles to the proper functioning of the internal market; and would be adopted under the ordinary legislative procedure according either to a regulation or to a directive.

---

395 Jürgen Basedow, *EU Private Law: Anatomy of a Growing Legal Order* (Intersentia 2021), 89.

396 Basedow (n.395), 89.

397 Basedow (n.395), 88, 89. On the contrary, see Report of the European Parliament with recommendations to the Commission on common minimum standards of civil procedure in the EU 2017) (2015/2084(INL)).

II) Art. 114 TFEU

Art. 114 TFEU[398] grants the EU legislative powers for adopting measures of harmonisation contributing to 'the establishment and functioning of the internal market'.

This general legal basis – it applies save where otherwise provided – aims at harmonising rules of national law in order to overcome differences which might hinder the proper functioning of the internal market. Its scope is not limited to cross-border settings (as is the case under Art. 81 TFEU), but generally concerns litigants in domestic and cross-border situations.

It should be noted that the possibility to build up legislation in civil procedure based on the internal market powers has historically been actively discussed in academia. In spite of favourable arguments led by the Storme group[399], the internal market competence has not been used for generally unifying and approximating laws in the procedural field. Developments in EU procedural law finally took place with the entry into force of the Amsterdam Treaty which provided the EU with a general competence in judicial cooperation in civil matters (i.e. Art. 65 EC and now Art. 81 TFEU)[400].

However, as the competence in this policy area is not full but restricted by certain criteria[401], debates on the possibility of using the internal market legal basis for filling in the gap left by Arts 65 EC and 81 TFEU are still ongoing. In this respect, one could reasonably argue in accordance with

398 Art. 114 TFEU finds its origin in Art. 100 EEC (introduced by the Treaty of Rome in 1957), Art. 100a EEC (provided for on the side of Art. 100 EEC by the Single European Act in 1986), and Art. 95 EC (amending Art. 100a EEC).

399 In particular, the Storme Group found that Arts 100, and 100(a) EEC provided sufficient support for the EU to promote a unification or approximation of laws in the procedural field. See Marcel Storme, *Approximation of Judiciary Law in the European Union* (Martinus Nijhoff 1994), 59; Jacques Normand, 'Le Rapprochement des Procedures Civiles dans l'Union Europeenne' (1998) 6 Eur. Rev. Private Law, 383–390.

400 An important impulse in this regard was given by the Tampere political programme of 1999, which established key political objectives for achieving relevant developments in the policy area of judicial cooperation in civil matters. See Tampere European Council Presidency Conclusions 200/1/99 of 16 October 1999.

401 Art. 81 TFEU is indeed limited to cases with cross-border implications and its territorial scope does not concern Denmark and Ireland. Under Art. 81 TFEU, the need to contribute to the internal market is not anymore a mandatory requirement – as happened under Art. 65 EC – for enacting legislation under Art. 81 TFEU; it has a mere optional character.

CJEU case law[402] – and as confirmed by the current EU law-making – that adopting general procedural law measures outside the scope of Art. 81 TFEU is not possible[403]. This would indeed circumvent the rationale and intention of the Lisbon Treaty's drafters, who deliberately decided to limit judicial cooperation in civil matters to a targeted category of cases[404].

1) Vertical dimension of EU procedural law

On a different note, the internal market legal basis (Arts 95 EC and 114 TFEU) finally justified the development of a vertical dimension of EU procedural law, which gained momentum together with the horizontal developments in judicial cooperation in civil matters. This is the 'sectoral' or 'vertical' approach[405] according to which the EU legislator introduces

---

402 It should be noted that this case law applies by analogy with respect to another case dealing with public health law matters. The CJEU in the Case C-376/98 *Federal Republic of Germany v European Parliament and Council of the European Union* (2000) EU:C:2000:544 stated that EU's internal market powers could not be used to circumvent a Treaty ban on harmonisation of public health law. Namely, it follows that 'other articles of the Treaty could not be used as a legal basis in order to circumvent the express exclusion of harmonisation'. This case law is deemed to deal as well with the policy area of judicial cooperation in civil matters. However, according to the opinion of AG Trstenjak Case C-265/07 *Caffaro Srl versus Azienda Unità Sanitaria Locale RM/C* (2007) EU:C:2008:496 there is no explicit ban in the policy area of judicial cooperation in civil matters – as happens with regard to public health – preventing the harmonisation of civil law according to the market law powers.

403 Peers (n.371), 353. On the other hand, some authors consider that there are no reasons for excluding approximation of national procedural laws under the internal market legal basis as long as the relationship between Art. 65-Art. 95 EC and Art. 81–114 TFEU would be regulated by the general principle *lex specialis derogat generali*. It would be in line with this principle to make use of the internal market competence where the one in judicial cooperation in civil matters is unavailable, provided that both legal bases aim at eliminating obstacles to the smooth functioning of the internal market – under Art. 81 measures to be adopted can still be linked to the internal market – caused by differences between domestic legal systems. Jona Israel, 'Conflict of Law and the EC after Amsterdam, A Change for the Worse?' (2000) 7 MJ, 90, 91; Partsch (n.371), fn 1367; Basedow (n.371), 699; Storskrubb (n.371), 36.

404 Peers (n.371), 353.

405 Hess, (n.51), 5–8; Hess (n.372), 5; Tulibacka, Sanz and Blomeyer (n.371), 58–60; Manko (n.371), 13.

procedural rules without legislating in the area of civil procedure, i.e. without relying on the competence granted under Art. 81 TFEU[406].

Such approach is premised on the two following related concepts. On the one hand, there is the general concept of EU law that the courts of the Member States must enforce EU law efficiently on the basis of their domestic procedures and, on the other hand, there is the related concept that specific substantive laws should be implemented efficiently, because an underlying public interest requires their efficient implementation[407].

In this respect, where the EU adopts instruments in specific areas of substantive law (e.g. IP rights, consumer law), the procedural element arises as annexed and ancillary to the substantive law-making. The influence of EU law in these areas might indeed be described as vertical: as national courts implement substantive EU law by virtue of their national procedures, the European lawmaker might intervene in order to guarantee or to improve the uniform interpretation of EU law by the courts of the Member States. This is the so-called phenomenon of 'proceduralisation through the back door'[408]: proceduralisation only concerns specific areas of EU law while the core parts of general procedural laws remain untouched.

2) Sectoral harmonisation of time limits

What arises from the above is that Art. 114 TFEU, even if it would have the great advantage of extending the scope of the harmonised rules also to national cases, cannot be used as the general legal basis for harmonising time limits in cross-border civil proceedings at the EU level.

On the other hand, vertical harmonisation is possible under Art. 114 TFEU: in specific areas of substantive law, a procedural matter like time limits could be harmonised being annexed to the substantive legislation. Harmonised time limits would then apply also to national litigation, however, their impact would be limited to the targeted sectoral area of substantive law.

---

406 See Gerhard Wagner, 'Harmonization of Civil Procedure: Policy Perspectives in Xandra Kramer and Remco Van Rhee (eds), *Civil Litigation in Globalising World* (Springer 2012), 101.

407 Hess (n.371), 164, 165.

408 Report on common minimum standards of civil procedure (n.397), 20; Wagner (n.406), 101–109.

III) Art. 81 TFEU as the most appropriate legal basis?

Provided that both horizontal (Art. 81 TFEU) and vertical (Art. 114 TFEU) harmonisation of time limits is possible, we shall explore which legal basis best fits the scope of the research.

The choice of the legal basis depends on the content, objective and purpose of the measure to be adopted. These factors cannot be easily discernible as the measures to be adopted might contain elements falling simultaneously both under the scope of Arts 81 and 114 TFEU, e.g. measures adopted under Art. 81 TFEU are generally meant to be beneficial to the proper functioning of the internal market overlapping with Art. 114 TFEU.

In this respect, 'if a measure pursues a twofold purpose or that it has a twofold component and, if one of these is identifiable as the main or predominant purpose or component whereas the other is merely incidental, the act must be based on a single legal basis, namely that required by the main or predominant purpose or component'[409]. This means that the EU legislator will concretely check if the content of the measure to be adopted is more related to the civil procedure or internal market element.

In principle, the identification of a dominant purpose either in Arts 114 or 81 TFEU is possible. However, under exceptional circumstances it could happen that the measure pursues several objectives which are inseparably linked without one being secondary and indirect in relation to the other. In such case, the measure must be founded on both Arts 114 and 81 TFEU[410].

In this respect, it should be noted that the issues which have been described under the scope of this research concern time limits under the Brussels Ibis, EEO, EPO and ESCP Regulations. The measures on time limits to be adopted aim then at tackling the mentioned issues emerging in a horizontal dimension regardless of the subject matter. The civil procedural element thus prevails over the internal market one.

For the purposes of this research, it could then be argued that the abovementioned factors weigh in favour of a legislative competence under Art. 81 TFEU. Concretely, this means that the regulatory competence of the EU to

409 Case C-211/01 *Commission of the European Communities v Council of the European Union* (2003) EU:C:2003:452, para 39.

410 Case C-336/00 *Republik Österreich v Martin Huber* (2002) EU:C:2002:509, para 31; Case C-281/01 *Commission of the European Communities v Council of the European Union* (2002) EU:C:2002:761, para 35, and Case C-2/00 *Opinions of the Court* (2001) EU:C:2001:664, para 23. However, it should be noted that this procedure never happened in practice.

deal with the time limits in civil proceedings will be limited to cross-border cases.

B) Desirability of EU action on time limits

Even if the EU possesses the legislative competences, one needs to consider whether it would be desirable to deal with the time limits at the EU level or, rather, whether this regime constitutes a national procedural matter where EU action would not be recommended.

When enacting legislation in civil procedure, the EU legislator must carefully assess its policy decision[411]. Harmonising civil procedure involves indeed the following competing considerations[412]: on the one hand, evaluating the impact of procedural divergences on the internal market and the need to protect procedural rights and, on the other hand, considering the very essence of procedural law which cannot be separated from national peculiarities and sensitivities[413].

I) The driving force

On the one hand, EU action on time limits in general civil proceedings could be supported by the following arguments.

411 Sophie Delabruyère, 'On "Legal Choice" and Legal Competition in a Federal System of Justice: Lessons for European Legal Integration' in Alain Marciano and Jean-Michel Josselin (eds), *From Economic to Legal Competition. New Perspectives on Law and Institutions in Europe* (Edward Elgar Publishing 2003), 22, 23.

412 Tulibacka (n.379), 1532.

413 Civil procedure is indeed perceived as one of the branches of law most closely linked to national environments, and should be studied and practiced as a purely national product; see Remo Caponi, 'Harmonizing Civil Procedure: Initial Remarks' in Burkhard Hess and Xandra Kramer, *From Common Rules to Best Practices in European Civil Procedure* (Nomos-Hart Publishing 2017), 46.

1) A level playing field in the internal market

The internal market has over the years been one of the main driving forces – a real 'impetus for legislation'[414] – contributing to the developments of the current *acquis communautaire* in EU procedural law[415].

In this respect, an economic analysis of the needs of the internal market will follow. Market implications must be assessed both from general macro and micro level perspectives, which will give insights on the actual effects which procedural diversity entails for citizens and companies operating in the EU common internal market.

From a general macro-level perspective, one could argue that 'procedural complexity creates barriers to trade, and also often discrimination, which entails that conditions are not equal for all the participants in the supranational market'[416].

On the other hand, from a general micro-level perspective, litigants 'will be faced with increased, even insurmountable, complexity, delay and costs, as soon as there is a cross-border element to transaction they undertake and they will therefore be less inclined to engage in transnational business'[417].

Undesired economic effects in the internal market could therefore follow from national procedural diversities distorting equal protection of parties' rights in the internal market. When litigating in cross-border disputes,

414 Eva Stroskrubb, 'Mutual Trust and the Dark Horse of Civil Justice' (2017) 20 Camb. Yearb. Eur. Leg. Stud., 192; Storskrubb (n.371), 306.

415 The importance of the market argument has risen since the adoption of the 1968 Brussels Convention. In particular, Mr Jenard in his report to the Convention highlighted that 'a true internal market between the Member States could be achieved only if adequate legal protection and, hence, legal security could be secured by providing for a satisfactory solution to the problem of the recognition and enforcement of judicial decisions beyond the boundaries of each national territory'. These findings were also reinforced at the end of 80's by the conclusions of the Storme group. Despite internal market pressures, procedural developments at the EU level occurred at a very slow pace as many doubts were cast on the compatibility between this project and the subsidiarity principle. With the entry into force of the Amsterdam Treaty in 1999, the link between the internal market and national procedural laws was concretely thrown into relief (see Arts 65 EC and 81 TFEU) leading to impressive developments in the policy area of judicial cooperation in civil matters. See Jenard Report (n.47).

416 Storskrubb (n.371), 79.

417 Storskrubb (n.371), 79.

creditors could find that they have 'fewer procedural rights or less procedural protection than in their home state'[418].

The presence of procedural rules of considerable divergent quality levels could distort competition in the internal market: 'cross-border or domestic operators competing in the internal market are on an unequal footing if one of them has access to efficient and effective procedure while the other does not'[419]. This is likely to cause fragmentation and even discrimination between litigants in the internal market preventing them from being able to litigate across the EU.

In such cases, divergent rules would prevent economic integration leading to a dichotomy between judicial practice and economic reality in the EU internal market. The risk is that law divides what economics unifies[420]. It follows that legal diversity hampers the smooth functioning of the internal market placing 'a tax on European businesses'[421], an onerous tax that does not create any benefits for the functioning of the internal market and leads to economic deceleration.

As arises from the case studies analysed under Chapter 2[422] of this work, divergences between national time limits could make cross-border dispute resolution particularly complicated, costly[423] and lengthy, thus negatively impacting, as such, on parties' access to justice. Under these circumstances, parties could refrain from litigating cross-border, and this is certainly an obstacle to the smooth functioning of the EU common internal market[424].

418 Storskrubb (n.371), 79.

419 Zampia Vernadaki, 'Civil Procedure Harmonization in the EU: Unravelling the Policy Considerations' (2013) 9 JCER, 300.

420 Francois Vincke, 'Les Enterprises Europeennes Ont Besoin de Rapprochement' in Marcel Storme (ed), *Procedural Laws in Europe. Towards Harmonisation* (Maklu 2003), 21.

421 Gerhard Wagner, 'The Economics of Harmonization: the Case of Contract Law' in 39 CMLR (2002), 1014.

422 See Chapter 2: Effective judicial cooperation in civil matters and the right to a fair trial

423 For instance, 'the costs of getting informed about the different legal systems may outweigh the gains from cross-border trade. And even if there were still such trade, it would become more expensive due to these legal differences'. See Louis Visscher, 'A Law and Economics View on Harmonisation of Procedural Law' in Xandra Kramer and Remco Van Rhee (eds), *Civil Litigation in Globalising World* (Springer 2012), 75.

424 Negative consequences would mainly affect occasional litigants, such as consumers and small and medium-sized companies, see Storskrubb (n.371), 80.

It could thus be argued that the incoherent mosaic of divergent national time limits across the EU is 'deconstructive'[425] and counter-productive to the smooth functioning of an integrated market[426]. EU legal intervention on the time limits would tackle these undesired effects and promote a level playing field in the internal market, notably improving market integration and citizens' economic freedoms[427]. This would challenge market failures[428] resulting from the vastly diverging rules on time limits, which might prevent parties from litigating in cross-border civil proceedings[429].

2) Fundamental rights perspective

The exercise of parties' rights in the proceedings, as embedded in Arts 6 ECHR and 47 CFR, firmly depends on the setting of time limits. As the cases described in Chapter 2 show[430], time limits vary with respect to their length, their *dies a quo* and depending on which act or event suspends or interrupts the time limit. These divergences could as such constitute an obstacle to judicial cooperation in civil matters.

Regulating time limits at the EU level would challenge this situation and increase legal certainty in the face of contrasting fragmentation and incoherence between Member States' procedural rules[431].

Uniform time limits, complying with the due process standards enshrined in Arts 6 ECHR and 47 CFR, would ensure equal protection of defendants' rights in cross-border proceedings, e.g. when first reacting to the claim or when challenging judgments. This would grant EU litigants involved in cross-border cases the possibility to rely on similar procedural guarantees in the proceedings.

Common time limits would therefore enhance the level of legal certainty strengthening the effectiveness and efficiency of each procedural system

425 Xandra Kramer, 'Strengthening Civil Justice Cooperation: the Quest for Model Rules and Common Minimum Standards of Civil Procedure in Europe' in Marco Antonio Rodrigues and Hermes Zaneti Jr (eds), *Coleção Grandes Temas do Novo CPC – v.13 – Cooperação Internacional* (Editora Juspodivm 2019), 596.

426 Kerameus (n.48), 928.

427 Vernadaki (n.419), 300; Visscher (n. 423), 67.

428 Visscher (n.423), 71.

429 Vernadaki (n.419), 300.

430 See Chapter 2: Effective judicial cooperation in civil matters and the right to a fair trial.

431 Vernadaki (n.419), 300.

within the EU framework[432]. Notably, this would reinforce mutual trust between Member States and positively affect EU economic growth, which might entail relevant economic benefits leading to more transactions and higher investment levels[433].

II) Assessment of the counterarguments

On the other hand, the assessment on the desirability question requires taking into account the following counterarguments supporting procedural diversity and thus challenging the valuable effects of EU action on time limits.

1) Procedural diversity as an advantage

First, according to some commentators, procedural diversity leads to inter-jurisdictional competition between Member States' legal systems, and could produce the following benefits.

Competition between national legal systems would both push Member States to look for the best solutions in their own jurisdiction[434] and enable them to learn from each other[435].

---

432 As time limits greatly influence the reasonable length of proceedings, this could have relevant implications on the choice of the forum. In principle, litigants could in certain cases abuse this possibility. Namely, companies might transfer their commercial activities to Member States with the least favourable procedural regime for consumers with negative consequences on their right of defence. In such circumstances, forum shopping would lead to a sort of competition between jurisdictions whereby the one with the lowest standards of protection – depending *inter alia* on the provisions on the time limits – would be the preferred one. This is the so-called 'Delaware effect'. Corporate regulation in this State ensured low quality standards in order to attract companies to litigate. In spite of these considerations, this effect is not considered a real issue in EU legal practice. See Vernadaki (n.419), 302.

433 Notably, this could entail relevant economic benefits leading to more transactions and higher investment levels, see Berns Hayo and Stefan Voigt, 'The Relevance of Judicial Procedure for Economic Growth' (2008) Cesifo Working Paper, 1.

434 'A race to the top rather than setting for the lowest common denominator standards' see Tulibacka (n.379), 1554.

435 Visscher (n.423), 78.

Moreover, procedural diversity grants litigants a wide range of choice between national legal systems within the EU[436] and generally avoids that pressure groups might promote their interests to the detriment of other groups when the EU introduces new legislation[437].

In this context, time limits are one of the main elements ensuring procedural diversity given its core role in proceedings. Litigants' preferences on the choice of forum therefore depend *inter alia* on how each national legal system shapes its own rules on time limits.

Nevertheless, it should be noted that for procedural diversity to be effective presupposes that litigants are aware of national procedural rules – in this case, time limits – and it is particularly burdensome for litigants within the EU territory to familiarize themselves with 27 different time limits.

Depending on the type of litigants involved in the dispute, actual implications will differ[438]. On the one hand, large international companies with the resources to engage expert lawyers would be able to take advantage of the efficiencies of inter-jurisdictional competition and discover the most beneficial procedural system for dispute resolution. On the other hand, individual litigants and small and medium-sized companies would probably not be able to make an appropriate choice of procedural rules due to lack of time, resources, or legal foundations. What arises is that different rules on time limits could accentuate inequalities between parties' rights which lead to a denial of parties' access to justice.

This does not comply with the right to a fair trial as guaranteed by Art. 6 ECHR and Art. 47 CFR. Hence, one could then argue that procedural diversity in this specific area of civil judicial cooperation is likely to cause more harm than benefits. Overall, a uniform European rule on time limits could therefore be regarded as a desirable outcome.

---

436 For instance, it has been argued that 'the greater the number of communities and the greater the variance among them, the closer the consumer will come to fully realizing his preference position', see Visscher (n.423), 77; Charles Tiebout, 'A Pure Theory of Local Expenditures' (1956) 64 JPE, 418.

437 Vernadaki (n.419), 302; Visscher (n.423), 78, 79.

438 Vernadaki (n.419), 307; Jon Johnsen, 'Vulnerable Groups at the Legal Service Market' in Alan Uzelac and Remco Van Rhee (eds), *Access to Justice and the Judiciary: Towards New European Standards of Affordability, Quality and Efficiency of Civil Adjudication* (Intersentia 2009), 33, 34

2) Time limits and national resistances

In addition to the above criticisms, it should be noted that dealing with time limits means considering some procedural rules which are deeply embedded in the national traditions of each Member State[439].

Cultural, historical, political, institutional, ethical and economic factors lead national procedural systems along very different paths[440]. National traditions therefore make the question of the acceptance by the Member States of uniform rules on time limits adopted at the EU level particularly sensitive[441].

It follows that this situation raises doubts as to the actual benefits produced by harmonised rules: 'cultural sensitivities reflected in the choice of procedural regimes may be so great that EU intervention into Member States' civil procedure law may be impossible, or so complicated, that its net results may not render it desirable for individual Member States'[442].

a) Time limits and national legal cultures

Against this backdrop, it is therefore necessary to determine whether between the 27 national legal systems, in spite of the structural differences underlying the setting of time limits at national level, there are common grounds enabling sufficient agreement on a certain degree of harmonisation to overcome any national resistance.

In this respect, the following analysis on how time limits are practically regulated by the Member States will give some relevant insights on the relationship between time limits and national legal cultures and on the possibility to overcome national resistances when enacting legislation at the EU level.

---

439 Biavati (n.367), 90, 91.

440 Michele Taruffo, 'Harmonisation in a Global Context: the Ali/UNIDROIT Principles' in Xandra Kramer and Remco Van Rhee (eds), *Civil Litigation in a Globalising World* (Asser 2012), 209; Caponi (n.413), 46.

441 Michele Angelo Lupoi, 'The Harmonization of Civil Procedural Law within the EU' in Orlando Frosini, Michele Angelo Lupoi and Michele Marchesiello (eds), *A European Space of Justice* (Longo, 2006), 209.

442 Vernadaki (n.419), 304.

aa) Calculation of time limits[443]

As a preliminary question for dealing with time limits, it is important to deal with the following rules on the calculation of time limits.

When calculating time limits, Member States establish a system based on the calculation of either working[444] or calendar[445] days.

Save for exceptions[446], the following principle generally applies when calculating time limits in days: *dies a quo non computatur in termino* and, on the contrary, *dies ad quem computatur in termino*[447].

In the same vein, time limits expressed in months and years are generally calculated *ex nominatione dierum* irrespective of the real number of days composing months and years[448]. The month (or year) of expiry of the time limit shall be determined by counting the number of months (or years) indicated in the time limit. Depending on the system at hand, Member States include[449] or exclude from the calculation the day[450] or month[451]

---

443 Regulation 1182/71 of 3 June 1971 determining the rules applicable to periods, dates and time limits already provides for uniform rules on the calculation of time limits, which, however, are not comprehensive. The Brussels Ibis Regulation does not refer to this regime for calculating time limits; the EPO, ESCP and EAPO Regulations refer to it, but the reference to Regulation 1182/71 still leaves open some interpretative questions. See for instance 1) Time limits for opposing the issuance of the EPO.

444 E.g. Spain.

445 Most of the Member States adopt this model of calculation, e.g. Italy, France, Germany, Belgium.

446 E.g. in Italy there is a specif category of time limits, the so called clear time limits ('termini liberi), whose regime is characterized by the fact that when calculating them neither the *dies a quo* nor the *dies ad quem* are taken into account in the calculation. See below i) Time to react in general first instance proceedings.

447 E.g. Art. 641 (1) French CPC; Section 187 (1) of the German BGB; Art. 155 (1) Italian c.p.c. In this respect, see also Art. 3 of Regulation 1182/71.

448 It follows that a time limit of 1 month will not always correspond to 30 days and a time limit of 1 year will not always correspond to 365 days. In principle, it does not matter if the time limit was running in a leap year. See Biavati (n.11), 258; Di Marzio (n.41), 92.

449 E.g. in France the *dies a quo* of a time limit expressed in month or years is the date when the act, event, decision or notification occurs. See Art. 641 (2) CPC. This is also the rule adopted by Art. 3 of Regulation 1182/71.

450 E.g. in Germany when calculating time limits in months or years the *dies a quo* of the time limit is not considered in the calculation. The time limit thus begins on the following day. See Section 222 (1) ZPO and Section 188 (2) of the BGB.

451 E.g. in Italy the month when the act occurred is not taken into account when calculating time limits in months and years. Thus, the time limit starts in the following month. See Art. 155 (2) Italian c.p.c.

when the act occurred. The *dies ad quem* is generally on the day that has the same date of the corresponding month (or year). Where the first month has more days than the last one and the starting day falls on a day not included in the last month, the *dies ad quem* expires on the last calendar day of the last month.

Generally, if the *dies ad quem* of the time limit occurs on a Saturday, Sunday or public holiday, this is postponed to the next working day[452]. This rule, however, usually does not concern time limits which are calculated backward as this might be counterproductive because it would abbreviate time limits[453]. In such a case, the *dies a quo* occurs chronologically later than the *dies ad quem*. Thus, the *dies a quo* – which shall not be taken into account – is the first day of backward calculation and, on the other hand the last day of backward calculation – which shall be taken into account – is the *dies ad quem*.

The list of public days is determined on a case-by-case basis by each Member State and referred to in Regulation 1182/71 of 3 June 1971[454].

Further, it should be noted that some Member States provide for an annual period of leave where the calculation of time limits is generally suspended[455].

It is also possible that Member States suspend, interrupt or put off time limits because of exceptional circumstances. This happened for instance to combat the spread of the coronavirus (Covid-19) where measures impacting on the management of the judicial workload and on the internal

452 See Art. 155 (4) Italian c.p.c.; in Germany see Section 222 (1) ZPO and Section 193 of the BGB; Art. 642 (2) French CPC. In this respect, see also Art. 3 of Regulation 1182/71.

453 See for instance the calculation of the time to react in Italy (see below i) Time to react in general first instance proceedings) or the rules on the calculation of backward time limits ('delais a rebours') under French law as interpreted by the French Supreme Court. See French Supreme Court 14-02-1990, n. 88-19.900 in Bull civ. 1990 II n. 33, 19 with case note of Roger Perrot in (1990) RTD civ., 557; French Supreme Court 04-02-1998, n. 95-21.479 in Bull civ. 1998 II n. 40, 25. See also Art. 3 of Regulation 1182/71 of 3 June 1971.

454 The list referred to by each Member State can be found in Regulation 1182/71.

455 E.g. in Italy (Art. 1 of the Law n. 1969/742) time limits are suspended by law during the annual period of leave between 1 and 31 August (a period of 31 days) of each year. It follows that the calculation of time limits breaks on 31 July and restarts on 1 September. The same happens in Greece where according to Art. 167 (7) Greek CPP the period from 1 to 31 August is not taken into account when calculating time limits. In Spain days in August are also considered non-working days.

organization of the judiciary were adopted by the Member States based on different legislative techniques[456].

---

456 For instance under Italian law, the Government' s Law Decree No 18 of 17 March 2020, then passed by the Parliament as Law No 27 of 24 April 2020, and the Government' s Law Decree No 23 of 8 April 2020, then passed by the Parliament as Law No 40 of 5 June 2020 suspended time limits in civil proceedings for the period 9/03 to 11/05. For a more detailed view on the measures adopted in Italy during the Covid-19 crisis see Vincenzo Lombardi, 'Sul Recente (e Caotico) Intervento Legislativo in Materia di Giustizia Civile' (Judicium.com 23 march 2020) https://www.judicium.it/emergenza-coronavirus-e-giustizia-civile/; Andrea Panzarola and Marco Farina, 'L'Emergenza Coronavirus ed il Processo Civile. Osservazioni a Prima Lettura' (Giustiziacivile.com 18 March 2020) https://giustiziacivile.com/arbitrato-e-processo-civile/editoriali/lemergenza-coronavirus-ed-il-processo-civile-osservazioni; Giovanni Chiapponi, 'The Impact of Corona Virus on the Management of Judicial Proceedings in Italy' (Eapilblog 13 March 2020) https://eapil.org/2020/03/13/the-impact-of-corona-virus-on-the-management-of-judicial-proceedings-in-italy/; Giuliano Scarselli, 'Interpretazione e Commento del Decreto Legge 8 marzo 2020 n. 11 di Differimento delle Udienze e Sospensione dei Termini Processuali Civili per Contrastare l'Emergenza da COVID 19' (Judicium.com 8 March 2020) https://www.judicium.it/decreto-legge-8-marzo-2020-n-11-differimento-delle-udienze-sospensione-dei-termini-processuali-civili-contrastare-lemergenza-covid-19/; Giovanni Chiapponi, 'Judicial Cooperation and Coronavirus: the Law Must Go on' (Judicium.com 23 may 2020) https://www.judicium.it/judicial-cooperation-and-coronavirus-the-law-must-go/.
Similarly, under French law, Ordonnance No 2020–306 of 25 March 2020 extended procedural time limits within civil proceedings expiring between 12/03 and the end of the state of emergency period (24/05) of 1 month, i.e. until 24/06. All the time limits having the dies ad quem expiring in the period between 12/03 and 24/06 were therefore legally protected. At the end of the aforementioned period, all time limits irrespective of their original length resumed normally, but from that moment they could run for a maximum period of 2 months, i.e. until 24/08, which worked thus as a 'delai butoir'. For a more detailed view on the measures adopted in France during the Covid-19 crisis see Loïc Cadiet, 'Un é État d'Exception pour la Procédure Civile Française à l'Épreuve du Coronavirus' (Judicium.com 20 April 2020) https://www.judicium.it/un-etat-dexception-pour-la-procedure-civile-francaise-lepreuve-du-coronavirus/; Romain Raffly and Mathieu Boccon-Gibod, 'L'Incertitude de la Fin de la "Période Juridiquement Protégée"' (Lescluddesjuristes.com 20 April 2020) https://blog.leclubdesjuristes.com/lincertitude-de-la-fin-de-la-periode-juridiquement-protegee/; Soraya Amrani-Mekki, 'La Part du Droit (et de la Justice) dans l'Angoisse Contemporaine. La Computation des Délais' (Leclubdesjuristes.com 30 March 2020); https://blog.leclubdesjuristes.com/la-part-du-droit-et-de-la-justice-dans-langoisse-contemporaine-la-computation-des-delais/; Betrand Poyet, 'L'Assouplissement des Règles de Communication des Conclusions et des Pièces en Temps de Crise Sanitaire' (Lescludesjuristes.com, 3 April 2020); https://blog.leclubdesjuristes.com/lassouplissement-des-regles-de-communication-en-temps-de-crise-sanitaire/.

bb) The time to react

Once the defendant has been served with the lawsuit or equivalent document instituting the proceedings[457], he must comply with specific time limits to react to the claim, whose meaning includes here, in compliance with the scope of Art. 45 (1)(b), both the time to react in general first instance proceedings and the time to oppose the issuance of payment orders[458]. However, where the defendant remains passive and fails to react, Member States generally provide for rules on default proceedings including some detrimental consequences on party's side and leading in principle to default judgments.

Rules on the defendant's first reaction (e.g. the time effectively granted to the defendant to react, the method of setting the time limit, the activities to accomplish when reacting, and the consequences attached to the expiry of the time limit) vary considerably from jurisdiction to jurisdiction depending on the assessment established by Member States when balancing the two following interests. On the one hand, the defendant must be granted enough time to become aware of the lawsuit, examine exhibited documents, and prepare his strategy of defence while, on the other hand, the time

On the other hand, under German law no specific legislative measure was taken. It was for the respective courts and judges to decide what measures should be taken in each individual case based on the provisions of the ZPO regulating the extension of time limits, stay of proceedings and the *restitutio in integrum.*

457 As traditionally affirmed in academia, the claim can be introduced according to the two following schemes. On the one hand, the claimant serves the lawsuit on the defendant who is summoned to appear at a scheduled hearing and then lodges it with the court. In this case, the first contact is between the parties and only at a later moment is the case filed with the court. For instance, this scheme is typical of Italian and French general first instance civil proceedings. On the other hand, the claimant addresses the claim to the court which fixes a hearing for the defendant to appear at. According to this scheme – typical e.g. of Italian and French payment order proceedings – proceedings are started *inaudita altera parte* and only later is the defendant informed of the claim initiated against him. See Giambattista Nappi, 'Dell'Introduzione della Causa' in Giambattista Nappi (ed), *Commentario al Codice di Procedura Civile*, vol 2 (Società Editrice Libraria 1942), 44.

458 Once the defendant has appeared before court (or in case of default) or opposed the issuance of payment orders, each national regulation establishes different rules concerning the scheduling of the proceedings. Those issues are mainly national issues and their impact on the fairness of litigation in a cross-border setting is limited. It follows that the time limits generally setting the development of national proceedings will not fall within the scope of this research as their impact on the Brussels Ibis grounds for refusal is limited.

limit to react should not be too long as this would hinder the speed and efficiency of proceedings.

Under these premises, the time to react and the time to oppose the issuance of payment orders will be analysed as follows:

i) Time to react in general first instance proceedings

The setting of the time to react in general first instance proceedings varies widely from one country to another based on the degree of complexity of the activities of defence that parties must accomplish when first reacting to the claim, e.g. appearing before the court[459], appointing a lawyer[460], stating the intention to defend the case[461], and filing defences[462]. What further influences the different choices of Member States when setting the time to react is the nature of the consequences attached to its expiry, i.e. their irreversible or reversible character.

The *dies a quo* of the time to react generally[463] starts to run from the day the defendant is effectively served with the lawsuit in order to not take into account the time necessary for carrying out service, which might unduly abbreviate the time to react when the lawsuit is served abroad.

Member States, to mitigate adversities deriving from the cross-border nature of the dispute, generally provide foreign defendants with longer deadlines than those laid down in purely national cases. Depending on the system at stake, such extension is granted either by law (e.g. France and Italy)[464] or on a case by case basis by courts (e.g. Germany)[465]. However,

459 E.g. in Austria (in district court proceedings); Belgium; The Netherlands; France (in front of the 'Tribunal de Commerce' or in oral hearings before the 'Tribunal Judiciaire'). See Gascón Inchausti and Requejo Isidro (n.95), para 125.

460 E.g. in France in general written proceedings before the 'Tribunal Judiciaire'. See below in this paragraph.

461 E.g. in Germany. See Gascón Inchausti and Requejo Isidro (n.95), para 125.

462 E.g. See in Austria (in regional court proceedings), Estonia, Greece, Latvia, Lithuania, Malta, Romania, Slovenia, Spain, Italy (see below in this paragraph). See Gascón Inchausti and Requejo Isidro (n.95), para 125.

463 Under specific circumstances, it could happen that this rule is not complied with and is disregarded by some national legislations, e.g. the situation under Luxemburgish law, see above α) Date of service under Art. 13.

464 See below in this paragraph.

465 E.g. see Section 274 (3) and Section 276 (1) sentence 3 ZPO which sets on a case by case basis the deadlines by which foreign defendants must submit their defences. See Gascón Inchausti and Requejo Isidro (n.95), para 127 fn 70.

it should be noted that there are also some Member States[466] which do not take into account the cross-border nature of the dispute when setting the time to react and retain a single, fixed deadline for all defendants, irrespective of the domestic or cross-border nature of the dispute[467].

Against this fragmented scenario, the following examples of the setting of the time to react in Italian and French proceedings will give some relevant indications on the practical differences which these time limits retain at national level.

Under French law in general written proceedings pending before the 'Tribunal Judiciaire' where representation by a lawyer is mandatory, the defendant must enter his appearance by appointing a lawyer and, this justifies short deadlines to react, i.e. a time limit of 15 days running from the date of service of the lawsuit (Art. 763 CPC)[468]. In light of the extension provided by law for foreign defendants (Art. 643 CPC), time limits to react are extended either by 1 month for defendants living in French oversea territories or 2 months for defendants living abroad.

There is no specific procedural sanction provided for if the defendant does not appoint a lawyer within the stated 15 days time limit. Provided that the expiry of the time to react does not entail any irremediable negative consequences on claimant's side and on judge's powers, nothing prevents the defendant from appointing a lawyer later in the proceedings. In particular, it seems possible to appoint a lawyer up until the judge has examined the content of the claimant's pleadings. However, if the defendant does not appoint a lawyer at all, proceedings will continue in default of his

466 E.g. Austria sets a 4 weeks fixed time limit to react or Spain provides for a 20 days time limit to react, which is reduced to 10 days for cases under €6,000. See Gascón Inchausti and Requejo Isidro (n.95), para 127 fn 80.

467 Regarding the rules on calculation see above aa) Calculation of time limits.

468 The lawsuit is generally served on the defendant by 'signification' which is a method of service which requires that the service is accomplished by the bailiff ('huissier de justice'). The date of service of the lawsuit is generally the date when this is served on the person (Art. 654 CPC), at his domicile or residence (Arts 655 and 656 CPC) or, in the case specified under Art. 659 CPC, the date of drafting of the official document recording service. See Héron, Le Bars, and Salhi (n.32), paras 170–185.

appearance and a final judgment will be rendered. This will be either a default judgment[469] or a judgment deemed to be defended[470].

The time to react is calculated according to calendar days. The *dies a quo* (the date of service of the lawsuit) is not counted in the calculation (Art. 641 (1) CPC); the *dies ad quem* happening at midnight on the last day of the time limit is instead considered (Art. 642 (1) CPC). When this time limit expires on a Saturday, Sunday, or public holiday, its *dies ad quem* is postponed to the next following working day (Art. 642 (2) CPC).

Under Italian law in ordinary civil proceedings pending before the 'Tribunale', the setting of the time to react depends on a specific mechanism which requires the claimant to indicate the date of the first hearing in the lawsuit ('citazione')[471]. In particular, when fixing the date of the first hearing, the claimant must comply with the following minimum requirements: clear time limits[472] of at least 120[473] (when the place of service is located in Italy) or 150 days (when the place of service is located abroad) must run between the date of the first hearing and the date of service of the lawsuit (Art. 163 bis (1) c.p.c.). The date of service of the lawsuit on the defendant[474] thus marks the *dies a quo* of the time to react.

---

469 A default judgment is rendered when the decision is given in the last instance and where the lawsuit has not been served on the defendant in person (Art. 473 (1) CPC). See Richard (n.60), 61.

470 A judgment is deemed to be defended if it is subject to appeal or has not been served on the defendant in person (Art. 473 (2) CPC). See Richard (n.60), 61.

471 It should be noted that at the beginning of each judicial year the president of the Tribunal, by decree approved by the president of the Court of Appeal, sets the days of the week and the hours of the hearings for the parties' first appearance before the judge (Art. 163 c.p.c.). According to Art. 168 c.p.c. (1) the president of the Tribunal thus designates the investigating judge before whom parties shall appear. If the designated judge does not hold hearings on the day indicated by the claimant, the judge *sua sponte* schedules the hearing for parties' appearance on the first date available on his agenda immediately after that day (Art. 168 (4) c.p.c.).

472 See above (fn 446) for further details on the definition of clear time limits.

473 It should be noted that this time period has recently been extended by the Legislative decree n. 150 of 10 October 2022 which implemented the Law n. 134 of 27 September 2021 (the so called 'Cartabia reform') from 90 to 120 days.

474 Service of the lawsuit on the defendant is accomplished by the bailiff ('ufficiale giudiziario'). The bailiff generally performs service in the hands of the addressee (Art. 138 c.p.c.), however under certain circumstances it could even proceed according to one of the following methods: postal service (Art. 149 c.p.c.), service by public proclamation (Art. 150 c.p.c.) and electronic certified service – 'PEC' – (Art. 149 bis c.p.c.).

Provided that these are clear time limits, the following special regime – contrary to the general principle where only the *dies a quo* is not taken into account – applies when calculating them according to calendar days: neither the *dies a quo* nor the *dies ad quem* is considered in the calculation; public holidays, shall, instead, be counted and if the *dies ad quem* falls on a holiday the time limit will expire on that day[475]. The rationale of these rules is to provide the defendant with a reasonable *spatium deliberandi* to effectively prepare his defences[476].

Once having been served with the lawsuit, for defendants to actively participate in the proceedings they must appear before the judge through a lawyer or in person, where this is allowed by the applicable law, at least 70 days before the date set for the first hearing (Art. 166 (1) c.p.c)[477]. Considering that this time limit is calculated backward, the *dies a quo* occurs chronologically later than the *dies ad quem*. Thus, the day of the hearing (the *dies a quo*) is not taken into account in the calculation[478].

It follows that defendants are generally granted at least either 50 (if the place of service is in Italy) or 70 days (if the place of service is abroad) to present their first reaction to the claim and appear before the judge[479].

Notably, defendants' reaction consists in a specific written statement of defence. In their answer, defendants must clearly and specifically file their defences aiming at denying the allegations made by the claimant in the lawsuit, identifying themselves, indicating the list of evidence they intend to submit and the documents exhibited, and finally briefly stating their conclusions and their position in the proceedings (Art. 167 (1) c.p.c.).

475 Provided that clear time limits do not require the accomplishment of any specific act related to the functioning of public offices, it does not matter if they expire on a non-working day.

476 Sergio Costa, 'Termini' in Antonio Azara e Ernesto Eula (eds), *Novissimo Digesto Italiano*, vol 19 (UTET Giuridica 1973) 120; Lupano (n.35), 657; Di Marzio (n.41), 93; Biavati (n.11), 258; Mandrioli and Carratta (n.9).

477 The reference to a period of at least 70 days has been recently introduced by the Cartabia Reform (see fn 473). Under the previous regime defendants had to appear at least 20 days before the date set for the first hearing.

478 The general rule postponing the expiry of the time limit falling on a holiday to the next working day (Art. 155 (4) c.p.c) does not apply with respect to time limits calculated backward (e.g. the time to react) as this would abbreviate the length of the time limits. Di Marzio (n.41), 98.

479 Compared to the previous regime where defendants where generally granted at least either 70 (if the place of service was in Italy) or 130 days (if the place of service was abroad) to react, the Cartabia reform ultimately abbreviated the general length of the time to react to 50 or 70 days.

The filing of these activities of defence is not provided under penalty of waiver; defendants may further specify or modify them pursuant to Art. 171 ter c.p.c.[480]. In addition, defendants in their statement of defense may, under penalty of waiver, file their counterclaims, raise procedural and on the merits objections and request a third party joinder (Art. 167 (2) and (3) c.p.c.). It follows that once the time to react expires, defendants are definitely (except in case of *restitutio in integrum*) prevented from filing counterclaims, raising objections and requesting third party joinder.

In light of the above, under Italian law the protection of the right of defence in the proceedings greatly depends on how the defendant manages his first reaction to the claim. This justifies the setting of rather long deadlines to react (i.e. 50 days for national litigants extended to 70 days for foreign ones) which are necessary to deal with the difficult preparation of their activity of defence and with the irreversible consequences attached to the expiry of the time to react.

What emerges from these examples is that even with two close legal systems belonging to the same legal tradition[481], it seems practically impossible to provide for uniform general time limits to react. There are indeed fundamental structural differences underlying the setting of time limits at national level. For instance, the method of setting the time limit is based on a different mechanism which in Italy depends on the date of the first hearing fixed in the lawsuit and in France is simply linked to the service of the lawsuit. The activities of defence which must be accomplished when first reacting to the claim, on the one hand (in France) simply consist of appointing a lawyer and, on the other hand (in Italy) require the filing of a relevant statement of defence. Further, the consequences attached to the expiry of the time to react in France do not entail any final effect and,

480 According to the new regime as introduced by the Cartabia reform (See fn 473) after the expiry of the 50 or 70 days time period, parties may, under penalty of waiver, accomplish the following supplementary activities of defence provided for by Art. 171 ter c.p.c. In particular, they may, at least 40 days before the date of the first hearing, file the claims and the objections which derive from the counterclaims or objections filed by the defendant and, also specifiy or modify the already submitted claims, objections and conclusions; they may, at least 20 days before the date of the first hearing, eventually answer to new or modified claims and objections filed by other parties and, indicate the list of evidence they intend to submit and the documents exhibited; they may, at least 10 days before the date of the first hearing, answer to the new objections and indicates the contrasting list of evidence.

481 When dealing with a larger pool of legal systems, differences are even more accentuated.

on the contrary in Italy entail the loss of some means of defence (counter-claims, procedural and on the merits objections, third party joinder) which must be exercised under penalty of waiver. Under these premises, such divergences can hardly be overcome and justify the setting of European uniform time limits to react.

ii) Time to oppose the issuance of payment orders

In light of the general structure of payment order proceedings[482], the need to grant the debtor sufficient time to oppose the issuance of a payment order is of utmost importance as this is the only possibility to contest it before having to bear the consequences attached to its enforcement. If time limits expire without any contestation, the payment order acquires indeed the *res judicata* effects and can accordingly be enforced across the EU. The debtor's lack of contestation becomes as such a tool to ensure finality of judgments and legal certainty[483].

Against this background, Member States generally implement either a documentary or a non-documentary payment order procedure and, this considerably impacts on the setting of time limits for opposing payment orders[484].

On the one hand, the documentary model[485] imposes on the claimant the requirement to produce evidence to justify the claim. Under this model, courts carry out a review of the documentation produced by the claimant, in order to dismiss unjustified or frivolous claims and to protect the defendant against such claims. The examination of evidence carried out by the judge represents a guarantee for the debtor against the issuance of unfound-

482 Payment orders are indeed premised on two different phases, a necessary one and another one, only eventual. First, the judge issues a payment order based only on the creditor's application without hearing the debtor or allowing him to submit any response or remarks, i.e. the order is pronounced *inaudita altera parte*. On the other hand, the debtor is informed of the procedure only after the issuance of the payment order. Only when he opposes the payment order, does the second phase takes place and opposition proceedings start. On the contrary, if the time limit expires without any opposition, the payment order becomes final and enforceable and enforcement proceedings can start immediately.

483 See Edoardo Garbagnati and Alberto Romano, *Il Procedimento d' Ingiunzione* (Giuffrè Editore 1991), 11; Vittorio Colesanti, 'Principio del Contraditorio e Procedimenti Speciali' (1975) 30 Riv. dir. proc., 583.

484 See Opinion of AG Sharpston in *Bondora* (n.230), para 70.

485 E.g. the Italian, French, Spanish and Slovenian systems.

ed payment orders. Opposition against these orders is generally brought within short time limits which are justified by the fact that evidence is produced.

On the other hand, the non-documentary model[486] is characterised by the complete absence of any examination on the merits of the claim by the court seized of an application for a payment order. Provided that an application is admissible and satisfies the basic formal requirements, that court issues an order for payment without any further assessment on the merits. Since this model does not involve any examination of the merits of the application, there is no need for documentary proof of the claim. In order to compensate for the summary nature of such a no evidence procedure, the time limit for lodging a statement of opposition against this order is generally twice as long, and more favourable than the one provided in the context of the documentary procedure[487].

Furthermore, the setting of time limits for opposing the issuance of payment orders is heavily influenced by the structure and complexity of the opposition procedure in national systems. Depending on if defendants file a mere[488] or grounded[489] opposition, Member States generally fix shorter or longer time limits for opposing payment orders (which could be extended[490] or not[491] in cross-border cases) running from the moment of their service on the respondent[492].

The following examples give a more detailed overview on these divergences at the EU level.

German law provides debtors with a 2 weeks time limit to oppose payment orders running from their service on them (Section 692 ZPO). The latter time limit is extended to 1 month in cross-border cases (Section 32 (3) AVAG). In any event, an opposition can still be made even after this deadline has expired if no enforcement order has been issued.

486 E.g. Germany, Austria, The Netherlands, Bulgaria.

487 Opinion of AG Sharpston in *Bondora* (n.230), fn 55.

488 E.g. France, Germany, the Netherlands.

489 E.g. Italy, Spain, Slovenia.

490 E.g. Germany, Italy and France, see below in this paragraph.

491 E.g. Spain and Slovenia, see below in this paragraph.

492 Regarding rules on their calculation, see above aa) Calculation of time limits.

Debtors (it is not necessary to be represented by a lawyer) shall simply lodge their opposition in writing without any other formal conditions being required (Section 694 ZPO)[493].

Days are calculated in calendar days according to the rule *dies a quo non computatur in termino* and, *dies ad quem computatur in termino.* If the time limit ends on a Saturday, Sunday, or public day, it is extended to the next working day (see Section 222 (1) ZPO. and Section 193 BGB).

Against this backdrop, if an opposition is lodged in due time, proceedings will continue, at the parties' request, according to the rules of ordinary litigation (Section 696 ZPO). However, if the payment orders remain uncontested after the expiry of the time limit, the court issues, upon the creditor's application, an order for enforcement (Section 699 ZPO).

Under French law, the debtor (representation of a lawyer is not mandatory) can contest the issuance of payment orders by merely stating an opposition without any further formalities and explanations required.

The opposition must be lodged within a general time limit of 1 month running from the service[494] of the payment order on the debtor (Art. 1416 (1) CPC). Nevertheless, if the order has not been served personally on the debtor, the opposition is admissible until the expiry of a 1 month time limit following the first act personally served on him, or, in absence thereof, following the first enforcement measure making the debtor's assets unavailable in part or in whole (Art. 1416 (2) CPC)[495]. This rule has been interpreted[496] in the sense that the time limit to oppose payment orders

493 It should be noted that when the order for payment is served, the debtor receives a pre-printed form that enables him to lodge his opposition; however, the use of this pre-printed form is only optional. See https://ejustice.europa.eu/41/EN/european_payment_order?GERMANY&init=true&member=1.

494 Service of the payment order is accomplished by the bailiff by 'signification'. See above fn 468.

495 The *dies a quo* of the time limits for opposing payment orders starts to run only under very strict conditions which are deemed to ensure debtors are protected from the involuntary expiry of time. This therefore excludes the debtors from any possibility of applying for relief.

496 French Supreme Court advice 16–09–2002, n. 02–00.003 in Bull. civ. 2002 Avis n.4; French Supreme Court 11–12–2008, n. 08–10141 in Bull. civ. 2008 II n. 262. See Héron, Le Bars, and Salhi (n.32). para 581; Cécile Chainais, Frédérique Ferrand, Lucie Mayer and Serge Guinchard, *Procédure Civile: Droit Commun et Spécial du Procès Civil, MARD et Arbitrage* (16th edn, Dalloz 2022), para 2039; François Melin, 'Procédure Écrite et Procédures Spécifiques devant le Tribunal Judciaire' in Serge Guinchard (ed), *Droit et Pratique de la Procédure civile: Droit Interne et Européen* (10th edn, Dalloz 2019) para 441.752.

starts running from the day the debtor becomes aware of the first enforcement measure, e.g. in the case of seizure of bank accounts the time limit starts from the announcement of the seizure to the debtor and not from the day of the seizure. The Court of Cassation thus accepts that the debtor is 'officially' aware – effective knowledge is not required[497] – of the enforcement measure which has been served on him, even at his domicile[498].

The French legislator does not explicitly provide any extension when the payment order is issued cross-border[499]. However, there would arguably be no reason to exclude the application of Art. 643 CPC extending the latter time limit either by 1 month for residents in French overseas territories or 2 months for residents in other EU countries[500]. The need to balance distance, linguistic deficiencies and inexperience with French law arises indeed also with regard to parties residing abroad against whom payment orders have been issued.

When calculating this time limit expressed in months according to calendar days, the *dies a quo* starts on the day of service of the order; its expiry is on the corresponding day of the following month(s) at midnight and if

---

497 The rationale of excluding effective knowledge is that, in certain cases, requiring effective knowledge of the first enforcement measure would indefinitely postpone the beginning of the time limits for opposing the issuance of payment orders. See See Héron, Le Bars, and Salhi (n.32), para 581.

498 See French Supreme Court 18-02-2016, n. 14-26.395; See Héron, Le Bars, and Salhi (n.32), para 581.

499 This is due to the fact that the payment order procedure is in principle meant to be a purely national procedure because there would not be any French court having jurisdiction to issue a payment order if the debtor is resident abroad without any domicile or residence in the French territory. Nevertheless, there does not exist any explicit provision – as is the case e.g. in Luxembourg and Belgium – forbidding the issuance of payment orders against debtors resident in other countries. According to some European special grounds of jurisdiction (e.g. Art. 7 (1) of the Brussels Ibis Regulation), it is therefore possible that the competence to issue payment orders is granted to French courts while debtors are resident abroad See Hélène Gaudemet-Tallon, 'Compétence Internationale: Matière Civile et Commerciale' (2019) Répertoire de droit international, para 202; Richard (n.60), 45. However, it has been argued that under these circumstances the competent French court must raise *ex officio* its lack of competence according to the rules of Art. 1406 CPC as long as this is a public policy clause, see André Huet, 'Compétence des Tribunaux Français à l'Égard des Litiges Internationaux, (2017) Fasc. 581–42 J-CL Droit international, para 34. Nevertheless, one could infer that this interpretation is contradicted by the rationale of the Brussels Ibis Regulation and by legal practice. The possibility that payment orders are issued cross-border will therefore be taken into account.

500 Melin (n.496), para 441.752.

it happens on a Saturday, Sunday, or public day it is put off to the next working day (Art. 642 CPC).

What follows is that if the debtor files his opposition, proceedings will continue according to the general rules governing ordinary proceedings; on the other hand, if the payment order remains uncontested, it becomes automatically enforceable as it already endorses the enforceable mention[501].

Under Italian law, upon service of the payment order[502], the debtor is generally granted a 40 days time limit - provided under penalty of waiver - for opposing its issuance. Where good reasons are at hand, these time limits can be reduced by the judge up to 10 days or increased up to 60 days[503]. Furthermore, the following extensions are automatically provided: if the defendant is resident in another EU country, the time limit for opposing payment orders is 50 days and can be reduced up to 20 days; if the defendant is resident in other States, the time limit is 60 days and, in any case, it cannot be shorter than 30 days or longer than 120 days.

The debtor (save for exceptional cases representation of a lawyer is mandatory) when opposing a payment order shall bring his challenge before the court that issued it, by filing the lawsuit ('citazione') which must

501 This change was introduced by Decree n. 2021-1322 of 11 October 2021 which modified the previous regime where the creditor, after the payment order became uncontested, had to request the registry to place the enforceable mention (previous Art. 1423 CPC).

502 The payment order (i.e. an authentic copy of the petition and the decree) is served on the defendant by the bailiff ('ufficiale giudiziario'). See fn 474. In particular, the service is accomplished by 60 days running from the issuance of the payment order where the place of service is in Italy and by 90 days where the place of service is abroad. However, if the service is not effected in compliance with the 60 or 90 days time limits, the payment order loses its validity (Art. 644 c.p.c.). See Biavati (n. 11), 589, 590; Crisanto Mandrioli and Antonio Carratta, *Diritto processuale civile*, vol 3 (21st edn, Giappichelli Editore, 2019), 24 fn 48.

503 Some academics have wondered about the consequences of fixing longer time limits than those allowed by law, i.e. more than 60 days. There is national case law to the effect that in such case opposition should be inadmissible because of the nature of final time limits which could not be extended. However, it has been argued in academia that the opponent should be relieved from the expiry of time limits because the fault is not attributable to him. The nature of the time limit for opposing the issuance of payment orders would indeed prevent any extension, see Claudio Consolo. 'Rigorismi Alterni e non Giustificati in Tema di Opposizione all'Ingiunzione per Sanzioni Amministrative' in (1984) 39 Riv. dir. proc., 823–844; Balbi (n.13), 429 and f.; Mandrioli and Carratta (n.502), 30 fn 64.

be served on the claimant at the address indicated in the application[504]. Despite having the same structure of the lawsuit, opposition has the same content as the first written statement of defence ('comparsa di risposta') in ordinary proceedings. The same system of preclusion provided for in Art. 167 c.p.c. therefore applies here[505].

These time limits are calculated in calendar days according to the general rule, not taking into consideration the *dies a quo,* but by applying the *dies ad quem* (Art. 155 c.p.c.). If the *dies ad quem* expires on a Saturday, Sunday, or public day, it is postponed to the next working day.

Under these premises, if the debtor contests the issuance of the payment order, proceedings will continue according to the general rules governing ordinary proceedings. On the contrary, if the opposition is not filed in time, the creditor can request the judge who originally issued the payment order to declare it enforceable.

Art. 815 LEC[506] fixes a 20 days time limit – which is reduced to 10 days for cases under €6,000 – running from the service of the payment order on the debtor. The opposition must be lodged in writing and the debtor[507] must briefly state the grounds of defence. The calculation of the time limit is made in accordance with working days (all days except for Saturday, Sunday and public holidays). It begins on the day following service of the payment order (*dies a quo non computatur*) and expires at midnight on the last day of the time limit (Art. 133 (1) LEC) In this respect, any documents that are subject to a time limit can be submitted up until 3 p.m. on the working day following that on which the time period expires and this also applies to the act of opposition (Art. 135 (5) LEC). If an opposition is lodged, the dispute will continue according to the rules for ordinary proceedings; however, if the time limit expires without any contestation

504 It should be noted that if the service is not finally carried out due to causes not attributable to the opponent, the opponent is allowed to renew the service according to the rules governing the specific regime for late oppositions (Art. 650 c.p.c.) which replace the general possibility to apply for relief. See Italian Supreme Court 4–05–2006, n. 10216 with case note of Luisa Biffi (2007) Giur. it, 1208–1211.

505 See Art. 167 c.p.c.; Mandrioli and Carratta (n.502), 34, 35.

506 The reform of this provision is currently discussed in Spanish academia. See Enrique Vallines Garcia, 'La Reforma Necesaria del Proceso Monitorio en España: Hacia una Generalización del Proceso Monitorio Europeo?' (2022) Estándares europeos y proceso civil Hacia un proceso civil convergente con Europa, 601. See also *Banco Espanol de Credito* (n.233).

507 Save for cases under €2,000, representation of a lawyer is mandatory.

the payment order becomes enforceable and the creditor can begin enforcement proceedings.

As mentioned above[508], under Slovenian law a grounded opposition to the issuance of a payment order must be lodged within 8 days of service of the order (Art. 9 ZIZ).

As is the case with the time to react in ordinary proceedings, these examples prove that the setting of the time limits for opposing payment orders can hardly be isolated from the type (documentary or non-documentary model) and structure (mere or grounded) of procedure within which these time limits are fixed. Against these divergent rules, it seems therefore that establishing common grounds for fully harmonising the setting of time limits for opposing payment orders at the EU level is hardly achievable.

cc) Appeal procedures

Fixing temporal limitations to the right to challenge judgments is a natural consequence of the need for finality and certainty (*res judicata* effects) which requires that the right to appeal cannot be pending indefinitely. In this respect, Member States fix time limits for challenging judgments based on their own balance between the need to achieve the *res judicata* effects and the need to correct errors. The expiry of time limits for appealing generally prevents parties from challenging first and second instance judgments that become as such *res judicata,* i.e. final and binding[509]

In light of their impact on the *res judicata,* the following analysis will thus deal both with time limits to appeal on factual and legal grounds.

i) Time limits for lodging an appeal on factual grounds

One can generally distinguish between countries providing a 'longer'[510] time limit for lodging an appeal on factual grounds and countries granting

508 See above (i) *LKW Walter*: open question on the length of the time limit) the procedural background surrounding the case *LKW Walter* (n.80).

509 Only under exceptional circumstances would it be possible to apply for relief.

510 E.g. Austria, Denmark; Estonia; Finland; Greece; Italy; Lithuania; Portugal; Romania; Belgium; France; Germany. See Cristoph Kern and Karol Weitz, 'Appeal and Third Instance' in Burkhard Hess and Pietro Ortolani (eds), *Impediments of Nation-*

a rather 'short'[511] period of time. This time limit could be extended (or not)[512] in cross-border cases either by law[513] or at the court's discretion[514].

Depending on the system at hand, the *dies a quo*[515] of time limits for lodging an appeal on factual grounds generally begins either on the date on which the judgment is served (*ex officio* or by the prevailing party) on the other party[516], or on the day of the rendering of the judgement[517].

In some Member States[518], before the expiry of the time limits for lodging an appeal on factual grounds parties should also have requested the suspension of enforcement proceedings of first instance judgments.

Furthermore, in some legal systems[519] the regime of incidental appeals is also subject to the general time limits for lodging an appeal on factual grounds.

The following examples will therefore show how these rules diverge practically across national systems.

---

al Procedural Law to the Free Movement of Judgments (Beck-Hart-Nomos, 2019), para 27 fn 66, 67, 68.

511 E.g. Ireland; Bulgaria; Cyprus; Poland; Czech Republic; Hungary; Slovakia; Slovenia. See Kern and Weitz (n.510), para 28 fn 71, 72, 73.

512 E.g. in Italy.

513 E.g. in Belgium, France, Greece time limits are extended by law because of the cross-border nature of the case. See Kern and Weitz (n.510), para 30 fn 76.

514 E.g. Cyprus, Denmark, Ireland, Lithuania. See Kern and Weitz (n.510), para 31 fn 81.

515 Regarding the rules on calculation see above aa) Calculation of time limits.

516 E.g. Austria; Belgium; Bulgaria; Czech Republic; Estonia; France; Germany; Greece; Italy; Luxembourg; Poland; Spain. See Kern and Weitz (n.510), para 24 fn 55.

517 E.g. the Netherlands, Sweden, Cyprus, Finland, Denmark, Latvia, Portugal, Malta. The day of the rendering of the judgment is regulated differently by national systems. In particular, 'in Sweden and the Netherlands, the parties are informed by the court when the judgment is orally pronounced or rendered; this moment triggers the time limit for lodging an appeal. In the other Member States belonging to this group, the time limit commences at the time when "the judgment or order becomes binding on the intending appellant" (Cyprus), (also) with the rendering of the judgment (Bulgaria in proceedings before the commercial court), with "the date of the judgment" (Denmark), "within 30 days of the judgment" (Finland), with the "announcement of the judgment" (Latvia), with the "date of the judgment" (Malta), with "notification" of the judgment to the parties (Portugal) or with the "communication of the decision" (Romania). In Belgium the time limit can also be triggered by notification by judicial letter'. See Kern and Weitz (n.510), para 25.

518 E.g. Italy.

519 E.g. Italy.

Under French law, a mechanism based on a double temporal dimension – short and long time limits – regulates the general filing of appeals on factual grounds including appeal and opposition.

On the one hand, there are 'short' time limits – 1 month (reduced to 15 days in non-contentious matters)[520] for appeal and opposition which is extended according to Art. 643 CPC either for 1 month for defendants living in French oversea territories or 2 months for defendants living abroad – running from the day of the notification of the judgment effected on parties' initiative[521] upon the losing parties[522] (Art. 528 (1) CPC). Service of the judgment will be carried out as follows depending if the first instance proceedings involved one or more parties in separable or non-separable cases. If cases are separable and parties stand independently from each other, each winning party serves the judgment on the losing party on his own initiative. Each service makes, as such, the time limits for appeal run separately based on each specific relationship at hand in the proceedings

520 It should be noted that the time limit to appeal has been object of considerable reforms during the years aimed at reducing uncertainties for the winning party in first instance proceedings. Traditionally, under ancient law it was 30 years; in 1667 it was reduced by order to 10 years; it became 3 months in the ancient code of civil procedure; it was shortened to 2 months in 1862; it was finally reduced to 1 month by the Decree of 30 October 1935. This length has been kept by the Decree of 28 August 1972 which became the current Art. 538 CPC; see Chainais, Ferrand, Mayer and Guinchard (n.496), para 1325.

521 Service is accomplished by the bailiff by 'signification', see fn 468. It should be noted that the time limits to appeal start running also for the party who served the judgment (Art. 528 (2) CPC). This rule reverses the traditional principle of the French code of civil procedure 'nul se forclot par soi meme' (nobody can waiver himself) which made the time limits to appeal run only for the party which had been served with the judgment and not for the one that served it. See Héron, Le Bars, and Salhi (n.32), para 707; Chainais, Ferrand, Mayer and Guinchard (n.496), para 1284.

522 The service which shall be taken into account is the one made personally on the party, not on his lawyer. French Supreme Court 19–05–1998, n. 96–17.349 in Bull. civ. (1998) II n. 158. Further, if the judgment was served multiple times, according to national and CJEU case law, the first service of the judgment (if it is valid) is the one causing the time limits to appeal start running, see Case C-473/04 *Plumex v Young Sports NV* (2006) EU:C:2006:96; French Supreme Court 07–10–2008, n. 06–20.093 in Bull. civ. (2008) IV n° 166; French Supreme Court 05–02–2009, n. 07–13.589 in Bull. civ. (2009) II n° 35; French Supreme Court 03–11–2010, n. 09–68.968 with case note of Roger Perrot, (2011) Procédures 4; French Supreme Court 14–03–2018, n 15–28.506; French Supreme Court 13–01–2022, n. 20–12.914. See Loïc Cadiet and Emmanuel Jeuland, *Droit Judiciaire Privé* (11th edn, LexisNexis 2020), para 811; Chainais, Ferrand, Mayer and Guinchard (n.496), para 1284.

between the serving parties and the addressee[523]. However, where cases are non-separable, the favourable or not favourable effects of the judgment on the parties' sides must be taken into account when serving it. Where a non-separable judgement has been rendered against several parties, the service of the judgment on one of them makes the time limits for appeal run only with respect to that party (Art. 529 (1) CPC). Where the judgement is, instead, favourable jointly or indivisibly to several parties, each of these parties can take advantage of the service made by[524] or against[525] one of them (Art. 529 (2) CPC).

On the other hand, if service of the judgment was not validly carried out[526], the filing of appeals on factual grounds is governed by 'long' time limits to appeal running irrespective of the service of the judgment[527]. Art. 528-1 (1) CPC[528] thus provides for a 2 years time limit running in any event from the day of the rendering of the judgment[529]. The mechanism of long time limits does not apply nevertheless to opposition proceedings where there would be a risk of sanctioning delays not attributable to the parties' fault if they did not appear[530].

523 See French Supreme Court 13-04-2010, n. 09-13.478 with case note of Roger Perrot, (2010) Procédures, 224. See also Héron, Le Bars, and Salhi (n.32), para 707

524 French Supreme Court 07-07-2005, n. 182, in Bull. civ. (2005) II n. 187, 165 with case note of François.Vinckel in Droit et procedures (2006), 33. Héron, Le Bars, and Salhi (n.32), para 707 fn 82.

525 French Supreme Court 06-05-1998, n. 96-19.014 in Bull. civ. (1998) II n. 146; Héron, Le Bars, and Salhi (n.32), para 707 fn 83.

526 Where the service of the judgment is null, it is deemed to have never been accomplished. French Supreme Court 10-11-1998, n. 96-42.749 in Bull. civ. (1998) V n. 487; French Supreme Court 07-07-2005, n. 03-15.469 in Bull. civ. (2005) II n. 164 with case note of Oscar Salati, (2005) Droit et procedures, 345. See also Héron, Le Bars, and Salhi (n.32), para 709 fn. 101; Chainais, Ferrand, Mayer and Guinchard (n.496), para 1282.

527 In this regard, it should be noted, as arises from Art. 503 CPC, that service of the judgment on the parties against whom enforcement is sought shall in any case be effected in order to proceed to its enforcement.

528 This rule was introduced by Decree n. 89-511 of 20 July 1989. It reversed the traditional solution which allowed an appeal to be filed without any temporal restriction as long as the time limits for appeal ran indefinitely. Héron, Le Bars, and Salhi (n.32), para 709.

529 The date of the rendering of the judgment is either the date it is given in open court or the date it is filed with the registry of the court, see Art. 453 CPC.

530 Héron, Le Bars, and Salhi (n.32), para 709.

Within the mentioned time limits, the appellants must therefore lodge their grounded appeal generally[531] by unilateral declaration ('declaration d'appel') before the competent court of appeal. The unilateral declaration[532] signed by the appellant's lawyer is filed with the registry of the court[533] together with a copy of the judgment and entails enrolment of the appeal in the court's registry ('inscription au role'). Incidental appeals are also generally lodged within the same time limits to appeal[534]. For default judgments, the defendants lodge their grounded opposition according to the general rules provided for initiating proceedings before the court that rendered the default judgment, i.e. in most cases, the first instance court.

In principle, the running of time limits for lodging appeals on factual grounds automatically suspends enforcement of first instance judgments, except where provisional enforcement has been ordered (Art. 539 CPC). Nevertheless, the practical impact of this rule is nowadays considerably limited as provisional enforcement of first instance judgments became the general rule with the entry into force of Art. 514 CPC[535].

Time limits to appeal are calculated in calendar days. The *dies a quo* starts on the date of service for short time limits and on the date of the

531 In exceptional cases, appeals can also be filed by joint petition ('requete conjointe'). A joint petition is admissible only if it is presented by all parties of the first instance proceeding. It must be handed over to the registry of the court in compliance with the time limits to appeal and it entails enrolment of the appeal in the court's registry. See Chainais, Ferrand, Mayer and Guinchard (n.496), para 1776.

532 Such declaration shall mention all the indications provided for in Art. 901 CPC.

533 The regsitry of the court will send straight away, generally by ordinary letter, to each of the respondents, a copy of the declaration of appeal stating their obligation to appoint a lawyer (Art. 902 (1) CPC). However, if the respondent is deemed to not be aware of the declaration of appeal the registry requires the appellant's lawyer to serve the declaration of appeal on the respondent through the bailiff. If eventually prior to service the respondent appoints a lawyer (Art. 902 (2) CPC), the declaration of appeal is served on the respondent's lawyer (Art. 902 (3) CPC). See Héron, Le Bars, and Salhi (n.32), para 775.

534 It should be noted that where incidental appeals have been brought before the expiry of the time limits to appeal, the inadmissibility of the main appeal does not have any impact on the type of the incidental one which is transformed as such into the main one. On the other hand, there is also the possibility to file incidental appeals after the expiry of the time limits to appeal, however their admissibility would depend on the one of the main appeal. See Héron, Le Bars, and Salhi (n.32), para 751.

535 See Decree n. 2019–1333 of 11 December 2019 (the so called 'reform Belloubet'); Jaques Pellerin, 'La Generalisation de l'Execution Provisoire de Droit' (2020) Gaz. Pal., 85; Chainais, Ferrand, Mayer and Guinchard (n.496), para 1363; Cadiet and Jeuland (n.522), para 830.

rendering of the judgment for long time limits. The *dies ad quem* is on the day of the last month or year bearing the same date when the act, the event, the decision or the notification that causes time to run, occurred. If the *dies ad quem* is on a Saturday, Sunday, or public holiday, it is extended until the first following working day.

Once the time limits to appeal have expired, the judgment becomes *res judicata*.

Under Italian law, the expiry of time limits for lodging an appeal on factual grounds is subject to two different regimes. On the one hand, there are 'short' time limits – 30 days (Art. 325 c.p.c) – running only if winning parties[536] take the initiative of serving the judgment upon losing parties (Art. 326 (1) c.p.c.)[537]. In particular, service of the judgment is performed upon parties' lawyers[538] at their elected or actual domicile[539].

---

536 It will generally be the winning party in first instance proceedings – having interest in achieving the *res judicata* effects as soon as possible – who will take the initiative of serving the judgment either by himself or through his lawyer. It should be noted that the service of the judgment on the addressee makes the time to appeal begin to run not only with respect to the addressee, but also with respect to the serving party who might partially lose with regard to some aspects of the judgment and might have an interest in partially challenging it. The effects of service therefore concern both parties in the proceedings, Italian Supreme Court (Sezioni Unite) 04–03–2019, n. 6278. Prior to the rendering of this judgment, such principle was highly discussed and it was argued that the time to appeal for the party serving the judgment starts from the date of delivery of the act to the bailiff. See Augusto Cerino Canova, 'Sulla Soggezione del Notificante al Termine Breve di Gravame' (1982) 37 Riv. dir. proc., 624–640; Francesco Amato, 'Termine Breve di Impugnazione e Bilateralita della Notificazione della Sentenza nel Processo con Due Sole Parti' (1985) 40 Riv. dir. proc., 330–385; Sergio Matteini Chiari, 'Termini per Impugnare' in Sergio Matteini Chiari and Mauro Di Marzio (eds), *Le Notificazioni e i Termini nel Processo Civile*, (Giuffrè Editore 2019), 481, 482; Mandrioli and Carratta (n.9), 417; Biavati (n.11), 454.

537 Where the challenged judgment has been issued against more parties in non-separable cases, its service, even if performed on the initiative of only one party, entails that the time for appeal starts running against all other parties of the proceedings (principle of unity of the time limits to appeal). This rule aims at preventing the losing party from challenging the judgment as he rethinks his procedural strategy against other winning parties during the running of long time limits to appeal. It follows that once the challenge upon one of the winning parties is served, short time limits will run also against other parties. It follows that on the one hand, if the judgment is not appealed against by some parties it will become *res judicata* with respect to that situation; however, if the judgment is finally appealed against by other parties, the challenges will be joined according to Art. 335 c.p.c. See Mandrioli and Carratta (n. 9), 436; Italian Supreme Court 09–02–2012, n. 1771; Italian Supreme Court 24- 06–2003, n. 10026.

On the other hand, where parties do not proceed to the notification of the judgment or if service is not valid, the regime of 'long' time limits to appeal – 6 months (Art. 327 (1) c.p.c.) – running from the publication of the judgment (i.e. when the judgment is filed with the registry of the court)[540] will apply. Nevertheless, as emerges from Art. 327 (2) c.p.c. this regime does not apply to defaulting defendants who prove that they were not informed of proceedings initiated against them because the lawsuit or its service was null[541]. This mechanism providing for a fixed period of time running independently of the notification of the judgment aims at preventing excessive delays in achieving the *res judicata* effects and legal uncertainty[542]. Without the provision of long time limits, the judgment would normally be subject to ordinary limitation periods. The mechanism of long time limits thus creates a *legal fictio* presuming legal knowledge of judgments, rather than requiring effective knowledge as it is the case with the short time limits.

Within these time limits, appellants must practically file their grounded act of appeal ('atto di appello') by serving[543] it upon all entitled parties. If

538 E.g. if service is accomplished at party's actual domicile, it is null, see Italian Supreme Court 01-02-2000, n. 1069; Italian Supreme Court 21-02-2017, n. 4374; Italian Supreme Court 25-09-2009, n. 20684. Further, it has also been considered that even if the judgment is served personally on the party (who elected domicile at lawyer's firm) and not on his lawyer, the time limit to appeal cannot start running, see Italian Supreme Court 14-01-1999 n. 239; Italian Supreme Court (Sezioni Unite) 13-06-2011, n. 12898; Italian Supreme Court 20-09-2016, n. 18356; Italian Supreme Court 11-07-2018, n. 2814. On a different opinion, in some cases it has been argued that personal service on the party at his lawyer's elected domicile is deemed to be equivalent to service on the lawyer, see Italian Supreme Court 11-06-2009, n. 13546; Italian Supreme Court 31-05-2011, n. 111971. Matteini Chiari (n.536), 487; Mandrioli and Carratta (n.9), 487.

539 It should be noted that this rule does not concern default judgments which must be served personally upon the party (Art. 292 c.p.c.).

540 The filing of the judgment in the registry of the court officially takes place when the regsitry enters the judgment in the chronological register of judgments attributing to it an identification number. See judgment of the Italian Constitutional court 22-02-2016, n. 3; Italian Supreme Court (Sezioni Unite) 01-08-2012, n. 13794; Italian Supreme Court 04-04-2013, n. 8216; Matteini Chiari (n.536), 523-526.

541 Under these circumstances, the 6 months time limit to appeal runs from the moment the defaulting defendant becomes effectively aware of the proceedings, provided that such knowledge is obtained differently than with service of the judgment. In any case, the burden of proof is on the defendant.

542 See Balbi (n.13), 334.

543 The act introducing appeal proceedings has the same form as the lawsuit ('citazione') and must contain the information required by Art. 163 c.p.c. The act

it happens that judgments are not challenged by service against all parties of the first instance proceedings, the judge shall order that the challenge is served upon all entitled parties who were not served with it. In this regard, consequences differ depending on if the first instance judgment was rendered against more parties either in separable or non-separable cases.

In the case of necessary third party joinder in non-separable or dependent claims (Art. 331 c.p.c.), the judge orders the party who filed the act of appeal to serve it also on the other entitled parties who were not served with it. If this order is not complied with, the challenge will be inadmissible as second instance judgments must necessarily be rendered against all parties whose claims depend on each other, which means that each decision affects the others. On the other hand, where claims are separable, if the appeal of a judgment has been filed only by or against a single party, the judge will order the latter act of appeal to be served also upon other parties who are entitled to challenge the judgment (Art. 332 c.p.c.). This mechanism thus 'provokes'[544] all served parties to make a choice, i.e. either to appeal or to accept the judgment.

If the parties served later with the act of appeal also decide to challenge the judgment, they must generally lodge their incidental appeals in the same proceedings in compliance with time limits to appeal; otherwise they will waive their right (Art. 333 c.p.c.)[545].

Furthermore, during the running of time limits to appeal the parties must eventually request the suspension of enforcement proceedings (the so-called 'inibitoria')[546], which might have already started given that first instance judgments (of conviction)[547] are already provisionally enforceable[548].

---

signed by appellant's lawyer is thus to be served on the defendant by the bailiff ('ufficiale giudiziario'). Once the service of the act of appeal has been accomplished, the claimant then appears before the Court of appeal by filing the act of appeal with the registry of the court ('iscrizione della causa a ruolo').

544 The service of the judgment has here the function of a *litis denuntiatio*, see Italian Supreme Court 18-04-2017, n. 9773; Mandrioli and Carratta (n.9), 437.

545 It should be noted that under exceptional circumstances there is a specific regime (Art. 334 c.p.c.) admitting late incidental appeals. In particular, late incidental appeals can be filed until the parties' appearance in appeal proceedings, however they are not independent as their nature depends on the type of main appeals.

546 The request of suspension is filed together with the act of appeal, however in practice it is independent and autonomous as it gives rise to a sub-proceedings within appeal proceedings which will generally be decided by the competent judge prior that the judgment of appeal. See Ernesto Brunori, 'Sulla Inibitoria' (1956) 11 Riv. dir. proc., 207; Edgardo Borselli, 'Inibitoria (Dir. Proc. Civ.)' in Antonio Azara e Ernesto

Time limits to appeal are calculated in calendar days according to the general *principle dies a quo non computatur in termino* (the day of service for short time limits and the month of the rendering of the judgment for long time limits) and *dies ad quem computatur in termino.* The *dies ad quem* is postponed to the next working day if it falls on Saturday, Sunday or public holiday.

Where parties do not appeal the judgment in time, the judgment will thus become *res judicata.*

What emerges when analysing these examples is that both the Italian and French systems of appeal on factual grounds provide a mechanism insisting on a double temporal dimension based on short and long time

---

Eula (eds), *Novissimo Digesto Italiano,* vol 19 (UTET Giuridica 1973), 701, 702; Aldo Frignani, 'Inibitoria (Azione)' in Francesco Calasso, Costantino Mortati, Salvatore Pugliatti, Francesco Santoro Passarelli, Mario Talamanca and Angelo Falzea (eds), *Enciclopedia del Diritto,* vol 19 (Giuffrè Editore 1971), 559–580; Federico Carpi, 'L' Inibitoria Processuale' (1975) 29 Riv. trim. dir. e proc. Civ., 93; Federico Carpi, *La Provvisoria Eecutorietà dela Sentenza* (Giuffrè Editore 1979), 225; Rosario Maccarone, 'Per un Profilo Strutturale dell'Inibitoria Processuale' (1981) 36 Riv. dir. proc., 274–329; Gianpaolo Impagnatiello, *La Provvisoria Esecuzione e l'Inibitoria nel Processo Civile* (Giuffrè Editore 2010); Mandrioli and Carratta (n.9), 310.

547 In this respect, Art. 282 c.p.c. generally refers to judgments without distinguishing between conviction and non-conviction judgments. Conviction judgments certainly fall within the scope of Art. 282 c.p.c., however some authors in academia wonder about a possible extension of immediate enforcement also to non-conviction judgments. See Carpi (n.546), 59; Gianpaolo Impagnatiello, 'La Provvisoria Esecutorietà delle Sentenze Costitutive' (1992) 45 Riv. trim. dir. e proc. civ., 47–91; Corrado Ferri, 'Effetti Dichiarativi e Costitutiivi Condizionati da Eventi Successivi alla sua Pronuncia' (2007) 57 Riv. dir. proc., 1393–1408 and f. The Court of Cassation solved this contrast stating that Art. 282 c.p.c. only applies with regard to conviction judgments, see Italian Supreme Court (Sezioni Unite) 22-02-2010, n. 4059 with case notes of Gianmpaolo Impagnatiello in Foro.it (2010), I, 2082 and of Maria Assunta Iuorio in Riv. es. forz. (2010), 267. In this regard, see also Italian Supreme Court 28-02-2011, n. 4907; Italian Supreme Court 29-07-2011, n. 16737; Italian Supreme Court 24-08-2016, n. 17311. See also Michele Fornaciari, 'La Provvisoria Efficacia delle Sentenze di Accertamento e Costitutive' (2012) 7 Giusto proc. civ., 383; Cesare Cavallini, 'L'Efficacia della Sentenza Impugnata' (2015) 65 Riv. dir. proc., 347; Mandrioli and Carratta (n.9), 509.

548 Enforcement is indeed not automatically suspended anymore, as was the case under the previous regime of appeal (previous version of Art. 337 c.p.c.) where judgments generally became enforceable only after second instance judgments. The running of time limits to appeal and the lodging of an appeal had therefore *ipso iure* a suspensive effect of enforcement proceedings. Nevertheless, Law n. 353/1990 granted enforceable character also to first instance judgments in order to prevent delaying tactics connected with mere dilatory appeals.

limits to appeal. At first glance, when considering these regimes, in spite of some minor divergences regarding the length of time limits[549] and the regime of default judgments[550], it seems possible to retain similar common foundations on the setting of time limits to appeal. Nevertheless, when looking at these systems in detail, it seems that appellants when filing their grounded act of appeal must deal with the preparation of complex activities of appeal specific to each system, which cannot be isolated from the national procedures at hand. For instance, in Italy and France the time limit to appeal is also the general temporal barrier to file incidental appeals. In Italy, parties within this time limit must also request suspension of enforcement proceedings. There are therefore specificities underlying the practical preparation of appeals that make the possibility of achieving common fixed time limits even between two similar systems belonging to the same legal tradition like the Italian and French one controversial.

Furthermore, when projecting this conclusion at the EU level and extending the analysis to a larger pool of systems, the scenario becomes more fragmented. The mechanism insisting on long and short time limits to appeal does not exist in each Member State[551] and the specificities linked to the preparation of appeals in each Member State further increase fragmentation.

Under these premises, establishing common grounds of harmonisation between the Member States on the time limits to appeal seems practically impossible. The method to fix these time limits and the practical filing of the act of appeal are indeed firmly connected with national considerations on legal certainty and protection of parties' rights defining and embedded in national identities.

549 I.e. in Italy there are short time limits of 1 month not extended in cross-border cases and long time limits of 6 months; in France there are short time limits of 30 days extended by 1 or 2 months because of distance and long time limits of 2 years.

550 Under French law, long time limits to appeal do not run if the judgment is rendered in default; under Italian law, long time limits run also if judgments are rendered in default and it is the defaulting defendant who has to prove that he was not aware of the proceedings initiated against him because service of the lawsuit was null.

551 As pointed out above (fn 517), there are Member States where the *dies a quo* starts from the rendering of the judgment, rather than service.

ii) Time limits for lodging an appeal on legal grounds

The same conclusions regarding appeals on factual grounds can be reiterated with respect to appeal on legal grounds. The length (these time limits are generally longer than the ones for lodging appeals on factual grounds), *dies a quo*, and extension of the time limits for lodging appeals on legal grounds vary widely between the Member States.

These time limits are as well premised on complex activities embedded in national procedures, which parties must accomplish when filing the appeal, e.g. filing a grounded appeal based on complex legal grounds, filing incidental appeals, requesting suspension of enforcement.

For instance, when looking at the time limit to lodge an appeal on legal grounds in Italy and France, it emerges that they are generally subject to the same regime of appeals on factual grounds analysed above. However, the most remarkable difference, compared to this regime, concerns the length of short limits for lodging an appeal on legal grounds which is respectively 60 days under Italian law and 2 months under French law.

These circumstances, as it was the case with respect to the time limits for lodging appeal on factual grounds, therefore prevent a uniform setting at the EU level of time limits for lodging appeals on legal grounds.

b) The setting of time limits embedded in national civil procedures

What emerges from this overall assessment is that time limits are premised on specific procedural activities (e.g. reacting to a claim, opposing a payment order, lodging an appeal) requiring different degrees of complexity which vary between the Member States. The setting of time limits is indeed firmly connected with the structure of national proceedings and the organization of parties' defences. Time limits are thus profoundly embedded in national legal backgrounds and cannot be considered in isolation from the procedure where they have been fixed. Setting one time limit rather than another is not casual, but depends on precise policy decisions taken by national lawmakers.

What follows is that, without a uniform European procedure at hand, opting for common fixed time limits for reacting, opposing payment orders, or lodging an appeal at the EU level would hardly be achievable.

c) The technical character of the rules on computation of time

On a different note, some rules regarding the regulation of time limits might be extrapolated from national backgrounds as not forming part of Member States' legal traditions. One could indeed argue that rules on the computation of time in civil litigation because of their prevalent technical character do not fall within the realm of those core procedural rules characterising national legal cultures[552]. Their source is more likely located in historical fate and is to a great extent, although not always entirely, attributable to chance rather than to reason linked to national identities[553].

Hence, regarding the issue of computation of time one could infer that the need for harmonisation overcomes national reticence. Within the area of computation of time, the three following types of issues can be distinguished[554]: the first group involves the calculation of periods of time (i.e. the computation of time in the strict sense of the term); the second category examines the extension or abridgment of time[555]; and the third set of problems deals with the *restitutio in integrum*[556] from the expiry of time limits.

Arising from the above, under the current legislative framework – save for the non-comprehensive rules provided for in Regulation 1182/71 – rules on the computation of time diverge across the EU and this could hinder judicial cooperation in civil matters.

In particular, when calculating time limits, Member States can use calendar (e.g. Italy, France, Germany) or working days (e.g. Spain); can consider or not the *dies a quo* in the counting (e.g. when time limits are expressed

552 Konstantinos Kerameus, 'Procedural Harmonization in Europe' (1995) *Am. J. Comp. L.*, 404; Vernadaki, (n.419), 307.

553 Kerameus (n.552), 415, 416.

554 Konstantinos Kerameus, 'Relevance and Computation of Time in Civil Procedure' in Franz Matscher, Oskar Ballon, Johann JosefHagen, *Verfahrensgarantien im Nationalen und Internationalen Prozessrecht: Festschrift Franz Matscher* (Manzsche Verlags- und Universitätsbuchhandlung 1993), 243.

555 As emerges from the above examples, the matter hardly has any practical relevance in cross-border cases. The possibility of providing uniform rules on abridgment of time therefore won't be dealt with. See Kerameus (n.554), 248.

556 It should be noted that Art. 22 (4) of the Service Regulation Recast already provides for uniform conditions for applying for relief. There is therefore no need to wonder here whether EU action on *restitutio in integrum* is desirable or not. However, the discussion, as we will see below, will be on the possibility to extend the scope of this provision.

in months or years Italy[557] does not take into account the month of the act, Germany[558] does not take into account the day of the act and France[559] includes the day of the act); can apply specific rules for calculating time limits backward[560]; can establish specific rules for calculating clear time limits (e.g. Italy does not count either the *dies a quo* or the *dies ad quem*); can take exceptional measures suspending or interrupting time limits under extraordinary circumstances (e.g. the covid-19 legislation). Establishing uniform rules for calculating time limits would address these relevant technical issues negatively affecting litigation across different Member States.

In addition, the above examples on the regulation of time limits at national level show that how Member States take into account the specificities of cross-border litigation varies widely. Member States generally extend deadlines for foreign litigants by law[561] or by judicial intervention[562]. However, not all Member States provide for the latter extensions and this is contrary to a fully integrated European single market[563]. For instance, Spanish and Austrian law does not extend the time to react in general first instance cross-border proceedings; Spanish and Slovenian law do not extend time limits to oppose payment orders in cross-border cases; Italian law does not extend time limits for foreign defendants to appeal. Providing uniform rules for extending deadlines for all cross-border litigants domiciled in the territory of the EU would offset the legislation of these Member States. This would allow foreign litigants to rely on similar procedural guarantees when dealing with the practical preparation of defences under a system they are not familiar with and facing linguistic barriers (e.g. requiring translation of documents, communicate with lawyers and courts).

Thus, harmonising rules on the calculation and extension of time limits would allow treatment at the EU level of some technical issues on time lim-

557 See above i) Time limits for lodging an appeal on factual grounds.

558 See above ii) Time to oppose the issuance of payment orders.

559 See above ii) Time to oppose the issuance of payment orders and i) Time limits for lodging an appeal on factual grounds.

560 See fn 453.

561 E.g. Italy extends the time to react and the time to oppose payment orders for foreign defendants; France provides for a general general extension of time limits in cross-border cases or Germany extends the time to oppose payment orders in cross-border cases. See above bb) The time to react.

562 E.g. This happens in Germany regarding the time to react in general first instance proceedings (see fn 461) or in the Member States mentioned in fn 514 with respect to the time to appeal on factual grounds,

563 Kerameus (n.554), 248.

its which might place foreign defendants in a weaker procedural position and negatively impact on the recognition and enforcement of judgments within the EU. It follows that the need for procedural harmonisation clearly emerges within the area of computation of time.

III) A concrete proposal for a EU action on time limits[564]

Against this background, it emerges that EU action on time limits is partially feasible and desirable in the area of computation of time. However, this action would not fully cover the issues which time limits raise under the Brussels Ibis Regulation and second generation instruments (EEO, EPO, ESCP and EAPO). These issues should be further tackled regulation by regulation in order to fill some of the gaps arising under the current regime of cross-border civil litigation and increase coordination between different laws at the EU level.

1) Umbrella instrument in EU civil procedure on the computation of time

A concrete proposal addressing the issue of computation of time in EU civil procedure could be the development of an 'umbrella instrument'[565] providing for a coherent and systematic set of rules on calculation and extension of time limits in cross-border proceedings[566]. For the purpose of calculating and extending procedural time limits in cross-border cases, such uniform rules shoud be applied under the scope of EU procedural law instruments, e.g. the Brussels Ibis Regulation or the second generation instruments (EEO, EPO, ESCP and EAPO). The model to follow might be,

564 Such proposal is not meant to be a final product but just a text for discussion. The elaboration of a final text of the proposal would indeed require taking into consideration how time limits are addressed in all the legal systems of the EU.

565 See Hess (n.371), 171; Tulibacka, Sanz and Blomeyer (n.371), 53.

566 It should be noted that, since these rules would apply only in the context of cross-border cases, this could create discrimination and confusion (for further details see above 3) Limitation to cases with cross-border implications) in those MS where the national way of calculating time limits ends up differing from the new European and harmonised way. In order to overcome this risk, national law-makers should be encouraged to make the necessary reforms to extend to domestic cases the new EU system of calculating time limits for cross-border cases, so that, at the end of the day, time limits would be calculated in the same way, irrespective of the cross-border or domestic nature of the case.

for instance, that of the Service Regulation governing a similar technical procedural issue.

According to the general practice at national[567] and EU[568] levels, rules on the calculation and extension of time limits in cross-border civil proceedings might reasonably be drafted as follows.

a) Proposed Regulation on the computation in the Member States of time limits in civil and commercial matters[569]

Article 1 (calendar days)

1. Time limits shall be counted in calendar days, which means that Saturdays, Sundays and public holidays are included in the calculation.
2. Time limits shall be suspended and interrupted according to the general[570] or exceptional[571] rules provided by the domestic law of the Member States.

Article 2 (*dies a quo*)

1. When determining the *dies a quo* of time limits expressed in days the principle *dies a quo non computar in termino* shall apply.
2. When determining the *dies a quo* of time limits expressed in weeks, months and years the starting point shall be on the date where the act, event, decision or notification occurs[572].

Art. 3 (*dies ad quem*)

1. The *dies ad quem* of time limits expressed in days shall be on the last day of the time limit.
2. The *dies ad quem* of time limits expressed in weeks, months or years shall expire on the day of last year, month or week bearing the same number or name as the one on which time began to run.

567 See the examples referred to above in aa) Calculation of time limits.
568 See Regulation 1182/71.
569 Such Regulation shall apply in compliance with the rules provided for in Regulation 1182/71.
570 E.g. suspension of time limits during summer vacation (see fn 455).
571 E.g. exceptional circumstances affecting the normal functioning of the judiciary (see fn 456).
572 Member States' solutions do not converge here. The latter rule has been chosen for sake of consistency with the solution adopted by Regulation 1182/72.

3. Where a corresponding date does not exist[573], as it occurs in leap years, the time limit shall expire on the last day of the last month.
4. Where time limits expire on Saturdays, Sundays or public holidays, the *dies ad quem* shall be postponed to the next following working day

Art. 4 (backward calculation)

1. Where time limits are calculated backward, the principle *dies a quo* (the first day of backward calculation) *non computatur in termino and dies ad quem* (the last day of backward calculation) *computatur in termino* shall apply.
2. However, the rule postponing the dies ad quem to the next working day if this falls on Saturdays, Sundays, or public holidays shall not apply.

Art. 5 (extension of time limits in cross-border cases)
National time limits to react, appeal, oppose payment orders, would be extended by law or by courts by at least 1 month for all persons domiciled in the territory of any Member State.

b) Benefit

Establishing a set of uniform rules for the calculation and extension of time limits would allow EU litigants to rely on a similar treatment of some technicalities, whose interpretation is crucial for succeeding in civil proceedings. This would simplify a practical aspect of EU cross-border litigation which would reinforce parties' procedural guarantees and legal certainty.

2) Addressing issues regulation by regulation

In addition to the introduction of the above umbrella instrument on computation of time in EU civil procedure, the issues further arising under the scope of the Brussels Ibis Regulation and second generation instruments, will be addressed separately as follows:

573 E.g. in a leap year.

a) Brussels Ibis Regulation

aa) Interpreting the notion of sufficient time under Art. 45 (1)(b)

As arises from the above, there is a need to clarify the notion of sufficient time – with respect to the time limits to react (including also the time to oppose payment orders), appeal (including appeals on factual and legal grounds) and relief – under the scope of Art. 45 (1)(b). In spite of the impossibility of achieving common fixed time limits to react, appeal and relief under Art. 45 (1)(b), it might be advisable to establish minimum deadlines, which would represent a uniform standard for national courts when interpreting the sufficiency of time. Together with minimum deadlines, some common elements that courts should necessarily take into account when checking the respect of defendants' rights under Art. 45 (1)(b), might also be indicated.

i) Amending Art. 45 (1)(b)

Art. 45(1)(b) could be reworded as follows (amendments in bold):

1. On the application of any interested party, the recognition of a judgment shall be refused:

   b) where the judgment was given in default of appearance, if the defendant was not served with the document which instituted the proceedings or with an equivalent document in sufficient time and in such a way as to enable him to arrange for his defence, unless the defendant failed to commence proceedings to challenge the judgment when it was possible for him to do so. **In particular, the notion of sufficient time shall be interpreted in the sense that time limits to react[574] cannot be shorter than 30 days[575]; time limits to appeal on factual grounds cannot be**

574 In order to apply uniformy this time limit it is necessary that the Regulation provides for a definition of the term 'react', otherwise, there will be many discrepancies in the application of the new rule across the different Member States. The following definition could be suggested: 'The term react refers to defendant's response to a claimant's statement of claim. The concrete form of the response shall be detemnied according to national law'.

575 Regarding the chosen minimum length of the time to react in general first instance proceedings see 'Rule 54' in European Law Institute and UNIDROIT (eds), *The ELI – UNIDROIT Model European Rules of Civil Procedure from Transnational*

shorter than 1 month[576], time limits to appeal on legal grounds cannot be shorter than 2 months[577], and time limits for applying for relief[578] cannot be shorter than 1 year[579]. In any case, when interpreting the notion of sufficient time, courts shall assess the degree of complexity of activities of defence in light of the following elements: the mere or grounded[580] nature of the statement of defence or act of appeal, the mandatory or optional character of legal representation, and the possibility to require translation of documents.

ii) Benefit

These minimum time limits combined with common criteria for assessing the complexity of defences would reduce the margin of appreciation of courts on the sufficiency of time under the Brussels Ibis regime, thus promoting a more consistent and uniform interpretation between the Member States on the grounds (including Art. 45 (1)(a)) for refusing recognition and enforcement. This would contribute to aligning a fundamental aspect of EU cross-border civil litigation allowing courts to rely on similar procedural guarantees when checking grounds for recognising and enforcing foreign

Principles to European Rules of Civil Procedure (Oxford University Press 2021) which refers to 30 days. With respect to the the chosen length of the time to oppose payment orders see Art. 16 (2) EPO Regulation.

576 Regarding the chosen minimum length of the time to appeal on factual grounds see 'Rule 156' in European Law Institute and UNIDROIT (eds), *The ELI – UNIDROIT Model European Rules of Civil Procedure from Transnational Principles to European Rules of Civil Procedure* (Oxford University Press 2021) referring to a 1 month time for appeals on factual grounds.

577 Regarding the chosen minimum length of the time to appeal on legal grounds see 'Rule 156' in European Law Institute and UNIDROIT (eds), *The ELI – UNIDROIT Model European Rules of Civil Procedure from Transnational Principles to European Rules of Civil Procedure* (Oxford University Press 2021) referring to a 2 month time limit for appeals on legal grounds.

578 In order to apply uniformly this time limit it is necessary that the Regulation provides for a definition of the term 'relief proceedings', otherwise, there will be many discrepancies in the application of the new rule across the different Member States. The following definition could be suggested: 'relief proceedings can be defined as those proceedings restoring time limits to challenge a judgment when the defendant was not made aware of a default judgments rendered against him and the time limits to appeal that judgment expired without any fault on his side'.

579 Regarding the chosen minimum length of time limits to apply for relief see Art. 22 (4) of the Service Regulation Recast.

580 If grounded, the level of detail shall also be taken into account.

judgments in the Member State of enforcement. Circulation of judgments would be less formalistic and characterised by more automatisms boosting a *pro creditore* approach.

bb) Time limits to proceed to enforcement as a condition of the enforceability of judgments

Under the current institutional framework of the Brussels Ibis Regulation, time limits to proceed to enforcement – in accordance with the *Al Bosco* ruling[581]– are governed by the law of the Member State addressed. This raises some uncertainties in enforcement settings, which might be addressed by including the time limits to proceed to enforcement as conditions for the enforceability of judgments, which shall be met under the law of the Member State of origin. Such information should thus be provided with the Art. 53 certificate, whose form (set out in Annex I of the Regulation) should include the following wording.

i) Amending the Art. 53 form

The following indications (in bold) should be included in Art. 53:

> **The applicable time limits to proceed to enforcement start on ... and expire on ... according to the law of the Member State of origin.**

ii) Benefit

By providing clear information regarding the time limits to proceed to enforcement of foreign judgments under the Brussels Ibis regime, this solution would increase legal certainty with respect to the *res judicata* effects attached to the judgment rendered in the Member State of origin (Art. 39). This would simplify the rapid and efficient cross-border enforcement of judgments across the EU.

581 See fn 170.

cc) Abolishing service of the Art. 53 certificate prior to the first enforcement measure

i) Deleting Art. 43 (1) and Recital 32

Regarding service of the Art. 53 certificate on the debtor prior to the first enforcement measure, the most recommended policy option is to remove this requirement from the Brussels Ibis Regulation by deleting Art. 43 (1) and, consequently Recital 32.

ii) Benefit

Deleting the requirement of serving the Art. 53 Certificate prior to the first enforcement measure would remove an intermediate step that causes the creditor additional delays and costs when proceeding to the cross-border enforcement of judgments. The free circulation of judgments under the Brussels Ibis regime would thus be less formalistic and faster.

b) Second generation instruments

The following proposals should be made to address the issues that time limits raise under the scope of the second generation instruments (EEO, EPO, ESCP and EAPO Regulations).

aa) Longer time limits for opposing payment orders for consumers within the EPO procedure

When dealing with the time limits for opposing the issuance of payment orders, it might be advisable to establish a specific regime for consumers' rights, which would ensure additional safeguards to the ones normally provided for. The introduction of a specific paragraph in Art. 16 EPO might be envisaged as follows:

i) Amending Art. 16 EPO

Art. 16 EPO could be reworded as follows (amendments in bold):

1. The defendant may lodge a statement of opposition to the European order for payment with the court of origin using standard form F as set out in Annex VI, which shall be supplied to him together with the European order for payment.
2. The statement of opposition shall be sent within 30 days of service of the order on the defendant.
3. **The statement of opposition shall be sent within 40 days[582] of service of the order on the consumer defendant.**

...

ii) Benefit

Providing consumers with longer time limits to oppose the issuance of payment orders would afford them an additional standard of protection within the EPO procedure. This further safeguard would thus strengthen consumers' right of defence in EU cross-border civil litigation.

bb) Uniform time limits for lodging appeals within the ESCP procedure

Time limits for lodging an appeal should be harmonised as follows under the scope of Art. 17 of the ESCP procedure. In addition, Art. 17 ESCP should also include uniform rules on the commencement, conduct, and conclusion of appeal procedures.

---

582 The length of this time limit has been chosen by drawing inspiration from the Italian and German payment order procedures, which are two of the most representative systems within the EU dealing respectively with a documentary and non-documentary model. Both payment order procedures can also be used against consumers. The time limits to oppose payment orders within these procedures are deemed to ensure consumers sufficient protection of their rights in cross-border cases. In particular, under Italian law, foreign defendants have 50 days to oppose a payment order; under German law, 1 month. By comparing these time limits with the EPO hybrid model, one could argue that the time limit granted to the consumer defendant for opposing an EPO should be 40 days, which is the average between the Italian and German time limits.

i) Amending Art. 17 ESCP

Art. 17 ESCP could be reworded as follows (amendments in bold):

1. **Against a judgment given in the framework of the European Small Claims Procedure, parties may lodge an appeal within 30 days from the service of the judgment performed in accordance with Article 13[583].**
2. **The appeal procedure shall be commenced, conducted and concluded through the use of specific standard forms[584] according to the following rules[585]...**

ii) Benefit

Harmonising the time limits for lodging an appeal and the appeal procedure itself in the context of the ESCP Regulation would promote uniformity in applying and interpreting this instrument. Notably, this would offset the current fragmentation which emerges from the application of different national rules on appeal proceedings when contesting a decision rendered within a uniform procedure.

cc) Uniform time limits to enforce the EAPO

The identification of the applicable time limits to enforce EAPOs across the Member States would be more straightforward if a reference to the expiry date of preservation orders were included among the information required by Art. 19 EAPO to fill in the form provided for in Annex 2 of Regulation 2016/1823. In addition, the temporal validity of EAPOs should be regulated uniformly under the scope of the EAPO Regulation. Art. 22 EAPO should

583 As is the case with respect to the time to apply for review (Art. 18 (2) ESCP Regulation), a uniform time limit could be established even if the appeal procedure is ultimately not harmonised. This would represent a common standard of protection for parties' rights against judgments rendered within the ESCP procedure.

584 In particular, the following forms should be created *ad hoc*: a form for filing the appeal, a form for completing or rectifying the appeal at the court's request, a form filed by the court and served on the addressee for answering the appeal.

585 The proposal is limited here to this general formulation and will not include a specific timeframe governing the commencement, conduct and conclusion of the appeal procedure.

provide for the following harmonized time limits to enforce EAPOs within the EU.

i) Amending Art. 19 EAPO[586]

Art. 19 EAPO could be reworded as follows (amendments in bold):

> ...
> 2. Part A shall include the following information:
> ....
> (i) the date of issue of the order **and its expiry date**
> ...

ii) Amending Art. 22 EAPO

Art. 22 EAPO could be reworded as follows (amendments in bold):

> A Preservation Order issued in a Member State in accordance with this Regulation shall be recognised in the other Member States without any special procedure being required and shall be enforceable in the other Member States without the need for a declaration of enforceability. **It shall be valid for a period of 1 month[587]running from the date of its issue.**

iii) Benefit

In order to better identify the time limits to enforce EAPOs and reinforce legal certainty, a reference to the expiry date of preservation orders should

586 This wording could be suggested both under the current legal framework where time limits to enforce EAPOs are regulated at national level and in the scenario where they would be finally hamonised under Art. 22 EAPO (see ii) Amending Art. 22 EAPO).

587 As for the suggested length of the time limits to enforce EAPOs, reference can be made to the *Al Bosco* judgment. In this ruling, the CJEU considered that the application of the 1 month time limit laid down in Section 929(2) ZPO did not undermine the effectiveness of the Brussels Ibis regime. One could argue that the circumstances under which a national preventive attachment order is enforced in a cross-border setting are similar to those for enforcing EAPOs across the Member States. A 1 month time limit could therefore be considered as a reasonable temporal restriction to the validity of EAPOs taking into account both the urgency of the protective measure and the protection of parties' rights.

be included among the information required by Art. 19 to fill in the form provided for in Annex II of Regulation 2016/1823. Furthermore, harmonising the time limits to enforce EAPOs under Art. 22 would have the advantage of overcoming fragmentation between national limits, which undermines the uniform character of the EAPO enforcement title.

cc) Aligning review procedures under the EEO, EPO and ESCP

The EU legislator should align review procedures under the scope of the EEO, EPO and ESCP Regulations in order to foster consistency across these instruments. The reference model for achieving this project is the review procedure provided for in Art. 18 ESCP Regulation, which under the current state of affairs seems to be more comprehensive than the respective procedures laid down in Arts 19 EEO and 20 EPO. The following proposals would also envisage the possibility to establish fully harmonised review procedures within the ESCP and EPO[588] Regulations. In this respect, it is necessary to provide for a specific timeframe governing, through the use of specific standard forms, the commencement, conduct and conclusion of these procedures at EU level.

i) Amending Art. 18 ESCP

Art. 18 ESCP concerning the review of judgments in exceptional cases could be reworded as follows (amendments in bold):

1. A defendant who did not enter an appearance shall be entitled to apply for a review of the judgment given in the European Small Claims Procedure before the competent court or tribunal of the Member State in which the judgment was given, where:
   (a) the defendant was not served with the claim form, or, in the event of an oral hearing, was not summoned to that hearing, in sufficient time and in such a way as to enable him to arrange for his defence; or
   (b) the defendant was prevented from contesting the claim by reason of force majeure or due to extraordinary circumstances without any fault on his part,

588 The possibility to provide for a uniform review procedures will not be considered under the scope of the EEO Regulation, see above fn 366.

unless the defendant failed to challenge the judgment when it was possible for him to do so.

2. The time limit for applying for a review shall be 30 days. It shall run from the day the defendant was effectively acquainted with the contents of the judgment and was able to react, at the latest from the date of the first enforcement measure having the effect of making the property of the defendant non-disposable in whole or in part. No extension of the time limit may be granted.
3. **The procedure for review shall be commenced, conducted and concluded through the use of specific standard forms[589] according to the following rules[590]...'**
4. If the court rejects the application for a review referred to in paragraph 1 on the basis that none of the grounds for a review set out in that paragraph apply, the judgment shall remain in force.
   If the court decides that a review is justified on any of the grounds set out in paragraph 1, the judgment given in the European Small Claims Procedure shall be null and void. However, the claimant shall not lose the benefit of any interruption of prescription or limitation periods where such an interruption applies under national law.

ii) Amending Art. 20 EPO

Art. 20 EPO concerning the review of European payment orders in exceptional cases could be reworded as follows (amendments in bold):

1. After the expiry of the time limit laid down in Article 16(2) the defendant shall be entitled to apply for a review of the European order for payment before the competent court in the Member State of origin where:
   (a) **the defendant was not served with the order for payment in sufficient time and in such a way as to enable him to arrange for his defence; or**

589 In particular, the following forms should be created *ad hoc*: a form for filing the review, a form for completing or rectifying the review at the court's request, a form filed by the court and served on the addressee for answering the review.

590 The proposal is limited here to this general formulation and will not include a specific timeframe governing the commencement, conduct and conclusion of the review procedure.

(b) the defendant was prevented from contesting the claim by reason of force majeure or due to extraordinary circumstances without any fault on his part,
unless the defendant failed to oppose the payment order when it was possible for him to do so.

2. After expiry of the time limit laid down in Article 16(2) the defendant shall also be entitled to apply for a review of the European order for payment before the competent court in the Member State of origin where the order for payment was clearly wrongly issued, having regard to the requirements laid down in this Regulation, or due to other exceptional circumstances.
3. **The time limit for applying for a review shall be 30 days. It shall run from the day the defendant was effectively acquainted with the contents of the order for payment and was able to lodge his opposition, at the latest from the date of the first enforcement measure having the effect of making the property of the defendant non-disposable in whole or in part. No extension of the time limit may be granted.**
4. **The procedure for review shall be commenced, conducted and concluded through the use of specific standard forms[591] according to the following rules[592]...**
5. If the court rejects the defendant's application on the basis that none of the grounds for review referred to in paragraphs 1 and 2 apply, the European order for payment shall remain in force.
If the court decides that the review is justified for one of the reasons laid down in paragraphs 1 and 2, the European order for payment shall be null and void. **However, the claimant shall not lose the benefit of any interruption of prescription or limitation periods where such an interruption applies under national law.**

iii) Amending Art. 19 EEO

Art. 19 EEO dealing with minimum standards for review in exceptional cases could be reworded as follows (amendments in bold):

591 In particular, the following forms should be created *ad hoc*: a form for filing the review, a form for completing or rectifying the review at the court's request, a form filed by the court and served on the addressee for answering the review.

592 The proposal is limited here to this general formulation and will not include a specific timeframe governing the commencement, conduct and conclusion of the review procedure.

1. Further to Articles 13 to 18, a judgment can only be certified as a European Enforcement Order if the debtor is entitled, under the law of the Member State of origin, to apply for a review of the judgment where:
   (a) the debtor was not served with the document instituting the proceedings or an equivalent document or, where applicable, the summons to a court hearing in sufficient time and in such a way as to enable him to arrange for his defence; or
   (b) the debtor was prevented from contesting the claim by reason of force majeure or due to extraordinary circumstances without any fault on his part,

   unless the defendant failed to challenge the judgment when it was possible for him to do so
2. **The debtor was granted a time limit not shorter than 30 days for filing his application for review. This time limit shall run from the day the defendant was effectively acquainted with the contents of the judgment and was able to react, at the latest from the date of the first enforcement measure having the effect of making the property of the defendant non-disposable in whole or in part.**
3. This Article is without prejudice to the possibility for Member States to grant access to a review of the judgment under more generous conditions than those mentioned in paragraph 1.

iiii) Benefit

Aligning the content of Arts 19 EEO and 20 EPO with Art. 18 ESCP would promote a consistent and uniform interpretation of the conditions for applying for review within these instruments. Adopting Art. 18 ESCP mechanism would also address some problematic interfaces between national and EU law (i.e. absolute lack of service of the documents instituting the proceedings and absence of a uniform time limit for review) that arise when applying Arts 19 EEO and 20 EPO. Finally, providing for a fully regulated review procedure in the context of the EPO and ESCP Regulations would further approximate the appreciation of national courts in assessing the EU standards of review, whose actual interpretation might be overshadowed by the application of national law.

Conclusions

The present study was designed to determine whether time limits in cross-border civil litigation might be considered as an obstacle to the judicial cooperation in civil matters. In particular, the analysis tackles problems that originate from the interplay between national procedural rules on time limits and the following five European Regulations on cross-border debt recovery across the Member States: the Brussels Ibis Regulation and the EEO, EPO, ESCP and EAPO Regulations.

The main findings of the research can be summarized as follows. The results highlight, on the one hand, the existence of significant enforcement deficiencies linked to the interaction between national and EU systems with respect to the regulation of time limits (Chapter 2: Effective judicial cooperation in civil matters and the right to a fair trial) and, on the other, the need to address these issues in future developments of EU civil procedure in order to reinforce the parties' right to a fair trial in cross-border civil proceedings (Chapter 3: Time limits from the perspective of the EU lawmaker).

The divergent time limits to react (including the ones to oppose the issuance of a payment order)[593] and appeal (including the ones for applying for relief)[594] at national level challenge the recognition and enforcement of judgments under the Brussels Ibis Regulation. In particular, practical issues in assessing and interpreting the notion of sufficient time under Art. 45 (1) (b) might follow with regard to the *dies a quo*[595], expiry[596] and length[597] of domestic rules on the time to react and appeal. The check on the sufficiency or insufficiency of time granted to the defendant to organize his defences in first instance and appeal proceedings is carried out by the enforcement court on a case by case basis. Many practical difficulties[598] arise in the

593 See b) Sufficient time.

594 See a) General time limits for challenging judgments and b) Restoring original time limits to challenge a judgment: the *Lebek* case.

595 See aa) *Dies a quo* of the time to react.

596 See bb) Expiry of the time to react.

597 See cc) The length of the time to react.

598 See for instance the examples referred to in dd) Practical cases on the lack of sufficient time.

Member State of enforcement due to the divergent standard under domestic case law regarding the question if the defendant was granted sufficient time in the Member State of origin where the judgment was rendered. The research has shown that there is a need for more coherent rules on the time limits to react and appeal in cross-border cases, which would allow more uniformity in interpreting the notion of sufficient time under Art. 45 (1)(b). In spite of the impossibility of achieving common fixed time limits due to the lack of similar structures between domestic procedures[599], the following legislative proposal has been envisaged for reforming Art. 45 (1) (b): still referring to a flexible notion of sufficient time, but combining it with common minimum time limits (i.e. to react, appeal and apply for relief) and common criteria which domestic courts must use as standards of reference when assessing on a case by case basis the sufficiency or insufficiency of time under Art. 45 (1)(b) and deciding on refusal of recognition and enforcement[600].

The applicable time limits to enforce foreign judgments under the Brussels Ibis Regulation are governed by the law of the Member State addressed (Art. 41 (2)). These time limits diverge widely (e.g. their length or *dies a quo)* across the Member States[601]. The application of a national enforcement rule (such as a time limit) that was designed for national cases to cross-border cases could lead to legal uncertainty and undermine the effectiveness of the Brussels Ibis Regulation, in particular, the recognition and enforcement of foreign judgments. This lack of legal certainty calls for an intervention of the EU lawmaker. The Recast of the Brussels Ibis Regulation should arguably consider that time limits to proceed to enforcement of foreign judgments pertains to the enforceability of judgments (Art. 39) and are governed by the law of the Member State of origin[602]. This would ensure that as time limits have not expired under the law of the State of origin, enforcement is still possible in the State addressed irrespective of what is the equivalent time limit provided for in this latter State.

According to the Brussels Ibis regime, a person seeking to enforce a judgment given in another Member State must serve the certificate issued pursuant to Art. 53 on the person against whom enforcement is sought

599 See above b) The setting of time limits embedded in national civil procedures.
600 See above aa) Interpreting the notion of sufficient time under Art. 45 (1)(b).
601 See above 2) Divergent time limits as obstacles to the free circulation of judgments.
602 See above bb) Time limits to proceed to enforcement as a condition of the enforceability of judgments.

within a reasonable time prior to the first enforcement measure (Art. 43 (1) read in conjunction with Recital 32). This condition adds an intermediate step for the cross-border enforcement of Member States' judgments charging the creditor with further delays and costs, which partially challenges the meaning of direct enforcement within the Brussels Ibis regime. In this respect, the time limits between the service of the Art. 53 certificate and the first enforcement measure are determined by national law and, should in principle ensure that the defendant has sufficient time to challenge the enforcement proceedings before suffering the effects of the first enforcement measure. The notion of reasonable time is interpreted widely by different domestic courts[603]. This goes so far that even 5 minutes have been deemed sufficient. If such a short time period does not violate defendant's right to a fair trial under national law, the rationale behind Art. 43 (1) is called into question as it is not an effective guarantee for the debtor and at the same it is a burden affecting creditor's rights. The EU legislator should step in and decide on prioritising a *pro creditore* or *pro debitore* approach. The best solution is to delete Art. 43 (1)[604].

Under the scope of the second generations instruments the following issues regarding the application of time limits in cross-border civil proceedings have been highlighted.

In particular, the 30 days time limit as foreseen by Art. 16 EPO Regulation for opposing the issuance of a European payment order is too short to protect the right to fair proceedings involving consumers in cross-border cases[605]. In light of the EU principles on consumer protection, the EU lawmaker should consider future legislative reforms to provide consumers with longer time limits under the EPO procedure as this would represent an additional safeguard strengthening their procedural rights[606].

Moreover, a uniform appeal procedure is lacking under the scope of the ESCP Regulation. National law governs the rules on appeal proceedings including the time limits for lodging an appeal against a judgment rendered in the context of the small claims procedure. This lack of uniformity regarding the time limits to appeal is undesirable[607]. Different national rules are

603 See above 1) Uncertain time limits.

604 See above cc) Abolishing service of the Art. 53 certificate prior to the first enforcement measure.

605 See above c) The alleged shortness of the time limits in consumer law proceedings.

606 See above aa) Longer time limits for opposing payment orders for consumers within the EPO procedure.

607 See above b) The lack of a unform time limit to appeal.

applicable to appeal judgments issued under the same procedure. The EU lawmaker should address this fragmentation and introduce common time limits for lodging an appeal which would apply either within a uniform appeal procedure (if this is hopefully implemented) or in the context of national appeal proceedings[608].

In addition, a specific rule governing the temporal validity of EAPOs is absent under the scope of the EAPO Regulation[609]. Under the current wording, a reference to the expiry date of the preservation order should be added among the information to fill in the standard form for issuing EAPOs in order to help identifying the time limits to enforce these orders which are (arguably) regulated by the law of the Member State of origin[610]. Neverthless, divergent national time limits undermine the rationale of the EAPO enforcement title. To ensure further efficiency the EU lawmaker should provide for a uniform rule governing the temporal validity of EAPOs across the Member States[611].

Further inconsistencies on the regulation of time limits in EU cross-border civil litigation arise with respect to the EEO, EPO and ESCP review proceedings. The models of review provided for under the scope of these Regulations are not consistent. The analysis of the EEO and EPO review procedures highlights, in particular, the following deficiencies related to time limits and their interplay with national law, which on the contrary do not emerge under the ESCP Regulation. First, where service is not accomplished in a manner consistent with the minimum standards laid down in the EEO and EPO Regulations (e.g. in case of absolute lack of service), the time to react does not start running[612]. The application of the Arts 19 EEO and 20 EPO review mechanisms is excluded and, the defendant must proceed according to the domestic law of the issuing court. In addition, Arts 19 EEO and 20 EPO do not provide for any uniform time limit for applying for review[613]; the length and *dies a quo* of the time limits for review are therefore governed by national law and must be investigated by the defendant in the systems at hand together with the available remedies. The reliance on national law leads to fragmentation which weakens rather

608 See above bb) Uniform time limits for lodging appeals within the ESCP procedure.

609 See above ff) Need to regulate the time limits to enforce the EAPO.

610 See above i) Amending Art. 19 EAPO.

611 See above ii) Amending Art. 22 EAPO.

612 See above aa) Absolute lack of service of the documents instituting the proceedings.

613 See above bb) Lack of uniform time limits for review.

than reinforcing the debtors' rights in cross-border proceedings[614]. The EU lawmaker should reform Arts 19 EEO and 20 EPO and draw on Art. 18 ESCP which deals both with the lack of service ('he was not served') and the time limits for review (30 days)[615].

Furthermore, courts should rely on European standards when reviewing the judgments (i.e. conditions regarding the sufficiency of time for preparing defences and the possibility to effectively challenge the judgment). European standards of review should not be overshadowed by a different pre-understanding of national time limits. In order to offset this undesired effect, the EU lawmaker should arguably opt within the EPO and ESCP Regulations for fully harmonised review proceedings.

In addition to the issues described above, it should be noted that rules on the computation of time entail further deficiencies under the scope of the Brussels Ibis, EEO, EPO[616], ESCP and EAPO Regulations. In particular, time limits are not calculated consistently within the EU and their identification is not easily discernible. Moreover, it happens that some national systems do not extend the time limits of parties litigating across the Member States. These circumstances undermine the right of access to justice in EU cross-border civil litigation. To face these practical difficulties, the EU legislator should establish a uniform set of rules dealing with computation of time in cross-border cases. Provided that rules on computation are mere technical rules not embedded in national legal cultures[617], it could be acceptable to harmonise these rules at EU level through an umbrella instrument[618] on the computation of time which would allow parties to rely on similar procedural guarantees in cross-border civil proceedings.

---

614 See above b) Different national pre-understandings of time limits when checking the grounds for review *in concreto*.

615 See above cc) Aligning review procedures under the EEO, EPO and ESCP.

616 See for instance b) Interruption and suspension of time limits according to national law (*C-18/21*).

617 See above c) The technical character of the rules on computation of time.

618 See above 1) Umbrella instrument in EU civil procedure on the computation of time.

Bibliography

A) Legal literature

I) Books

Amrani-Mekki Soraya, *Le Temps et le Procès Civil* (Dalloz 2002).

Balbi Carlo Edoardo, *La Decadenza nel Processo di Cognizione* (Giuffrè Editore 1983).

Barbaud Roger, *Dictionnaire des Délais: de Procédure de Prescriptions et de Formalités* (Sansovini imprimerie *1960)*.

Basedow Jürgen, *EU Private Law: Anatomy of a Growing Legal Order* (Intersentia 2021).

Biavati Paolo, *Europa e Processo Civile: Metodi e Prospettive* (Giappichelli Editore 2003).

Biavati Paolo, *Argomenti di Diritto Processuale Civile* (5th edn, Bononia University Press 2020).

Biavati Paolo, *Argomenti di Diritto Processuale Civile* (6th edn, Bononia University Press 2023).

Bonomi Andrea, *Diritto Internazionale Privato e Cooperazione Giudiziaria in Materia Civile* (Giappichelli Editore 2008).

Cadiet Loïc and Jeuland Emmanuel, *Droit Judiciaire Privé* (11th edn, LexisNexis 2020).

Calamandrei Piero, *Istituzioni di Diritto Processuale Civile,* vol 1 (Cedam 1941).

Caponi Remo, *La Rimessione in Termini nel Processo Civile* (Giuffrè Editore 1996).

Carbone Sergio and Tuo Chiara, *Il Nuovo Spazio Giudiziario Europeo in Materia Civile e Commerciale. Il Regolamento UE n. 1215/2012* (Giappichelli Editore 2016).

Carnelutti Francesco, *Istituzioni del Processo Civile Italiano*, vol 1 (Foro Italiano 1956).

Carpi Federico, *La Provvisoria Esecutorietà della Sentenza* (Giuffrè Editore 1979).

Chainais Cécile, Ferrand Frédérique, Mayer Lucie and Guinchard Serge, *Procédure civile: Droit Commun et Spécial du Procès Civil, MARD et Arbitrage* (16th edn, Dalloz 2022).

Chiovenda Giuseppe, *Saggi di Diritto Processuale Civile 1894–1937* (Giuffrè Editore 1993).

Cornu Gérard and Foyer Jean, *Procédure Civile* (11th edn, P.U.F. 1996).

Crifò Carla, *Cross-Border Enforcement of Debts in the European Union, Default Judgments, Summary Judgments and Orders for Payment* (Kluwer Law International 2009).

Cuniberti Gilles and Migliorini Sara, *The European Account Preservation Order: A Commentary* (Cambridge University Press 2018).

D'Alessandro Elena, *Il Riconoscimento delle Sentenze Straniere* (Giappichelli Editore 2007).

D'Alessandro Elena, *Il Procedimento Uniforme per le Controversie di Modesta Entità* (Giappichelli Editore 2008).

De Santis Francesco, *La Rimessione in Termini nel Processo Civile* (Giappichelli Editore 1997).

Diana Antonio Gerardo, *Termini Processuali* (Key, 2017).

Goldschmidt James, *Zivilprozessrecht* (Springer 1932).

Dickinson Andrew, *The Rome II Regulation. The Law Applicable to Non-Contractual Obligations* (Oxford University Press 2009).

Farina Marco, *Titoli Esecutivi Europei ed Esecuzione Forzata in Italia* (Aracne Roma 2012).

Garbagnati Edoardo and Romano Alberto, *Il Procedimento d'Ingiunzione* (Giuffrè Editore 1991).

Gaudemet-Tallon Hélène and Ancel Marie-Élodie, *Compétence et Exécution des Jugements en Europe: Matières Civile et Commerciale: Règlements 44/2001 et 1215/2012, Conventions de Bruxelles (1968) et de Lugano (1988 et 2007)* (6th edn, LGDJ 2018).

Giugliano Valeria, *Le Opposizioni all'Esecuzione della Decisione Straniera nel Regolamento (UE) 1215/2012* (PhD thesis Università degli Studi di Milano 2017/2018).

Giussani Andrea, *Cross-Border Enforcement of Monetary Claims – Interplay of Brussels I A Regulation and National Rules*, National Report: Italy (University of Maribor Press 2018).

Gomez Amigo Luiz, *El Proceso Monitorio Europeo* (Thomson Reuters Aranzadi 2008).

Grossi Simona and Pagni Maria Cristina, *Commentary on the Italian Code of Civil Procedure* (Oxford University Press 2010).

Héron Jacques, *Droit Judiciaire Privé* (Montchrestien 1991).

Héron Jacques, Le Bars Tristan and Salhi Karim, *Droit Judiciaire Privé* (7th edn, LGDJ 2019).

Hess Burkhard, *Europäisches Zivilprozessrecht* (2nd edn, De Gruyter 2021).

Hess Burkhard, Jauernig Othmar, Roig Molés Eduard, Lent Friedrich, *Manual de Derecho Procesal Civil* (Marcial Pons 2015).

Huet Danièle Alexandre and Huet André, *Compétence Judiciaire et Effets des Décisions dans l'Union Européenne. Matière Civile et Commerciale* (Dalloz 2020),

Hutchinson Terry, *Researching and Writing in Law* (4th edn, Thomson Reuters 2018).

Impagnatiello Gianpaolo, *La Provvisoria Esecuzione e l'Inibitoria nel Processo Civile* (Giuffrè Editore 2010).

Kennett Wendy, *Enforcement of Judgments in Europe* (Oxford University Press 2000).

Kramer Xandra, *Procedure matters: Construction and Deconstructivism in European Civil Procedure* (Eleven International Publishing [u.a.] 2013).

Layton Alexander and Mercer Hugh, *European Civil Practice*, vol 1 (2nd edn, Thomson, Sweet and Maxwell 2004).

López de Tejada Maria, *La Disparition de l'Exequatur dans l'Espace Judiciaire Européen* (LGDJ 2013).

Lupoi Michele Angelo, *Civil Procedure in Italy* (Wolters Kluwer 2019).

Mandrioli Crisanto and Carratta Antonio, *Diritto Processuale Civile*, vol 1, 2, 3 (21st edn, Giappichelli Editore 2019).

Murray Peter L and Stürner Rolf, *German Civil Justice* (Carolina Academic Press 2004)

Ontanu Elena Alina, *Cross-Border Debt Recovery in the EU. A Comparative and Empirical Study on the Use of the European Uniform Procedures* (Intersentia 2017).

Partsch Philippe Emmanuel, *Le Droit International Privé Européen: De Rome a Nice* (Larcier 2003).

Picardi Nicola, *La Successione Processuale*, vol 1 (Giuffrè Editore 1964).

Raworth Philip, *The French Code of Civil Procedure in English* (Thomson Reuters, 2022).

Richard Vincent, *Le Jugement par Défaut dans l'Espace Judiciaire Européen* (Droit Université Panthéon-Sorbonne – Paris I 2019).

Ritz Nico, *Vorläufige Kontenpfändung in Europa* (Peter Lang 2019).

Rocco Ugo, *Trattato di Diritto Processuale Civile* (2nd edn, UTET Giuridica 1966).

Romano Alberto, *Il Procedimento Europeo di Ingiunzione di Pagamento* (Giuffrè Editore 2009).

Saracini Eugenio, *Il Termine e le sue Funzioni* (Giuffrè Editore 1979).

Salerno Francesco, *Giurisdizione ed Efficacia delle Decisioni Straniere nel Regolamento (UE) n. 1215/2012 (Rifusione)* (4th edn, Wolters Kluwer Cedam 2015).

Schlosser Peter and Hess Burkhard (eds), *EU-Zivilprozessrecht: mit EuGVVO, EuMahnVO, EuBagVO, EuZVO, EuBVO* (5th edn, Beck 2021).

Senés Motilla Carmen, *La Orden Europea de Retención de Cuentas: Aplicación en Derecho Español del Reglamento (UE) Núm. 655/2014 de 15 de Mayo de 2014* (Aranzadi 2015).

Storskrubb Eva, *Civil Procedure and EU law. A Policy Area Uncovered* (Oxford Univeristy Press 2008).

Storme Marcel, *Approximation of Judiciary Law in the European Union* (Martinus Nijhoff 1994).

Trocker Nicolò, *La Formazione del Diritto Processuale Europeo* (Giappichelli Editore 2011).

Tuo Chiara Enrica, *La Rivalutazione della Sentenza Straniera nel Regolamento Bruxelles I: tra Divieti e Reciproca Fiducia* (Cedam 2012).

Vallines Garcia Enrique, *La Preclusión en el Proceso Civil* (Civitas 2004).

Von Hoffmann Bernd, *Internationales Privatrecht: Einschließlich der Grundzüge des Internationalen* (Verlag C.H. Beck 2022).

Zanzucchi Marco Tullio, *Diritto Processuale Civile*, vol 1 (6th edn, Giuffrè Editore 1964).

II) Book chapters

Achermann Alberto, "Asylum and Immigration Policies: from Cooperation to Harmonization" in Bieber Roland and Monar Jörg (eds), *Justice and Home Affairs in the European Union: The Development of the Third Pillar* (European Interuniversity Press 1995), 127–140.

Barrett Gavin, 'Cooperation in Justice and Home Afffairs in the European Union - An Overview and a Critique' in Barrett Gavin (ed), *Justice Cooperation in the European Union* (Institute of European Affairs 1997), 3–48.

Basedow Jürgen, 'EC Regulations in European Private Law' in Basedow Jürgen, Meier Isaak, Girsberger Daniel, Einhorn Talia and Schnyder Anton K (eds), *Private Law in the International Arena: from National Conflict Rules Towards Harmonization and Unification. Liber Amicorum Kurt Siehr* (T.M.C. Asser Press 2000), 17–33.

Besso Chiara and Lupano Matteo, 'Atti processuali. Disposizioni generali Art. 121–162' in Chiarloni Sergio (ed), *Commentario Codice di Procedura Civile* (Zanichelli 2016), 608–644.

Biavati Paolo, 'Is Flexibility a Way to the Harmonization of Civil Procedural Law in Europe?' in Carpi Federico and Lupoi Michele Angelo (eds), *Essays on Transnational and Comparative Civil Procedure* (Giappichelli Editore 2001), 85–105.

Biavati Paolo, 'L'Organizzazione della Giustizia Civile' in Biavati Paolo, Guarnieri Carlo, Orlandi Renzo and Zanon Nicolò (eds), *La Giustizia Civile e Penale in Italia* (Il Mulino 2008), 137–196.

Biavati Paolo, 'L'Incidenza del Diritto dell'Unione Europea sul Diritto Processuale Civile' in Rossi Lucia Serena and Di Federico Giacomo (eds), *L'Incidenza del Diritto dell'Unione Europea sullo Studio delle Discipline Giuridiche* (Editoriale Scientifca 2008), 325–338.

Biavati Paolo, 'Gli Obblighi dello Stato Membro verso l'Unione Europea nella Cooperazione Giudiziaria Civile', in Perlingieri Pietro and Ruggeri Lucia (eds), *Diritto Privato Comunitario* (Edizioni Scientifiche Italiane 2008), 363–375.

Biavati Paolo, 'Some Remarks about the European Regulation Creating an Enforcement Order for Uncontested Claims' in National and Kapodistrian University of Athens (eds), *Essays in Honour of Konstantinos Kerameus* (Bruylant 2009), 75–90.

Biavati Paolo, 'Il Regolamento (CE) n. 1896/2006 del Parlamento Europeo e del Consiglio del 12 dicembre 2006, che Istituisce un Procedimento Europeo d'Ingiunzione di Pagamento' in Taruffo Michele e Varano Vincenzo (eds), *Manuale di Diritto Processuale Civile Europeo* (Giappichelli Editore 2011), 311–336.

Biavati Paolo, 'L'Esecutorietà delle Decisioni nell'Unione Europea alla Luce del Reg. UE n. 1215/2012' in Tiscini, Roberta Capponi Bruno, Sassani Bruno, Storto Alfredo (eds), *Il Processo Esecutivo (Liber Amicorum Romano Vaccarella)* (UTET Giuridica 2014), 189–196.

Bolzanas Darius, Tamošiuniene Egidija, Vasariene Dalia and Jokubauskas Remigijus, 'Certification of Enforceability in Member State of Origin: Service of Certificate' in Rijavec Vesna, Kennett Wendy, Keresteš Tomaž and Ivanc Tjaša (eds), *Remedies Concerning Enforcement of Foreign Judgments Brussels I Recast* (Wolters Kluwer 2018), 113–130.

Bonomi Andrea, 'Il Diritto Internazionale Privato dell'Unione Europea: Considerazioni Generali' in Bonomi Andrea (ed), *Diritto Internazionale Privato e Cooperazione Giudiziaria in Materia Civile* (Giappichelli Editore 2009), 1–51.

Borselli Edgardo, 'Inibitoria (Dir. Proc. Civ.)' in Azara Antonio e Eula Ernesto (eds), *Novissimo Digesto Italiano*, vol 19 (UTET Giuridica 1973), 701–702.

Caponi Remo, 'Transnational Litigation and Elements of Fair Trial' in Gottwald Peter and Hess Burkhard (eds), *Procedural Justice* (Gieseking 2014), 493–536.

Caponi Remo, 'Harmonizing Civil Procedure: Initial Remarks' in Hess Burkhard and Kramer Xandra (eds), *From Common Rules to Best Practices in European Civil Procedure* (Nomos-Hart Publishing 2017), 43–62.

Carpi Federico, 'Dal Riconoscimento delle Decisioni all'Esecuzione Automatica' in Colesanti Vittorio and Attardi Aldo (eds), *Il Diritto Processuale Civile nell'Avvicinamento Giuridico Internazionale: Omaggio ad Aldo Attardi*, vol 2 (CLEUP 2009), 701–724.

Chiapponi Giovanni, 'Time Limits to React under the Brussels Ibis and EEO Regulations: Need for Harmonisation?' in Ligeti Katalin and Kei Hannah Brodersen (eds), *Studies on Enforcement in Multi-Regulatory Systems* (Nomos 2022), 143–163.

Chiapponi Giovanni, 'Art. 39' in Requejo Isidro Marta (ed), *Brussels I Bis. A Commentary on Regulation (EU) No 1215/2012* (Edward Elgar Publishing 2022), 577–586.

Chiapponi Giovanni, 'Art. 41' in Requejo Isidro Marta (ed), *Brussels I Bis. A Commentary on Regulation (EU) No 1215/2012* (Edward Elgar Publishing 2022), 596–606.

Chiapponi Giovanni, 'Art. 43' in Requejo Isidro Marta (ed), *Brussels I Bis. A Commentary on Regulation (EU) No 1215/2012* (Edward Elgar Publishing 2022), 617–627.

Chynoweth Paul, 'Legal Research', in Knight Andrew, Ruddock Les (eds), *Advanced Research Methods in the Built Environment* (Wiley-Blackwell 2008), 28–39.

Costa Sergio, 'Termini' in Azara Antonio e Eula Ernesto (eds), *Novissimo Digesto Italiano,* vol 19 (UTET Giuridica 1973), 117–121.

Crifo Carla, 'Trusted with a Muzzle and Enfranchised with a Clog: The British Approach to European Civil Procedure' in Hess Burkhard, Bergström Maria and Storskrubb Eva (eds), *EU Civil Justice Current Issues and Future Outlook* (Bloomsbury 2016), 81–97.

Cuniberti Gilles, 'The Promotion of Best Practices in European Civil Procedure: Some Introductory Remarks' in Hess Burkhard and Kramer Xandra (eds), *From Common Rules to Best Practices in European Civil Procedure* (Nomos-Hart Publishing 2017), 439–450.

Cuniberti Gilles, 'Making Cross-Border Enforcement More Effective for Creditors' in Von Hein Jan and Kruger Thalia (eds), *Informed Choices in Cross-Border Enforcement. The European State of the Art and Future Perspectives* (Intersentia 2021), 413–426.

Cuniberti Gilles, 'Art. 41' in Magnus Ulrich and Mankowski Peter (eds), *Commentary Brussels I bis Regulation* (2nd edn, Ottoschmidt 2023), 824–827.

Cuniberti Gilles, 'Art. 43' in Magnus Ulrich and Mankowski Peter (eds), *Commentary Brussels I bis Regulation* (2nd edn, Ottoschmidt 2023), 835–838.

Cuniberti Gilles and Rueda Isabelle, 'Art. 41' in Magnus Ulrich and Mankowski Peter (eds), *Commentary Brussels I bis Regulation* (1st edn, Ottoschmidt 2016), 845–849.

Cuniberti Gilles and Rueda Isabelle, 'Art. 43' in Magnus Ulrich and Mankowski Peter (eds), *Commentary Brussels I bis Regulation* (1st edn, Ottoschmidt 2016), 857–859.

D'Alessandro Elena, 'L'Armonia tra Decisioni nello Spazio Giudiziario Europeo nel Sistema del Regolamento UE n. 1215/2012', in Biagioni Giacomo (ed), *Il Principio dell'Armonia delle Decisioni Civili e Commerciali nello Spazio Giudiziario Europeo*, (Giappichelli Editore 2016), 145–160.

D'Alessandro Elena, 'Italy: European Small Claim Procedure' in Von Hein Jan and Kruger Thalia (eds), *Informed Choices in Cross-Border Enforcement. The European State of the Art and Future Perspectives* (Intersentia 2021), 262–265.

D'Alessandro Elena, 'I Mezzi di Ricorso e la Protezione dei Terzi' in Franzina Pietro and Leandro Antonio (eds), *Il Sequestro Europeo di Conti Bancari* (Giuffrè Editore 2015), 87–118.

D'Alessandro Elena, 'Art. 22' in D'Alessandro Elena and Gascón Inchausti Fernando (eds), *Commentary of Regulation No 655/2014* (Edward Elgar Publishing 2022), 218–223.

D'Alessandro Elena, 'Art. 23' in D'Alessandro Elena and Gascón Inchausti Fernando (eds), *Commentary of Regulation No 655/2014* (Edward Elgar Publishing 2022), 224–229.

D'Alessandro Elena, 'Art. 46' in D'Alessandro Elena and Gascón Inchausti Fernando (eds), *Commentary of Regulation No 655/2014* (Edward Elgar Publishing 2022), 381–384.

D'Alessandro Elena and Sandrini Lidia, *Italy: European Account Preservation Order* in Von Hein Jan and Kruger Thalia (eds), *Informed Choices in Cross-Border Enforcement. The European State of the Art and Future Perspectives* (Intersentia 2021), 265–271.

Dalla Bontà Silvana, 'Art. 36' in D'Alessandro Elena and Gascón Inchausti Fernando (eds), *Commentary of Regulation No 655/2014* (Edward Elgar Publishing 2022), 317–328.

Dalla Bontà Silvana, 'Art. 37' in D'Alessandro Elena and Gascón Inchausti Fernando (eds), *Commentary of Regulation No 655/2014* (Edward Elgar Publishing 2022), 329–336.

De Cristofaro Marco, 'Ordine pubblico "Processuale" ed Enucleazione dei Principi Fondamentali del Diritto Processuale "Europeo"' in Colesanti Vittorio and Attardi Aldo (eds), *Il Diritto Processuale Civile nell'Avvicinamento Giuridico Internazionale: Omaggio ad Aldo Attardi*, vol 2 (CLEUP 2009), 893–976.

Delabruyère Sophie, 'On "Legal Choice" and Legal Competition in a Federal System of Justice: Lessons for European Legal Integration' in Marciano Alain and Josselin Jean-Michel (eds), *From Economic to Legal Competition. New Perspectives on Law and Institutions in Europe* (Edward Elgar Publishing 2003), 19–43.

Di Marzio Mauro, 'La Disciplina dei Termini in Matteini Chiari Sergio and Di Marzio Mauro (eds), *Le Notificazioni e i Termini nel Processo Civile* (Giuffrè Editore 2019), 61–101.

Esders Elke, 'The European Parliament's Committee on Civil Liberties and Internal Affairs – the Committee Responsible for Justice and Home Affairs', in Bieber Roland and Monar Jörg (eds), *Justice and Home Affairs in the European Union: The Development of the Third Pillar* (European Interuniversity Press 1995), 259–275.

Ferrand Frédérique, 'Injonction de Payer Européenne' in Guinchard Serge (ed), *Droit et Pratique de la Procedure Civile* (10th edn, Dalloz 2021), 1406–1426.

Ferrand Frédérique, 'Procédure Européenne de Règlement des Petits Litiges' in Guinchard Serge (ed), *Droit et Pratique de la Procedure Civile* (10th edn, Dalloz 2021), 1427–1448.

Fitchen Jonathan, 'Art. 45'. in Dickinson Andrew and Lein Eva (eds), *The Brussels I Regulation Recast* (Oxford University Press 2015), 432–480.

Fortescue John Adrian, 'First Experiences with the Implementation of Third Pillar Provisions' in Bieber Roland and Monar Jörg (eds), *Justice and Home Affairs in the European Union: The Development of the Third Pillar* (European Interuniversity Press 1995), 19–28.

Francq Stéphanie, 'Art. 45' in Magnus Ulrich and Mankowski Peter (eds), *Commentary Brussels I bis Regulation* (1st edn, Ottoschmidt 2016), 863–926.

Frignani Aldo, 'Inibitoria (Azione)' in Calasso Francesco, Mortati Costantino, Pugliatti Salvatore, Santoro-Passarelli Francesco, Talamanca Mario and Falzea Angelo (eds), *Enciclopedia del Diritto*, vol 19 (Giuffrè Editore 1971), 559–580

Gascón Inchausti Fernando, 'La Reconnaissance et l'Exécution des Décisions dans le Règlement Bruxelles I bis' in Guinchard Emmanuel (ed), *Le Nouveau Règlement Bruxelles I bis Règlement n°1215/2012 du 12 Décembre 2012 Concernant la Compétence Judiciaire, la Reconnaissance et l'Exécution des Décisions en Matière Civile et Commerciale* (Bruylant 2014), 205–247.

Gascón Inchausti Fernando and Hess Burkhard, 'Introduction' in Gascón Inchausti Fernando and Hess Burkhard (eds), *The Future of the European Law of Civil Procedure: Coordination or Harmonisation?* (Intersentia 2020), 1–9.

Gascón Inchausti Fernando, 'Have the EU Regulations on Judicial Cooperation Fostered Harmonization of National Procedures' in Gascón Inchausti Fernando and Hess Burkhard (eds), *The Future of the European Law of Civil Procedure: Coordination or Harmonisation?* (Intersentia 2020), 91–108.

Gascón Inchausti Fernando, 'Ensuring Adequate Protection in Cross-Border Enforcement for Debtors' in Von Hein Jan and Kruger Thalia (eds), *Informed Choices in Cross-Border Enforcement. The European State of the Art and Future Perspectives* (Intersentia 2021), 429–455.

Gascón Inchausti Fernando and Requejo Isidro Marta, 'A Classic Cross-border Case: the Usual Situation in the First Instance' in Hess Burkhard and Ortolani Pietro (eds), *Impediments of National Procedural Law to the Free movement of Judgments* (Beck-Hart-Nomos, 2019), 5–88.

Gascón Inchausti Fernando. 'Art. 10' in D'Alessandro Elena and Gascón Inchausti Fernando (eds), *Commentary of Regulation No 655/2014* (Edward Elgar Publishing 2022), 99–110.

Gascón Inchausti Fernando. 'Art. 28' in D'Alessandro Elena and Gascón Inchausti Fernando (eds), *Commentary of Regulation No 655/2014* (Edward Elgar Publishing 2022), 263–271.

Giussani Andrea, 'Il Regolamento (CE) n. 44/2001 del Consiglio, del 22 Dicembre 2000, Concernente la Competenza Giurisdizionale, il Riconoscimento e l'Esecuzione delle Decisioni in Materia Civile e Commerciale. Riconoscimento ed Esecuzione" in Taruffo Michele e Varano Vincenzo (eds), *Manuale di Diritto Processuale Civile Europeo* (Giappichelli Editore 2011), 77–105.

Giussani Andrea, 'Remedies' in Rijavec Vesna, Kennett Wendy, Keresteš Tomaž, Ivanc Tjaša (eds), *Remedies Concerning Enforcement of Foreign Judgments Brussels I Recast* (Wolters Kluwer 2018), 179–194.

Grossi Dante, 'Termine (Diritto Procesuale Civile)' in Calasso Francesco, Mortati Costantino, Pugliatti Salvatore, Santoro-Passarelli Francesco, Talamanca Mario and Falzea Angelo (eds), *Enciclopedia del Diritto*, vol 44 (Giuffrè Editore 1992), 234–252.

Hailbronner Kay, 'Migration Law and Policy within the Third Pillar of the Union Treaty' in Bieber Roland and Monar Jörg (eds), *Justice and Home Affairs in the European Union: The Development of the Third Pillar* (European Interuniversity Press 1995), 95–126.

Hau Wolfgang, 'Europeanisation of Civil Procedure: Overcoming Follow-up Fragmentation through Bottom-up Harmonisation' in Nylund Anna and Strandberg Magne (eds), *Civil Procedure and Harmonisation of Law* (Intersentia 2019), 61–76.

Hau Wolfgang, 'The Dialogue on the European Law of Civil Procedure' in Hess Burkhard and Lenaerts Koen (eds), *The 50th Anniversary of the European Law of Civil Procedure* (Nomos 2020), 161–174

Hess Burkhard, 'Procedural Harmonization in a European Context' in Kramer Xandra and Van Rhee Remco (eds), *Civil Litigation in Globalising World* (Springer 2012), 159–173.

Hess Burkhard, 'The State of the Justice Union' in Hess Burkhard, Bergström Maria and Storskrubb Eva (eds), *EU Civil Justice Current Issues and Future Outlook* (Bloomsbury 2016), 1–22.

Hess Burkhard and Kramer Xandra, 'From Common Rules to Best Practices in European Civil Procedure: an Introduction' in Hess Burkhard and Kramer Xandra (eds), *From Common Rules to Best Practices in European Civil Procedure* (Nomos-Hart Publishing 2017), 9–30.

Hess Burkhard, 'Seminal Judgments (les Grands Arrets) in the Case Law of the European Court of Justice' in Hess Burkhard and Lenaerts Koen (eds), *The 50th Anniversary of the European Law of Civil Procedure* (Nomos-Hart Publishing 2020), 11–46

Hess Burkhard, 'Towards a More Coherent EU Framework for the Cross-Border Enforcement of Civil Claims' in Von Hein Jan and Kruger Thalia (eds), *Informed Choices in Cross-Border Enforcement. The European State of the Art and Future Perspectives* (Intersentia 2021), 389–412.

Hess Burkhard and Raffelsieper Katharina, 'Eckpunkte der Kontenpfändungsverordnung' in Hess Burkhard (ed), *Die Anerkennung im Internationalen Zivilprozessrecht: Europäisches Vollstreckungsrecht* (Gieseking 2014), 214–222

Hutchinson Terry, 'Doctrinal Research: Researching the Jury' in Watkins Dawn and Burton Mandy (eds), *Research Methods in Law* (Routledge Taylor and Francis Group 2013), 7–34.

Johnsen Jon, 'Vulnerable Groups at the Legal Service Market' in Uzelac Alan and Van Rhee Remco (eds), *Access to Justice and the judiciary: Towards New European Standards of Affordability, Quality and Efficiency of Civil Adjudication* (Intersentia 2009), 31–43.

Kennet Wendy, 'Different National Enforcement Structures and their Consequences for Cross-Border Enforcement' in Rijavec Vesna, Kennett Wendy, Keresteš Tomaž, Ivanc Tjaša (eds), *Remedies Concerning Enforcement of Foreign Judgments Brussels I Recast* (Wolters Kluwer 2018), 301–358.

Kerameus Konstantinos, 'Relevance and Computation of Time in Civil Procedure' in Matscher Franz, Ballon Oskar, Josef Hagen Johann (eds), *Verfahrensgarantien im Nationalen und Internationalen Prozessrecht: Festschrift Franz Matscher* (Manzsche Verlags- und Universitätsbuchhandlung 1993), 241–250.

Kern Cristoph and Weitz Karol, 'Appeal and Third Instance' in Hess Burkhard and Ortolani Pietro (eds), *Impediments of National Procedural Law to the Free Movement of Judgments* (Beck-Hart-Nomos 2019), 163–205.

Kessedjian Catherine, 'L'Avenir de la Coopération Judiciaire Transfrontière' in Menetrey Séverine and Hess Burkhard (eds), *Les Dialogues des Juges en Europe* (Larcier 2014), 349–359.

Kramer Xandra, 'Article 41' in Dickinson Andrew and Lein Eva (eds), *The Brussels I Regulation Recast* (Oxford University Press 2015), 415–421.

Kramer Xandra, 'Art. 43'. in Dickinson Andrew and Lein Eva (eds), *The Brussels I Regulation Recast* (Oxford University Press 2015), 425–429.

Kramer Xandra, 'Judicial Cooperation in Civil Matters' in Kuijper Pieter Jan, Amtenbrink Fabian, Curtin Deirdre, De Witte Bruno, McDonnell Alison and Van den Bogaert Stefaan (eds), *The Law of the European Union* (Kluwer Law International 2018), 673–691.

Kramer Xandra, 'Specific Instruments' in Hess Burkhard and Ortolani Pietro (eds), *Impediments of National Procedural Law to the Free movement of Judgments* (Beck-Hart-Nomos 2019), 207–240.

Kramer Xandra, 'Strengthening Civil Justice Cooperation: the Quest for Model Rules and Common Minimum Standards of Civil Procedure in Europe' in Rodrigues Marco Antonio and Zaneti Jr Hermes (eds), *Coleção Grandes Temas do Novo CPC – v.13 – Cooperação Internacional* (Editora Juspodivm 2019), 591–607.

Kramer Xandra and Hoevenaars Jos, 'European Civil Procedure and the Dialogue between National Courts and the European Court of Justice', in Hess Burkhard and Lenaerts Koen (eds), *The 50th Anniversary of the European Law of Civil Procedure* (Nomos-Hart Publishing 2020), 175–202.

Kruger Thalia and Van Overbeeke Fieke, 'European Enforcement Order' in Von Hein Jan and Kruger Thalia (eds), *Informed Choices in Cross-Border Enforcement. The European State of the Art and Future Perspectives* (Intersentia 2021), 51–63.

Leandro Antonio, 'La Circolazione dell'Ordinanza Europea di Sequestro Conservative dei Conti Bancari' in Franzina Pietro and Leandro Antonio (eds), *Il Sequestro Europeo di Conti Bancari* (Giuffrè Editore 2015), 119–145.

Linton Marie, 'Abolition of Exequatur, All in the Name of Mutual Trust!' in Hess Burkhard, Bergström Maria and Storskrubb Eva (eds), *EU Civil Justice Current Issues and Future Outlook* (Bloomsbury 2016), 257–282.

Lugani Katharina, 'Art. 25' in D'Alessandro Elena and Gascón Inchausti Fernando (eds), *Commentary of Regulation No 655/2014* (Edward Elgar Publishing 2022), 243–248.

Lupoi Michele Angelo, 'The Harmonization of Civil Procedural Law within the EU' in Frosini Orlando, Lupoi Michele Angelo and Marchesiello Michele (eds), *A European Space of Justice* (Longo 2006), 201–228.

Lupoi Michele Angelo, 'Regolamento (UE) n. 1215/2012 del Parlamento e del Consiglio del 12 dicembre 2012 Concernente la Competenza Giurisdizionale, il Riconoscimento e l'Esecuzione delle Decisioni in Materia Civile e Commerciale' in Carpi Federico and Taruffo Michele (eds), *Commentario Breve al Codice di Procedura Civile. Ultimissime sul processo civile* (Cedam 2013), 137–177.

Lupoi Michele Angelo, 'L'Attuazione negli Altri Stati Membri dei Provvedimenti Provvisori e Cautelari nel Reg. UE 1215/2012 (Bruxelles I *bis*)' in Tiscini Roberta, Capponi Bruno, Sassani Bruno, Storto Alfredo (eds), *Il Processo Esecutivo (Liber Amicorum Romano Vaccarella)* (UTET Giuridica 2014), 1517–1547.

Lupoi Michele Angelo, 'Prefazione' in Lupoi Michele Angelo (ed), *Il Tempo nel Diritto, il Diritto nel Tempo* (Bonomo Editore 2020), 7–9

Lupoi Michele Angelo, 'Competenza Giurisdizionale, Riconoscimento ed Esecuzione delle Decisioni in Materia Civile e Commerciale: il Regolamento n. 1215 del 2012" in Biavati Paolo and Lupoi Michele Angelo (eds), *Regole Europee e Giustizia Civile* (4th edn, Bologna University Press 2022), 23–97.

Malatesta Alberto and Nisi Nicolò, 'Le Novità in Materia di Riconoscimento ed Esecuzione delle Decisioni' in Malatesta Alberto (ed), *La Riforma del Regolamento di Bruxelles I. Il Regolamento (UE) n. 1215/2012 sulla Giurisdizione e l'Efficacia delle Decisioni in Materia Civile e Commerciale* (Giuffrè Editore 2016), 135–162.

Mankowski Peter, 'Art. 45' in Magnus Ulrich and Mankowski Peter (eds), *Commentary Brussels I bis Regulation* (2nd edn, Ottoschmidt 2023), 842–918.

Marinelli Marino, '"Note sul Regolamento CE n. 1896/2006" in Tema di Procedimento Ingiuntivo Europeo' in Colesanti Vittorio and Attardi Aldo, *Il Diritto Processuale Civile nell'Avvicinamento Giuridico Internazionale: Omaggio ad Aldo Attardi*, vol 1 (CLEUP 2009), 579–606.

Matteini Chiari Sergio, 'Termini per Impugnare' in Matteini Chiari Sergio and Di Marzio Mauro (eds), *Le Notificazioni e i Termini nel Processo Civile* (Giuffrè Editore 2019), 473–538.

Melin François, 'Procédure Écrite et Procédures Spécifiques Devant le Tribunal Judciaire' in Guinchard Serge (ed), *Droit et Pratique de la Procédure Civile: Droit Interne et Européen* (10th edn, Dalloz 2019), 1270–1328.

Menetrey Séverine, 'La "Communication des Juges" en Droit Judiciaire Européen' in Monjal Pierre-Yves, Jan Pascal et Geslot Christophe, *La Concurrence des Juges en Europe: le Dialogue des Juges en Question(s)* (Clément Juglar Éditions juridiques et économiques 2018), 95–103.

Moccia Luigi, 'European Law: from "Market" to "Citizenship" in Moccia Luigi (ed), *The Making of European Private Law: Why, How, What, Who* (Sellier European Law Publishers 2017), 47–65.

Monar Jörg, 'Democratic Control of Justice and Home Affairs: the European Parliament and the National Parliaments', in Bieber Roland and Monar Jörg (eds), *Justice and Home Affairs in the European Union: The Development of the Third Pillar* (European Interuniversity Press 1995), 243 -258.

Monar Jörg, 'The Evolving Role of the Union Institutions in the Framework of the Third Pillar' in Roland Bieber and Monar Jörg (eds), *Justice and Home Affairs in the European Union: The Development of the Third Pillar* (European Interuniversity Press 1995), 75- 80.

Monar Jörg, 'European Union – Justice and Home Affairs: a Balance Sheet and an Agenda for Reform' in Edwards Geoffrey, Pjpers Alfred (eds), *The Politics of European Treaty Reform. The 1996 Intergovernmental Conference and Beyond* (Pinter 1997), 328–331

Muller-Graff Peter-Christian, 'The Legal Bases of the Third Pillar and its Position in the Framework of the Union Treaty' in Morgan Roger and Monar Jörg (eds), *The Third Pillar of the European Union: Cooperation in the Fields of Justice and Home Affairs* (European Interuniversity Press 1995), 21–37.

Nappi Giambattista, 'Dell'Introduzione della Causa' in Nappi Giambattista (ed), *Commentario al Codice di Procedura Civile*, vol 2 (Società Editrice Libraria 1942), 35–54.

Neuwahl Nanette, 'Judicial Control in Matters of Justice and Home Affairs: what Role for the Court of Justice?' in Bieber Roland and Monar Jörg (eds), *Justice and Home Affairs in the European Union: The Development of the Third Pillar* (European Interuniversity Press 1995), 301–320.

Nylund Anna and Strandberg Magne. 'Conclusions on Civil Procedure and Harmonisation of Law' in Nylund Anna and Strandberg Magne (eds), *Civil Procedure and Harmonisation of Law* (Intersentia 2019), 231–241.

Nowak Janek and Richard Vincent, 'Art. 45' in Requejo Isidro Marta (ed), *Brussels I Bis. A Commentary on Regulation (EU) No 1215/2012* (Edward Elgar Publishing 2022), 638–678.

O'Keefe James, 'A Critical View of the Third Pillar', in Pauly Alexis (ed), *De Schengen à Maastricht: Voie Royale et Course d'Obstacles* (European Institute of Public Administration 1996), 1–16.

Olivieri Giuseppe, II Titolo Esecutivo Europeo. Qualche Considerazione sul Regolamento CE n. 805/2004 del 21 Aprile 2001' in Colesanti Vittorio and Attardi Aldo (eds), *Il Diritto Processuale Civile nell'Avvicinamento Giuridico Internazionale: Omaggio ad Aldo Attardi*, vol 2 (CLEUP 2009), 725–747.

Ontanu Elena Alina, 'Art. 24' in D'Alessandro Elena and Gascón Inchausti Fernando (eds), *Commentary of Regulation No 655/2014* (Edward Elgar Publishing 2022), 228–242.

Oro Martinez Cristian, 'The Small Claims Regulation: on the Way to an Improved European Procedure' in Hess Burkhard, Bergström Maria and Storskrubb Eva (eds), *EU Civil Justice Current Issues and Future Outlook* (Bloomsbury 2016), 123–142.

Pataut Etienne, 'Notifications Internationales et Règlement Bruxelles I' in Azzi Tristan and Gaudemet Tallon Hélène (eds), *Vers de Nouveaux Équilibres entre Ordres Juridiques: Liber Amicorum Hélène Gaudemet-Tallon* (Dalloz, 2008), 377–395.

Payan Guillaume, 'Art. 18' in D'Alessandro Elena and Gascón Inchausti Fernando (eds), *Commentary of Regulation No 655/2014* (Edward Elgar Publishing 2022), 99–110.

Peers Steve, 'Civil Cooperation' in Peers Steve (ed), *EU Justice and Home Affairs Law – EU Criminal Law, Policing, and Civil Law,* vol 2 (Oxford University Press 2016), 338–394.

Picardi Nicola, 'Art. 152' in Allorio Enrico (ed), *Commentario del Codice di Procedura Civile*, vol 1 book 2 (2nd edn, UTET Giuridica 1973), 1532–1575.

Picardi Nicola and Martino Roberto, 'Termini' in *Enciclopedia Giuridica Treccani*, vol 31 (Giuffrè Editore 1994).

Pipkorn Jörn, 'Les Méthodes de Rapprochement des Législations à l'Intérieur de la CEE', in Bourel Pierre, Drobnig Ulrich and Droz Georges (eds), *L'Influence des Communautés Européennes sur le Droit International Privé des États Membres* (Larcier 1981), 13–48.

Pocar Fausto, 'The Brussels Convention: 50 Years of Contribution to European Integration' in Hess Burkhard and Lenaerts Koen (eds), *The 50th Anniversary of the European Law of Civil Procedure* (Nomos-Hart Publishing 2020), 248–258.

Redenti Enrico, 'Atti Processuali Civili' in Calasso Francesco, Mortati Costantino, Pugliatti Salvatore, Santoro-Passarelli Francesco, Talamanca Mario and Falzea Angelo (eds), *Enciclopedia del Diritto*, vol 4 (Giuffrè Editore 1959), 105–140.

Requejo Isidro Marta, 'On the Abolition of Exequatur' in Hess Burkhard, Bergström Maria and Storskrubb Eva (eds), *EU Civil Justice Current Issues and Future Outlook* (Bloomsbury 2016), 283–299.

Requejo Isidro Marta, 'The Enforcement of Monetary Final Judgments under the Brussels Ibis Regulation (A Critical Assessment)', in Lazić Vesna and Stuij Steven (eds), *Brussels Ibis Regulation Changes and Challenges of the Renewed Procedural Scheme* (Springer 2017), 71–97.

Requejo Isidro Marta, 'Do We Need Harmonisation to Achieve Harmonious Cooperation?' in Hess Burkhard and Kramer Xandra (eds), *From Common Rules to Best Practices in European Civil Procedure* (Nomos-Hart Publishing 2017), 77–118.

Rijavec Vesna, 'Final Assessment of Brussels I Recast', in Rijavec Vesna, Kennett Wendy, Keresteš Tomaž, Ivanc Tjaša (eds), *Remedies Concerning Enforcement of Foreign Judgments Brussels I Recast* (Wolters Kluwer 2018), 359–422.

Rouchaud Anne-Marie, 'Le Renforcement de la Coopération Judiciaire' in Storme Marcel (ed), *Approximation of Judiciary Law in the European Union* (Maklu 2003.), 449–460.

Scholz Florian, Auernig Katharina, Schumann Julius, Oberhammer Paul, 'Default Procedures and Judgments in Cross-border Settings' in Hess Burkhard and Ortolani Pietro (eds), *Impediments of National Procedural Law to the Free movement of Judgments* (Beck-Hart-Nomos 2019), 89–130.

Storme Marcel, 'Closing Comments: Harmonisation or Globalisation of Civil Procedure' in Kramer Xandra and Van Rhee Remco (eds), *Civil Litigation in Globalising World* (Springer 2012), 379–387.

Storme Marcel, 'Approximation of Procedural Law in Europe' in Hess Burkhard and Kramer Xandra (eds), *From Common Rules to Best Practices in European Civil Procedure* (Nomos-Hart Publishing 2017), 481–484.

Storskrubb Eva, 'Civil Justice: Constitutional and Regulatory Issues Revisited' in Fletcher Maria, Herlin-Karnell Ester and Matera Claudio (eds), *The European Union as an Area of Freedom, Security and Justice* (Routledge 2017), 303–336.

Storskrubb Eva, 'EU Civil Justice at the Harmonisation Crossroads?' in Nylund Anna and Strandberg Magne (eds), *Civil Procedure and Harmonisation of Law (Intersentia 2019), 11–28*

Storskrubb Eva, 'Civil Justice Extending its Tentacles' in Craig Paul and De Búrca Gráinne (eds), *The Evolution of EU Law* (3rd edn, Oxford University Press 2021), 770–792.

Taruffo Michele, 'Harmonisation in a Global Context: the Ali/UNIDROIT Principles' in Kramer Xandra and Van Rhee Remco (eds), *Civil Litigation in a Globalising World* (Asser 2012), 207–222.

Tarzia Giuseppe, 'L'Ordine Europeo del Processo Civile' in Colesanti Vittorio and Attardi Aldo (eds), *Il Diritto Processuale Civile nell'Avvicinamento Giuridico Internazionale: Omaggio ad Aldo Attardi*, vol 1 (CLEUP 2009), 65–104.

Toader Camelia, 'La Confiance Mutuelle, Fondement et Temoignage de la Valeur de l'Union Europeenne' in Hess Burkhard and Lenaerts Koen (eds), *The 50th Anniversary of the European Law of Civil Procedure* (Nomos-Hart Publishing 2020), 47–58.

Ulrici Bernhard, 'Art. 20 EG-MahnVO' in Krüger Wolfgang and Rauscher Thomas (eds), *Münchener Kommentar zur Zivilprozessordnung: mit Gerichtsverfassungsgesetz und Nebengesetzen*, vol 3 (5th edn, C.H. Beck 2022), 18–19.

Vallines Garcia Enrique, 'Art. 21' in D'Alessandro Elena and Gascón Inchausti Fernando (eds), *Commentary of Regulation No 655/2014* (Edward Elgar Publishing 2022), 204–214.

Vallines Garcia Enrique, 'Art. 53' in Requejo Isidro Marta (ed), *Brussels I Bis. A Commentary on Regulation (EU) No 1215/2012* (Edward Elgar Publishing 2022), 724–734.

Van Rhee Remco, 'Harmonization of Civil Procedure: An Historical and Comparative Perspective', in Kramer Xandra and Van Rhee Remco (eds), *Civil Litigation in Globalising World* (Springer 2012), 40–64.

Villamarín López María Luisa, 'Art. 33' in D'Alessandro Elena and Gascón Inchausti Fernando (eds), *Commentary of Regulation No 655/2014* (Edward Elgar Publishing 2022), 297–305.

Villamarín López María Luisa, 'Art. 34' in D'Alessandro Elena and Gascón Inchausti Fernando (eds), *Commentary of Regulation No 655/2014* (Edward Elgar Publishing 2022), 306–313.

Vincke Francois, 'Les Enterprises Europeennes Ont Besoin de Rapprochement' in Storme Marcel (ed), *Procedural Laws in Europe. Towards Harmonisation* (Maklu 2003), 15–25.

Visscher Louis, 'A Law and Economics View on Harmonisation of Procedural Law' in Kramer Xandra and Van Rhee Remco (eds), *Civil Litigation in Globalising World* (Springer 2012), 65–92.

Von Hein Jan, 'EU Competence to Legislate in the Area of Private International Law and Law Reforms at the EU level' in Beaumont Paul, Danov Mihail, Trimmings Katarina and Yuksel Burku (eds), *Cross-Border Litigation in Europe* (Bloomsbury 2017), 19–35.

Wagner Gerhard, 'Harmonization of Civil Procedure: Policy Perspectives' in Kramer Xandra and Van Rhee Remco (eds), *Civil Litigation in Globalising World* (Springer 2012), 93–120.

III) Journal articles

Adam Roberto, 'La Cooperazione in Materia di Giustizia e Affari Interni tra Comunitarizzazione e Metodo Intergovernativo' (1994) Riv. dir. eu., 504–520.

Amato Francesco, 'Termine Breve di Impugnazione e Bilateralità della Notificazione della Sentenza nel Processo con Due Sole Parti' (1985) 40 Riv. dir. proc., 330–385.

Arenas García Rafael, 'Plazo para la Ejecución en un Estado Miembro de una Medida Cautelar Dictada en Otro Estado' (2018) 65 La Ley Unión Europea, 86–102.

Basedow Jürgen, 'The Communitarization of the Conflict of Laws under the Treaty of Amsterdam' (2000) 37 CMLR, 687–708.

Beaumont Paul and Johnston Emma, 'Abolition of the Exequatur in Brussels I: Is a Public Policy Defence Necessary for the Protection of Human Rights?' (2010) 30 IPRax, 105–110.

Beaumont Paul and Walker Lara, 'Recognition and Enforcement of Judgments in Civil and Commercial Matters in the Brussels I Recast and Some Lessons from it and the Recent Hague Conventions for the Hague Judgments Project' (2015) 11 JPIL, 31–63..

Beraudo Jean-Paul and Beraudo Marie-Josèphe, 'Convention de Bruxelles, Conventions de Lugano, Règlement (CE) No 44/2011, Règlement (UE) No 1215/2012 – Exécution des Décisions Judiciaires, des Actes Authentiques et des Transactions Judiciaires' (2020) Fasc. 633 J-CL Droit International.

Biagioni Giacomo, 'L'Abolizione dei Motivi Ostativi al Riconoscimento e all'Esecuzione nella Proposta di Revisione del Regolamento Bruxelles I' (2011) 47 RDIPP, 971–986.

Biavati Paolo, 'Diritto Comunitario e Diritto Processuale Civile Italiano fra Attrazione, Autonomia e Resistenze' (2000) 5 Il Diritto dell'Unione europea, 717–748.

Biavati Paolo, 'Gli Interventi Normativi dell'Unione Europea in Ambito Processuale e le Prospettive di un Diritto Processuale Comune Europeo' (2003) Bologna Forense, 21–27.

Biavati Paolo, 'Art. 1' in Biavati Paolo 'Reg. CE n. 1896/2006 del Parlamento europeo e del Consiglio che Istituisce un Procedimento Europeo d'Ingiunzione di Pagamento' (2010) 33 Le nuove leggi civili commentate, 387–394.

Biavati Paolo, 'Il Colloquio di Bruxelles del 26–27 Ottobre 2001 sull'Incontro dei Diritti Processuali Civili in Europa' (2002) 66 Riv. trim. dir. e proc. civ., 357–359.

Biavati Paolo, 'Il Futuro del Diritto Processuale di Origine Europea' (2010) 74 Riv. trim. dir. e proc. civ., 859–874.

Biavati Paolo, 'Judicial Cooperation in Europe: is Exequatur Still Necessary?' (2011) 1 IJPL, 403–431.

Biavati Paolo, 'Il Sequestro Conservativo Europeo su Conti Bancari: alla Ricerca di un Difficile Equilibrio (2015) 79 Riv. trim. dir. e proc. civ., 855–872.

Brunori Ernesto, 'Sulla Inibitoria' (1956) 11 Riv. dir. proc., 207–229.

Carpi Federico, 'L'Inibitoria Processuale' (1975) 29 Riv. trim. dir. e proc. civ., 93–187.

Cavallini Cesare, 'L'Efficacia della Sentenza Impugnata' (2015) 70 Riv. dir. proc., 339–352.

Cerino Canova Augusto, 'Sulla Soggezione del Notificante al Termine Breve di Gravame (1982) 37 Riv. dir. proc., 624–640.

Chalmers Damian, 'The Court of Justice and the Third Pillar' (2004) E.L. Rev., 773–774

Chiapponi Giovanni, 'Can Harmonized Time Limits in European Civil Procedure Enhance the Effectiveness and Enforcement of EU law?' (2020) 12 Cuad. der. trans., 543–548.

Chiapponi Giovanni, 'Time Limits and Default Judgments in European Cross-Border Civil Litigation: Minimum Standards?' (2020) 12 Cuad. der. trans., 971–978.

Consolo Claudio. 'Rigorismi Alterni e non Giustifcati in Tema di Opposizione all'Ingiunzione per Sanzioni Amministrative' in (1984) 39 Riv. dir. proc., 823–844.

Consolo Claudio, 'La Tutela Sommaria e la Convenzione di Bruxelles: la "Circolazione" Comunitaria dei Provvedimenti Cautelari e dei Decreti Ingiuntivi' (1991) 27 RDIPP, 593–628.

Colesanti Vittorio, 'Principio del Contraddittorio e Procedimenti Speciali' (1975) 30 Riv. dir. proc., 578–619.

Cuniberti Gilles and Rueda Isabelle, 'Abolition of the Exequatur. Addressing the Commission's Concerns' (2011) 75 Rabels Zeitschrift für ausländisches und internationales Privatrecht, 286–316.

Curtin Deirdre, 'The Constitutional Structure of the Union: a Europe of Bits and Pieces', (1993) 30 CMLR, 17–71.

De Burca Gráinne, 'The Quest for Legitimacy in the European Union' (1996) 59 MLR, 349–376.

De Miguel Asensio Pedro Alberto, 'La Evolución del Derecho Internacional Privado Comunitario en el Tratado de Ámsterdam' (1998) 58 REDI, 373–376.

D'Alessandro Elena, 'Prime Applicazioni Giurisprudenziali del Regolamento n. 805 del 21 Aprile 2004 che Istituisce il Titolo Esecutivo Europeo per i Crediti non Contestati, con Particolare Riferimento alla Possibilità di Proporre Opposizione ex Art. 615 c.p.c. Qualora lo Stato Richiesto dell'Esecuzione Sia l'Italia' (2010) 10 Riv. es. forz., 197–204.

D'Alessandro Elena, 'Irregolare Notifica del Decreto Ingiuntivo e Possibilità di Invocare, nello Stato Richiesto dell'Esecuzione, il Motivo di Diniego di Riconoscimento di cui all'Art. 34 n. 2 Reg. n. 44/2001: il Punto di Vista del Bundesgerichtshof Tedesco, Nota a BGH, Beschluss 21 Gennaio 2010 – IX ZB 193/07' (2010) 3/4 INT'L LIS, 141–146.

D'Alessandro Elena, 'Il Titolo Esecutivo Europeo nel Sistema del Regolamento n. 1215/2012' (2013) 68 Riv. dir. proc., 1044–1065.

D'Alessandro Elena, 'Il Procedimento Monitorio Europeo con Particolare Riferimento alla Fase di Opposizione ex Art. 17 Reg. n. 1896/2006' (2011) 6 Giusto proc. civ., 719–738.

D'Alessandro Elena, 'Titolo Esecutivo Europeo e Opposizione all'Esecuzione' (2016) 80 Riv. trim. e dir. proc.civ., 565–591.

D'Alessandro Elena, 'Opposizione all'Ingiunzione di Pagamento Europea e Modalità di Prosecuzione del Giudizio' (2020) GIur. it., 484–488.

De Cristofaro Marco, 'The Abolition of Exequatur Proceedings: Speeding up Free Movement of Judgments While Preserving the Rights of the Defense' (2011) 1 IJPL, 432–451.

Di Blase Antonietta, 'Esecuzione di Sentenze Straniere e Provvedimenti Provvisori in Base alla Convenzione di Bruxelles 27 Settembre 1968' (1986) 35 Giust. civ., 319–320.

Dickinson Andrew, 'Surveying the Proposed Brussels I *bis* Regulation: Solid Foundations but Renovation Needed' (2010) 12 Yb. PIL, 247–311.

D'Avout Louis, 'L'Efficacité Internationale des Jugements. Après la Refonte du Règlement Bruxelles I' (2015) 5 IJPL, 239–259.

Farina Marco, 'L'Ordinanza Europea di Sequestro Conservativo su Conti Bancari' (2015) Le nuove leggi civili commentate, 495–523.

Ferri Corrado, 'Effetti Dichiarativi e Costitutiivi Condizionati da Eventi Successivi alla sua Pronuncia (2007) 57 Riv. dir. proc., 1393–1408.

Fornaciari Michele, 'La Provvisoria Efficacia delle Sentenze di Accertamento e Costitutive' (2012) 7 Giusto proc. civ., 383.

Foussard Dominique, 'Délai d'Exécution d'une Ordonnance de Saisie Conservatoire Émise par un État Membre et Revêtue du Caractère Exécutoire sur le Territoire d'un Autre État Membre' (2019) 109 RCDIP, 160–177.

Ferrand Frédérique, 'Titre Exécutoire Européen' (2019) Répertoire de procédure civile, para 128.

Gascón Inchausti Fernando, 'Service of Proceedings on the Defendant as a Safeguard of Fairness in Civil Proceedings: in Search of Minimum Standards from EU Legislation and European Case-Law' (2017) 13 JPIL, 475–518.

Gaudemet-Tallon Hélène, 'Compétence Internationale: Matière Civile et Commerciale' (2019) Répertoire de droit international, para 20.

Gaudemet-Tallon Hélène and Kessedjian Catherine, 'La Refonte du Règlement Bruxelles I' (2013) 49 RTD eur., 435–454.

Giussani Andrea, 'Decreto Ingiuntivo non Opposto di Liquidazione di Misura Coercitiva Accessoria a Provvedimento Cautelare e Sospensione della sua Esecuzione ex Art. 23 Regolamento (CE) n. 805/2004' (2014) 14 Riv. es. forz., 85–95.

Giussani Andrea, 'A General Overview of Enforcement in Commercial and Civil Matters in Italy' (2016) 16 Riv. es. forz., 55–62.

Giussani Andrea, 'Grounds for Refusal of Recognition of Foreign Judgment: Developments and Perspectives in EU Member States on Public Order and Conflicting Decisions' (2018) 2 Judicium, 357–368.

Giussani Andrea, 'Controversie di Modesta Entità e Rifusione dei Compensi di Difesa nel Regolamento UE n. 2421/2015' (2020) 75 Riv. dir. proc., 690–697.

Goldman Berthold, 'Un Traité Fédérateur: La Convention entre États membres de la CEE sur la Reconnaissance et l'Exécution des Décisions en Matière Civile et Commerciale' (1971) 7 RTD eur, 1–39.

Guarnieri Guerino, 'Esecuzione di Sentenza Straniera e Sequestro Conservativo – Il Commento' *(1988) 5* Cor. giur., 38–40.

Hayo Berns and Voigt Stefan, 'The Relevance of Judicial Procedure for Economic Growth' (2008) Cesifo Working Paper, 1–36.

Hess Burkhard, 'The Brussels I Regulation: Recent Case Law of the Court of Justice and the Commission's Proposed Recast' (2012) 49 CMLR, 1075–1112.

Hess Burkhard, 'Reforming the Brussels Ibis Regulation: Perspectives and Prospects' (2021) 8 Max Planck Research Paper Series, 1–17.

Hess Burkhard and Raffelsieper Katharina, 'Shuldnerschutz bei Fehlender Zustellung eines EU-Mahnbescheids: Regelungslucken der EUMahnVO (2015) 35 IPRax, 401–403.

Hess Burkhard, Althoff David, Bens Tess, Elsner Niels, and Järvekülg Inga, 'The Reform of the Brussels Ibis Regulation' (2022) 9 Max Planck Research Paper Series, 1–35.

Hoscheit Thierry, 'La Transmission des Actes vers l'Étranger' (2013) 28 Journal des tribunaux (Luxembourg), 89–98.

Hovaguimian Philippe, 'The Enforcement of Foreign Judgments under Brussels I bis: False Alarms and Real Concerns (2015) 11 JPIL, 213–251.

Huet André, 'Compétence des Tribunaux Français à l'Égard des Litiges Internationaux, (2017) Fasc. 581-42 J-CL Droit international.

Hurka Steffen and Steinebach Yves, 'Legal Instrument Choice in the European Union' (2021) 59 JCMS, 278-296.

Kennet Wendy, 'Reviewing Service: Double Check or Double Fault' (1992) 11 C.J.Q., 115.

Kerameus Konstantinos, 'Procedural Harmonization in Europe' (1995) *Am. J. Comp. L.*, 401–416.

Kerameus Konstantinos, 'Political Integration and Procedural Convergence in the European Union' (1997) 45 (4) Am. J. Comp. L, 919–930.

Koechel Felix, 'Harmonisation and Unification of Civil Procedural Law: Prospects for Further Development' (2016) 6 IJPL 86–102.

Kohler Christian, 'Interrogations sur les Sources du Droit International Privé Européen après le Traité d'Amsterdam' (1999) 89 RCDIP, 191–217.

Kramer Xandra, 'The Rome II Regulation on the Law Applicable to Non-Contractual Obligations: The European Private International Law Tradition Continued' (2008) NIPR, 414–424.

Kramer Xandra, 'Abolition of Exequatur under the Brussels I Regulation: Effecting and Protecting Rights in the European Judicial Area' (2011) NIPR, 633–649.

Kramer Xandra, 'The Structure of Civil Proceedings and Why it Matters: Exploratory Observations on Future ELI-UNIDROIT European Rules of Civil Procedure' (2014) 19 Unif. L. Rev., 218–238.

Idot Laurence, 'Motifs de Refus de Reconnaissance' (2016) 10 Europe, 40–41.

Impagnatiello Gianpaolo, 'La Provvisoria Esecutorietà delle Sentenze Costitutive' (1992) 45 Riv. trim. dir. e proc. civ., 47–91.

Israel Jona, 'Conflict of Law and the EC after Amsterdam, A Change for the Worse?' (2000) 7 MJ, 81–99.

Leroy Etienne, 'L'Exequatur aux Confins de la Coopération Judiciaire Européenne et du Respect des Droits de l'Homme ou le Paradigme de l'Homme Avisé mais pas Informé' (2016) Ius & Actores, 439–453.

Lopez de Tejada Maria, 'Titre Exécutoire Européen. Règlement (CE) n. 805/2004 Portant Création d'un Titre Exécutoire Européen pour les Créances Incontestées' (2020) J-CL Europe Traité, para 39.

Lupoi Michele Angelo, 'Di Crediti non Contestati e Procedimenti di Ingiunzione: le Ultime Tappe dell'Armonizzazione Processuale in Europa' (2008) 71 Riv. trim. dir. e proc. civ., 171–206.

Lupoi Michele Angelo, 'Art. 18' in Biavati Paolo 'Reg. CE n. 1896/2006 del Parlamento Europeo e del Consiglio che Istituisce un Procedimento Europeo d'Ingiunzione di Pagamento' (2010) 33 Le nuove leggi civili commentate, 447–449.

Lupoi Michele Angelo, 'Art. 19' in Biavati Paolo 'Reg. CE n. 1896/2006 del Parlamento Europeo e del Consiglio che Istituisce un Procedimento Europeo d'Ingiunzione di Pagamento' (2010) 33 Le nuove leggi civili commentate, 449–450.

Lupoi Michele Angelo, 'Il Punto su: il Regolamento n. 44 del 2001 (Bruxelles I)' (2012) 65 Riv. trim. dir. e proc. civ., 1275–1296.

Lupoi Michele Angelo, 'La Circolazione delle Decisioni Giudiziarie nel Sistema del Regolamento Bruxelles I bis' (2019) Le Pagine de l'Aula Civile, 51–68.

Maccarone Rosario, 'Per un Profilo Strutturale dell'Inibitoria Processuale' (1981) 36 Riv. dir. proc., 274–329.

Menetrey Séverine and Richard Vincent, 'Le Silence dans le Procès International: Paroles de Droit Judiciaire Européen' (2016) 56 Les Cahiers de Droit, 491–524.

Moccia Luigi, 'Du "Marché" à la "Citoyenneté": à la Recherche d'un Droit Privé Européen Durable et de sa Base Juridique' (2004) 56 RIDC, 291–327.

Normand Jacques, 'Le Rapprochement des Procedures Civiles dans l'Union Europeenne' (1998) 6 Eur. Rev., 383- 390.

Nourissat Cyril, 'Reconnaissance et Exécution: la Cour de justice de l'Union Européenne Conforte sa Nouvelle Construction sur la Purge des Procédures dans l'État d'Origine' (2016) 12 Procédures, 24–25.

Nuyts Arnaud, 'La Refonte du Reglement Bruxelles I' (2013) 103 RCDIP, 1–65.

Pellerin Jaques, 'La Generalisation de l'Execution Provisoire de Droit' (2020) Gaz. Pal., 85.

Picardi Nicola, 'Per una Sistemazione dei Termini Processuali' (1963) 18 IUS, 209–233.

Porcelli Giacomo, 'Art. 16' in Biavati Paolo 'Reg. CE n. 1896/2006 del Parlamento Europeo e del Consiglio che Istituisce un Procedimento Europeo d'Ingiunzione di Pagamento' (2010) 33 Le nuove leggi civili commentate, 440–442.

Rentsch Bettina, 'Die Grenzüberschreitende Vollziehung Einstweiliger Maßnahmen: Im Zweifel für Die Lex Fori' (2020) 40 IPRax, 337–342.

Requejo Isidro Marta, 'On Exequatur and the ECHR: Brussels I Regulation before the ECtHR' (2015) 35 IPRax, 69–74.

Richard Vincent, 'La Refonte du Règlement sur la Notification des Actes Judiciaires et Extrajudiciaires' (2021) 111 RCDIP, 349–360.

Rossi Lucia Serena, 'L'Incidenza dei Principi di Diritto Comunitario sul Diritto Internazionale Privato: dalla "Comunitarizzazione" alla "Costituzionalizzazione"' (2004) 40 RDIPP, 63–84.

Silvestri Caterina, 'L'Esecuzione Forzata nella Prospettiva UE. Il Caso Al Bosco: Sovvertiti i Principi alla Base dello Spazio Giudiziario Europeo?' (2019) Le Pagine de l'Aula Civile, 824–826.

Stroskrubb Eva, 'Mutual Trust and the Dark Horse of Civil Justice' (2017) 20 Camb. Yearb. Eur. Leg. Stud., 179–201.

Steinmetz Alexander, 'Anwendbarkeit der Ausschlussfrist in der Spanischen ZPO auch auf Ausländische Vollstreckungstitel?' (2009) 55 RIW, 304.

Tarzia Giuseppe, 'Modelli Europei per un Processo Civile Uniforme' (1999) 54 Riv. dir. proc., 947–962.

Tiebout Charles, 'A Pure Theory of Local Expenditures' (1956) 64 JPE, 416–424.

Trevor Hartley, 'Procedure for Obtaining Protective Measures' (1986) 11 E.L. Rev., 95–99.

Tulibacka Magdalena, 'Europeanisation of Civil Procedure: in Search of a Coherent Approach' (2009) 46 CMLR, 1527–1565.

Vallines Garcia Enrique, 'Proceso Monitorio Europeo: la Revisión de un Requerimiento de Pago Ejecutivo no Procede Cuando se Basa en Circunstancias que el Demandado Pudo Haber Tenido en Cuenta para Presentar un Escrito de Oposición' (2017) 9 Cuad. der. trans., 725–736.

Vallines Garcia Enrique, 'La Reforma Necesaria del Proceso Monitorio en España: Hacia una Generalización del Proceso Monitorio Europeo?' (2022) Estándares europeos y proceso civil Hacia un proceso civil convergente con Europa, 601–649.

Velicogna Marco, Lupo Giampiero and Ontanu Elena Alina, 'Simplifying Access to Justice in Cross-Border Litigation, the National Practices and the Limits of the EU Procedures. The Example of the Service of Documents in the Order for Payment Claims' (2017) 7 IJPL, 93–130.

Vernadaki Zampia, 'Civil Procedure Harmonization in the EU: Unravelling the Policy Considerations' (2013) 9 JCER, 298–312.

Wagner Gerhard, 'The Economics of Harmonization: the Case of Contract Law' in 39 CMLR (2002), 995–1022.

Wilderspin Michael, 'The Rome II Regulation: Some Policy Observations' (2008) NIPR, 408–413.

IV) Studies and Reports

Buzzoni Marco, *Collection of French Implementation Rules in Towards More Effective EnFORcemenT of ClaimS in Civil and Commercial Matters within the EU EFFORTS (Project JUST-JCOO-AG-2019–881802).*

Buzzoni Marco, *Report on National Case-Law: France in Towards More Effective EnFORcemenT of ClaimS in Civil and Commercial Matters within the EU EFFORTS (Project JUST-JCOO-AG-2019–881802).*

Buzzoni Marco and Santaló Goris Carlos, *Report on Practices in Comparative and Cross-Border Perspective in Towards More Effective EnFORcemenT of ClaimS in Civil and Commercial Matters within the EU EFFORTS (Project JUST-JCOO-AG-2019–881802).*

Buzzoni Marco, Mariottini Cristina M., Casi Michele and Santaló Goris Carlos, *Report on EU Policy Guidelines in Towards More Effective EnFORcemenT of ClaimS in Civil and Commercial Matters within the EU EFFORTS (Project JUST-JCOO-AG-2019–881802).*

European Law Institute and UNIDROIT (eds), *The ELI – Unidroit Model European Rules of Civil Procedure from Transnational Principles to European Rules of Civil Procedure* (Oxford University Press 2021).

Hess Burkhard, *Study No. JAI/A3/2002/02 on Making More Efficient the Enforcement of Judicial Decisions within the European Union: Transparency of a Debtor's Assets, Attachment of Bank Accounts, Provisional Enforcement and Protective Measures. Version of 2/18/2004* (http://www2.ipr.uni-heidelberg.de/studie/).

Hess Burkhard and Pfeiffer Thomas, *Interpretation of the Public Policy Exception as Referred to in EU Instruments of Private International and Procedural Law (Study 15–06–2011 on the interpretation of the public policy exception).*

Hess Burkhard, *Harmonized Rules and Minimum Standards in the European Law of Civil Procedure* (Policy Department C: Citizens' Rights and Constitutional Affairs 2016).

Hess Burkhard, Pfeiffer Thomas and Schlosser Peter, *The Brussels I-Regulation (EC) No 44/2001: The Heidelberg Report on the Application of Regulation Brussels I in 25 Member States (Study JLS/C4/2005/03)* (Beck 2008).

Jenard Paul, *Report on the Convention on Jurisdiction and the Enforcement of Judgments in Civil and Commercial Matters* (Signed at Brussels, 27 September 1968) (OJ C-59/1 1979).

Kramer Xandra, *Current Gaps and Future Perspectives in European Private International Law: Towards a Code on Private International Law?* (Policy Department C: Citizens' Rights and Constitutional Affairs 2012).

Manko Rafal, *Europeanisation of Civil Procedure: Towards Common Minimum Standards?* (European Parliamentary Research Service 2015).

Tulibacka Magdalena, Sanz Margarita and Blomeyer Roland, *Common Minimum Standards of Civil Procedure* (European Added Value Assessment Annex I 2016).

Villata Francesca, Sandrini Lidia, Farina Marco, Molinaro Gabriele, Giugliano Valeria, Casi Michele and Docaj Denisa, *Collection of Italian Implementation Rules in* Efforts' *in Towards More Effective EnFORcemenT of ClaimS in Civil and Commercial Matters within the EU EFFORTS (Project JUST-JCOO-AG-2019–881802),* 30.

Villata Francesca, Sandrini Lidia, Farina Marco, Molinaro Gabriele, Giugliano Valeria, Casi Michele and Docaj Denisa, *Report on Italian Case-Law in Towards More Effective EnFORcemenT of ClaimS in Civil and Commercial Matters within the EU EFFORTS (Project JUST-JCOO-AG-2019–881802).*

V) Websites and Blog

Amrani-Mekki Soraya, 'La Part du Droit (et de la Justice) dans l'Angoisse Contemporaine. La Computation des Délais' (Leclubdesjuristes.com 30 March 2020) https://blog.leclubdesjuristes.com/la-part-du-droit-et-de-la-justice-dans-langoisse-contemporaine-la-computation-des-delais/.

Cadiet Loïc, 'Un État d'Exception pour la Procédure Civile Française à l' Épreuve du Coronavirus' (Judicium.com 20 April 2020) https://www.judicium.it/un-etat-dexception-pour-la-procedure-civile-francaise-lepreuve-du-coronavirus/.

Chiapponi Giovanni, 'The Impact of Corona Virus on the Management of Judicial Proceedings in Italy' (Eapilblog 13 March 2020) https://eapil.org/2020/03/13/the-impact-of-corona-virus-on-the-management-of-judicial-proceedings-in-italy/.

Chiapponi Giovanni, 'Judicial Cooperation and Coronavirus: the Law Must Go on' (Judicium.com 23 may 2020) https://www.judicium.it/judicial-cooperation-and-coronavirus-the-law-must-go/.

Chiapponi Giovanni, 'Postponing the *Dies a quo* of Domestic Time Limits to Ensure Effectiveness of the Right to Refuse Service of Documents: Some Insights from LKW WALTER (C-7/21)' (EU Law Live 27 July 2022) https://eulawlive.com/analysis-postponing-the-dies-a-quo-of-domestic-time-limits-to-ensure-effectiveness-of-the-right-to-refuse-service-of-documents-some-insights-from-lkw-walter-c-7-21-by-giovanni-ch/.

Cuniberti Gilles, 'French Supreme Court Rules Certificate Provided for in Article 53 Brussels I bis May Be Served 5 Minutes before Enforcement' (EAPIL Blog 21 February 2023) https://eapil.org/2023/02/21/french-supreme-court-rules-certificate-provided-for-in-article-53-brussels-i-bis-may-be-served-5-minutes-before-enforcement/.

D'Alessandro Elena, 'Ingiuntivo e Europeo. Procedimento' (Enciclopedia Treccani. Il diritto online 2017) https://www.treccani.it/enciclopedia/ingiuntivo-europeo-procedimento_%28Diritto-on-line%29/.

D'Alessandro Elena, 'Titolo Esecutivo Europeo' (Enciclopedia Treccani. Il diritto on-line 2017) https://www.treccani.it/enciclopedia/titolo-esecutivo-europeo_%28Diritto-on-line%29/.

Poyet Betrand, 'L'Assouplissement des Règles de Communication des Conclusions et des Pièces en Temps de Crise Sanitaire' (Lescludesjuristes.com, 3 April 2020) https://blog.leclubdesjuristes.com/lassouplissement-des-regles-de-communication-en-temps-de-crise-sanitaire/.

Raffly Romain and Boccon-Gibod Mathieu, 'L'Incertitude de la Fin de la "Période Juridiquement Protégée"' (Lescluddesjuristes.com 20 April 2020) https://blog.leclubdesjuristes.com/lincertitude-de-la-fin-de-la-periode-juridiquement-protegee/.

Lombardi Vincenzo, 'Sul Recente (e Caotico) Intervento Legislativo in Materia di Giustizia Civile' (judicium.com 23 march 2020) https://www.judicium.it/emergenza-coronavirus-e-giustizia-civile/.

Panzarola Andrea and Farina Marco, 'L'Emergenza Coronavirus ed il Processo Civile. Osservazioni a Prima Lettura' (Giustiziacivile.com 18 March 2020) https://giustiziacivile.com/arbitrato-e-processo-civile/editoriali/lemergenza-coronavirus-ed-il-processo-civile-osservazioni.

Scarselli Giuliano, 'Interpretazione e Commento del Decreto Legge 8 Marzo 2020 n. 11 di Differimento delle Udienze e Sospensione dei Termini Processuali Civili per Contrastare l'Emergenza da COVID 19' (Judicium.com 8 March 2020) https://www.judicium.it/decreto-legge-8-marzo-2020-n-11-differimento-delle-udienze-sospensione-dei-termini-processuali-civili-contrastare-lemergenza-covid-19/.

Viola Luigi, 'La Perentorietà Tollerante dei Termini Ordinatori' (Judicium.com 26 September 2013) https://www.judicium.it/la-perentorieta-tollerante-dei-termini-ordinatori-processuali/.

B) Case law

I) CJEU

Case C- 42/76, 30 November 1976, *Jozef de Wolf v Harry Cox BV*, ECLI:EU:C:1976:168.

Case C-125/79, 21 May 1980, *Bernard Denilauler v SNC Couchet Frères*, ECLI:EU:C:1980:130.

Case C-166/80, 16 June 1981, *Peter Klomps v Karl Michel,* ECLI:EU:C:1981:137

Case C-119/84, 3 October 1985, *Capelloni and Aquilini v. Pelkmans,* ECLI:EU:C:1985:388.

Case C- 145/86, 4 February 1988, *Horst Ludwig Martin Hoffmann v Adelheid Krieg,* ECLI:EU:C:1988:61.

Case C-49/84, 11 June 1985, *Leon Emile Gaston Carlos Debaecker and Berthe Plouvier v Cornelis Gerrit Bouwman,* ECLI:EU:C:1985:252.

Case C-123/91, 12 November 1992, *Minalmet GmbH v Brandeis Ltd,* ECLI:EU:C:1992:432.

Case C-414/92, 2 June 1994, *Solo Kleinmotoren GmbH v Emilio Boch,* ECLI:EU:C:1994:221.

Case C-474/93, 13 July 1995, *Hengst Import BV v Anna Maria Campese,* ECLI:EU:C:1995:243.

Case C-78/95, 10 October 1996, *Bernardus Hendrikman and Maria Feyen v Magenta Druck & Verlag GmbH,* ECLI:EU:C:1996:380.

Case C-391/95, 17 November 1998, *Van Uden Maritime BV, trading as Van Uden Africa Line v Kommanditgesellschaft in Firma Deco-Line and Another,* ECLI:EU:C:1998:543.

Case C-99/96, 27 April 1999, *Hans-Hermann Mietz v Intership Yachting Sneek BV,* ECLI:EU:C:1999:202.

Case C- 267/97, 29 April 1999, *Eric Coursier v Fortis Bank and Martine Coursier, née Bellami,* ECLI:EU:C:1999:213.

Case C-7/98, 28 March 2000, *Dieter Krombach v André Bamberski,* ECLI:EU:C:2000:164.

Case C-38/98, 11 May 2000, *Régie nationale des usines Renault SA v Maxicar SpA and Orazio Formento,* ECLI:EU:C:2000:225,

Case C-376/98, 5 October 2000, *Federal Republic of Germany v European Parliament and Council of the European Union,* ECLI:EU:C:2000:544.

Case C-2/00, 6 December 2001, *Opinions of the Court,* ECLI:EU:C:2001:664.

Case C-336/00, 19 September 2002, *Republik Österreich v Martin Huber,* ECLI:EU:C:2002:509.

Case C-281/01, 12 December 2002, *Commission of the European Communities v Council of the European Union,* ECLI:EU:C:2002:761.

Case C-211/01, 11 September 2003, *Commission of the European Communities v Council of the European Union,* ECLI:EU:C:2003:452.

Case C-39/02, 14 October 2004, *Mærsk Olie & Gas A/S v Firma M. de Haan en W. de Boe,* ECLI:EU:C:2004:615.

Case C-473/04, 9 February 2006, *Plumex v Young Sports NV,* ECLI:EU:C:2006:96

Case C-3/05, 16 February 2006, *Gaetano Verdoliva v J. M. Van der Hoeven BV Banco di Sardegna and San Paolo IMI SpA,* ECLI:EU:C:2006:113.

Case C-283/05, 14 December 2006, *ASML Netherlands BV v Semiconductor Industry Services GmbH (SEMIS),* ECLI:EU:C:2006:787.

Case C-14/07, 8 May 2008, *Ingenieurbüro Michael Weiss und Partner GbR v Industrie- und Handelskammer Berlin*, ECLI:EU:C:2008:264.

Opinion of AG Trstenjak, 11 September 2008, Case C-265/07 *Caffaro Srl versus Azienda Unità Sanitaria Locale RM/C*, ECLI:EU:C:2008:496

Case C-394/07, 2 April 2009, *Marco Gambazzi v DaimlerChrysler Canada Inc. and CIBC Mellon Trust Company*, ECLI:EU:C:2009:219.

Case C-420/07, 28 April 2009, *Meletis Apostolides v David Charles Orams and Linda Elizabeth Orams*, ECLI:EU:C:2 009:271.

Case C-139/10, 13 October 2011, *Prism Investments BV v Jaap Anne van der Meer*, ECLI:EU:C:2011:653.

CJEU Case C-618/10, 14 June 2012, *Banco Español de Crédito, SA v Joaquín Calderón Camino*, ECLI:EU:C:2012:349.

Case C-629/10, 6 September 2012, *Trade Agency Ltd v Seramico Investments Ltd*, ECLI:EU:C:2012:531.

Case C-144/12, 13 June 2013 *Goldbet Sportwetten GmbH v. Massimo Sperindeo*, ECLI:EU:C:2013:393.

Cases C-119/13 and C-120/13, 4 September 2014, *Eco cosmetics GmbH & Co. KG and Raiffeisenbank St. Georgen reg. Gen. mbH v Virginie Laetitia Barbara Dupuy and Tetyana Bonchyk*, ECLI:EU:C:2014:2144.

Case C-300/14, 17 December 2015, *Imtech Marine Belgium NV v Radio Hellenic SA*, ECLI:EU:C:2015:825.

Case C-112/13, 11 September 2014, *A v B and others*, ECLI:EU:C:2014:2195,

Case C-519/13, 16 September 2015, *Alpha Bank Cyprus Ltd v Dau Si Senh and Others*, ECLI:EU:C:2015:603.

Case C- 245/14, 22 October 2015 *Thomas Cook Belgium NV v Thurner Hotel GmbH*, ECLI:EU:C:2015:715.

Opinion of AG Kokott, 7 April 2016, Case C-70/15, *Emmanuel Lebek v Janusz Domino*, ECLI:EU:C:2022:777.

Case C-384/14, 28 April 2016, *Alta Realitat SL v Erlock Film ApS and Ulrich Thomsen*, ECLI:EU:C:2016:316.

Case C-559/14, 25 May 2016 *Rudolfs Meroni v Recoletos Limited*, ECLI:EU:C:2016:349.

Case C-511/14, 16 June 2016 *Pebros Servizi Srl v Aston Martin Lagonda Ltd*, ECLI:EU:C:2016:448.

Case C-70/15, 7 July 2016, *Emmanuel Lebek v Janusz Domino*, ECLI:EU:C:2016:524.

Case C-612/15, 5 June 2018, *Criminal proceedings against Nikolay Kolev and Others*, ECLI:EU:C:2018:392.

Opinion of AG Szpunar, 20 June 2018 Case C-379/17 *Proceedings brought by Società Immobiliare Al Bosco Srl*, ECLI:EU:C:2018:472.

Case C-21/17, 6 September 2018 *Catlin Europe SE v O. K. Trans Praha spol. s.r.o.*, ECLI:EU:C:2018:675.

Case C-176–17, 13 September 2018, *Profi Credit Polska S.A. w Bielsku Białej v Mariusz Wawrzosek*, ECLI:EU:C:2018:711.

Case C-379/17, 4 October 2018, *Proceedings brought by Società Immobiliare Al Bosco Srl,* ECLI:EU:C:2018:806.

Opinion of AG Sharpston, 31 October 2019, Cases C-453/18 and C-494/18, *Bondora AS v Carlos V. C. and XY,* ECLI:EU:C:2019:921.

Case C-386/17, 16 Janaury 2019, *Stefano Liberato v Luminita Luisa Grigorescu,* ECLI:EU:C:2019:24.

Case C-579/17, 28 February 2019, *BUAK Bauarbeiter-Urlaubs- u. Abfertigungskasse v Gradbeništvo Korana d.o.o.*, ECLI:EU:C:2019:162.

Case C-555/18, 7 November 2019, *KHK v BAC abd EEK,* ECLI:EU:C:2019:937.

Case C-453/18, 19 December 2019 *Bondora AS v Carlos V. C. and XY,* ECLI:EU:Ć:2019:1118.

Opinion of AG Pikamäe, 10 March 2022, Case C-7/21 *LKW WALTER Internationale Transportorganisation AG v CB and Others,* ECLI:EU:C:2022:185.

Case C-7/21, 7 July 2022, *LKW WALTER Internationale Transportorganisation AG v CB and Others,* ECLI:EU:C:2022:527.

CJEU C-18/21, 15 September 2022, *Uniqa Versicherungen AG v VU,* ECLI:EU:C:2022:682.

II) ECtHR

Avotiņš v Latvia App no 17502/07 (ECtHR 25 February 2014)

Avotiņš v Latvia App no 17502/07 (ECtHR 23 May 2016)

III) National case law

1) Italy

Court of Appeal of Milan, 28-09-1976, Soc. Ingg. S and Agostino Belotti S.r.l v Veeder Root GmbH.

Court of Appeal of Milan, 29-09-1978, Officina Costruzioni Meccaniche S.r.l. v S.A. Ets Jean Ivens in (1980) 26 RDIPP, 53-56.

Court of Appeal of Naples, 20-02-1982, Trans-Atlantica S.p.A. v Soc. Vertom Shipping and Trading Corporation B.V. in (1983) 19 RDIPP, 128-135.

Italian Supreme Court, 14-01-1999, n. 239.

Italian Supreme Court, 01-02-2000, n. 1069.

Italian Supreme Court, 24- 06-2003, n. 10026.

Italian Supreme Court, 4-05-2006, n. 10216 with case note of Biffi Luisa (2007) Giur. it., 1208-1211.

Italian Supreme Court, 11-06-2009, n. 13546.

Italian Supreme Court 25-09-2009, n. 20684.

Italian Supreme Court (Sezioni Unite), 22-02-2010, n. 4059 with case notes of Gianpaolo Impagnatiello (2010) Foro. it., 2082 and of Maria Assunta Iuorio (2010) Riv. es. forz., 267.

Court of Appeal of Milan, 26.04.2010 Trading Corpora B.V. in (2010) 46 RDIPP, 764.

Italian Supreme Court, 28-02-2011, n. 4907.

Italian Supreme Court, 31-05-2011, n. 11971.

Italian Supreme Court (Sezioni Unite), 13-06-2011, n. 12898.

Italian Supreme Court, 29-07-2011, n. 16737.

Italian Supreme Court, 09-02-2012, n. 1771.

Italian Supreme Court (Sezioni Unite), 01-08-2012, n. 13794.

Italian Supreme Court, 04-04-2013, n. 8216.

Italian Supreme Court, 16-07-2014, n. 16272.

Italian Constitutional Court, 22-02-2016, n. 3.

Italian Supreme Court, 24-08-2016, n. 17311.

Italian Supreme Court, 20-09-2016, n. 18356.

Italian Supreme Court), 18-11-2016, n. 23561.

Italian Supreme Court, 21-02-2017, n. 4374.

Italian Supreme Court, (Sezioni Unite) 20-03-2017, n. 7075.

Italian Supreme Court, 18-04-2017, n. 9773.

Italian Supreme Court, 11-07-2018, n. 2814.

Italian Supreme Court (Sezioni Unite), 04-03-2019, n. 6278.

2) France

Court of Appeal of Lyon, 18-04-1978 with case note of Holleaux Dominique (1979) JDI, 380.

French Supreme Court, 10-11-1998, n. 96-42.749 in Bull. civ. (1998) V n. 487.

French Supreme Court, 14-02-1990, n. 88-19.900 in Bull. civ. (1990) II n. 33 with case note of Perrot Roger in RTD civ. (1990), 557.

French Supreme Court, 04-02-1998, 95-21.479 in Bull. civ. (1998) II n. 40.

French Supreme Court, 06-05-1998, n. 96-19.014 in Bull. civ. (1998) II n. 146.

French Supreme Court, 19-05-1998, n. 96-17.349 in Bull. civ. (1998) II n. 158.

French Supreme Court, 10-11-1998, n. 96-42.749 in Bull. civ. (1998) V n. 487.

French Supreme Court advice, 16-09-2002, n. 02-00.003 in Bull. civ. (2002) Avis n. 4.

French Supreme Court, 07-07-2005, n. 03-15.469 in Bull. civ. (2005) II n. 164 with case note of Salati Oscar (2005), Droit et procédures, 345.

French Supreme Court, 07-07-2005, n. 182 in Bull. civ. (2005) II n. 187. with case note of Vincke François (2006) Droit et procedures, 33.

French Supreme Court, 07-10-2008, n. 06-20.093 in Bull. civ. (2008) IV n° 166.

French Supreme Court, 11-12-2008, n. 08-10.141 in Bull. civ. 2008 II n. 262.

French Supreme Court, 05-02-2009, n. 07-13.589 in Bull. civ. (2009) II n° 35.

French Supreme Court, 13-04-2010, n. 09-13.478 (not published in Bull. civ.) with case note of Perrot Roger (2010) Procédures, 224.

French Supreme Court, 03-11-2010, n. 09-68.968 (not published in Bull. civ.) with case note of Perrot Roger (2011) Procédures, 4.

French Supreme Court, 18-02-2016, n. 14-26.395 (not published in Bull. civ.)

Court of appeal of Bordeaux, 31-03-2016, n. 14/05833.

French Supreme Court, 14-03-2018, n 15-28.506 (not published in Bull. civ.).

Court of Appeal of Metz, 20-03-2018, n. 16/04164.

Court of Appeal of Paris, 14.02.2019, n. 17/22771.

Court of Appeal of Versailles, 09-01-2020 n. 17/08693.

Tribunal of Paris, 01-07-2021, n. 21/80506.

French Supreme Court, 13-01-2022, n. 20-12.914 in Bull. civ. (2022) I.

French Supreme Court, 11-01-2023 n. 21-17092 in Bull. civ. (2023) I.

3) Germany

Higher Regional Court of Hamm, 07-03-1979, n. 20 W 29/78.

German Supreme Court, 23-01-1986, n. 9 ZB 38/85.

Higher Regional Court of Dusseldorf, 11-10-1999, n. 3 W 258/99.

Higher Regional Court of Nurnberg, 14-04-2014, n. 2 W 1488/11.

4) Spain

Spanish Supreme Court, 16-10-2014 (Sala Civil, Sección 1a).